older & wiser

Brilliant Puzzles

older & wiser

Brilliant Puzzles

To keep your mind active!

ARCTURUS

ARCTURUS

This edition published in 2015 by Arcturus Publishing Limited
26/27 Bickels Yard, 151–153 Bermondsey Street,
London SE1 3HA

ISBN: 978-1-78404-798-6
AD004640NT

Printed in China

INTRODUCTION

How many of us have blamed 'old age creeping on' for the fact that we can never remember where we left the car keys, or what we climbed the stairs to get, let alone what day of the week it is? Proof indeed that we need to keep our minds active, even if our bodies refuse to climb stairs at the speed they used to.

However, this book may help you regain confidence in your powers of reasoning, which probably have never really diminished - after all, you may be able to work out sums in your head that today's youth needs a calculator to accomplish. And your mind is less likely to be cluttered with those trivial matters that once seemed so important, such as the latest fashions, who's number one in the hit parade, and so on.

The book contains puzzles that start off fairly easy to solve, and then progress to becoming harder; however, once your brain is accustomed to solving a few, you may not notice the difference, as your mind will be more active and more quickly able to work out the answers.

But there aren't just puzzles in the book: we've also included some quips quotations that might make you smile, and that you can slip into a lull in any conversation (to prove that you weren't asleep, after all), and various ways to challenge you to think or act slightly differently. And as for your powers of recall, we've included quizzes that might dredge up a few memories, as well as a few 'short-term' memory tests, too!

So curl up on the couch, sharpen a pencil, and prepare to sharpen your mind. Don't worry if you get stuck solving a puzzle: all the answers are at the back of the book, but do try not to peek!

Eric Saunders

WORDSEARCH: THINGS YOU CAN LOSE

Can you find all of the listed things you can lose hidden in the grid below? Words run forwards or backwards, in either a horizontal, vertical or diagonal direction.

```
E T E C A P S R S Q Q E T U T
E H E R M B P G E D C A M T A
U G S L I C N E P A C W J A L
B I N V Y I A P V Z S X R J G
T E E Z R S K U W O Y O H P J
I W S A E F M R S B I I N N S
H M E K B N O S A E H C E Y F
Y B B P Y E O E N U B C E I U
Q T I X M Q W H H S A K O N U
M A R B L E S Q P L S H A P E
C E T E R E W O P H T W D E H
V I D N P C D G J E A E X H T
V U F I A O G L E F V N C N I
P Y Y R R R R T O R I P E A A
L E Z P H P P P P T F W L F F
```

BEARINGS	KEYS	REASON
CAR	MARBLES	SENSE
CAT	PENCIL	SHAPE
CAUSE	PLACE	SPACE
CELL PHONE	POWER	TEETH
FACE	PRIDE	TRIBE
FAITH	PROPERTY	VOICE
GAME	PURSE	WEIGHT

BREAK-TIME CROSSWORD

Across

1 Feeling of annoyance or anger (11)
9 Gave a military gesture (7)
10 Returned from the dead (5)
11 Graphic symbol (4)
12 Precious blue gemstone (8)
14 Popular spice (6)
16 Strike out (6)
18 Delighted (8)
19 In addition (4)
22 Transmitting live from a studio (2,3)
23 Apprentice (7)
24 Plant grown for its pungent, edible root (11)

Down

2 Inuit dwelling (5)
3 Feeling of sympathy and sorrow (4)
4 Make attractive or lovable (6)
5 Missile filled with fragments (8)
6 Breathe (7)
7 Secret rendezvous (11)
8 Needless (11)
13 Expresses strong disapproval (8)
15 Whirlwind (7)
17 Basement (6)
20 Connections (5)
21 Without hair (4)

HEXAFIT

Place the listed words into the hexagons, one letter per cell, starting in any of those surrounding a black circle, so that words read clockwise. Some letters are already in place.

The letter is the same in any cell that shares a common border with a cell in a touching hexagon.

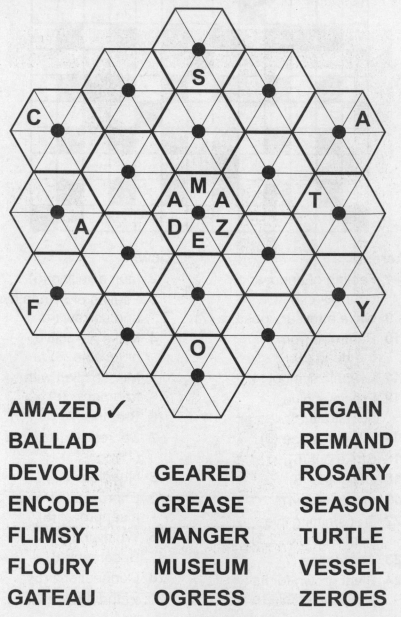

AMAZED ✓

BALLAD

DEVOUR

ENCODE

FLIMSY

FLOURY

GATEAU

GEARED

GREASE

MANGER

MUSEUM

OGRESS

REGAIN

REMAND

ROSARY

SEASON

TURTLE

VESSEL

ZEROES

KAKURO

Fill the grid so that each block adds up to the total in the box above or to the left of it.

You can only use the digits 1-9, one per square, but the same digit must not be used twice in a block. The same digit may occur more than once in any row or column, but it must be in a separate block.

Whenever I feel the need to exercise, I lie down until it goes away.

Paul Terry

SUDOKU

Place one of the numbers from 1 to 9 into every empty cell so that each row, each column and each 3x3 block contains all the numbers from 1 to 9.

1	5			7	2	6		
8		6			5			1
					8	9	3	
	1	4	8					7
	2		4		6		9	
3					9	8	1	
	4	7	2					
5			6			4		2
		9	5	3			7	6

DOMINO PLACEMENT

A standard set of twenty-eight dominoes has been laid out as shown below. Can you draw in the edges of them all? One is already in place.

It may be helpful to use the check-box to tick off the dominoes as they are found.

1	0	1	1	2	3	3	1
2	0	0	1	2	6	6	3
6	6	1	2	5	1	4	1
0	6	4	5	5	6	0	6
5	5	4	6	4	3	0	0
2	3	5	2	0	4	4	3
3	2	5	5	4	3	4	2

0-0	0-1	0-2	0-3	0-4	0-5	0-6	1-1
				✓			

1-2	1-3	1-4	1-5	1-6	2-2	2-3	2-4	2-5	2-6

3-3	3-4	3-5	3-6	4-4	4-5	4-6	5-5	5-6	6-6

ALPHAFILL

Place 25 different letters of the alphabet, one per circle, in order to spell out the listed words. Words are formed by moving between adjacent circles along the connecting lines, either horizontally, vertically or diagonally in any direction.

Begin by crossing out the letters already in place, together with the one letter which doesn't appear in any of the words.

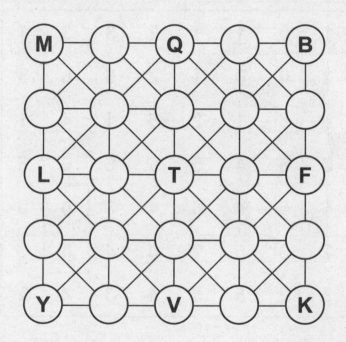

A B C D E F G H I J K L M

N O P Q R S T U V W X Y Z

BUNTING	LARVA	NOTHING
FIX	MONTH	PUNT
GLAD	MOSQUITO	TICKET
HAVE	MOTIF	TOLD
JOT	NOTARY	WHITE

NUMBER FILLER

Can you fit all of the listed numbers into the grid? One is already in place, to get you off to a good start!

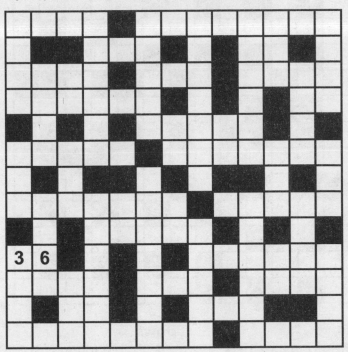

2 digits	3 digits	4 digits	5 digits	7 digits
10	253	1066	16344	1252383
36 ✓	279	1561	43921	3890735
49	458	2652	62829	4687914
57	554	2905	63014	7188961
60	597	3050	68482	
63	647	3229	86806	
85	700	3937		**8 digits**
86	790	5823	**6 digits**	45105752
94	915	6128	293563	94770449
96	938	6674	343897	
		7308	436112	
		7780	563040	
		7817	820118	
		8719	887247	

BREAK-TIME CROSSWORD

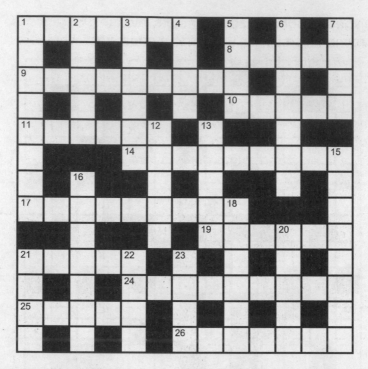

Across

1 Afternoon theatrical performance (7)
8 Pear-shaped tropical fruit (5)
9 Deadlock (9)
10 Empty area (5)
11 Reddish-brown (6)
14 Having no definite form (9)
17 Sale or purchase of goods by post (4,5)
19 Perplexing riddle (6)
21 Make different in some respect (5)
24 Exaggerate (9)
25 Turbulent or highly emotional episode (5)
26 Line touching a curve (7)

Down

1 Edible fungus (8)
2 Snares (5)
3 Female relatives (6)
4 Biblical son of Isaac and Rebecca (4)
5 Grows old (4)
6 Floor show at a nightclub (7)
7 Front of the head (4)
12 In that place (5)
13 Distressed (5)
15 Most intelligent (8)
16 Country, capital Hanoi (7)
18 Motive (6)
20 Digging implement (5)
21 Presidential assistant (4)
22 Highway (4)
23 Held back, retained (4)

CODEWORD

Every letter in this puzzle has been replaced by a number, the number remaining the same for that letter wherever it occurs. Every letter of the alphabet has been used. Substitute numbers for letters to complete the codeword.

It may help to cross off the letters beneath the grid to keep a track of progress, and to use the reference box showing which numbers have been decoded. Three letters have already been entered into the grid, to help you on your way.

1	20	4	4	18	5		6	21	6	19	9	1
23		20		20				11		11		25
24	10	4	20	8	6		25	1	9	8	25	18
3		4		6	22	6	8	9		15		20
6	23	6			19		25	18	11	6		9
18	6	9	16	25	18		17	6	23	25	8	6
	18		6		20 U	1 S	6 E		6		25	
26	18	11	8	24	2		1	6	2	25	9	6
18		5	6	9	24		12			2	6	15
25		1		1	15	11	20	9		8		14
15	20	9	10	6	7		6	20	18	11	7	5
13		6		18				17		24		10
1	19	8	20	26	26		17	6	6	9	18	6

A B C D E F G H I J K L M

N O P Q R S T U V W X Y Z

1 S	2	3	4	5	6 E	7	8	9	10	11	12	13
14	15	16	17	18	19	20 U	21	22	23	24	25	26

ROUND DOZEN

First solve the clues. All of the solutions begin with the letter in the central circle, and some others are already in place. When the puzzle is complete, you can then go on to discover the twelve-letter hyphenated word reading clockwise around the outermost ring of letters.

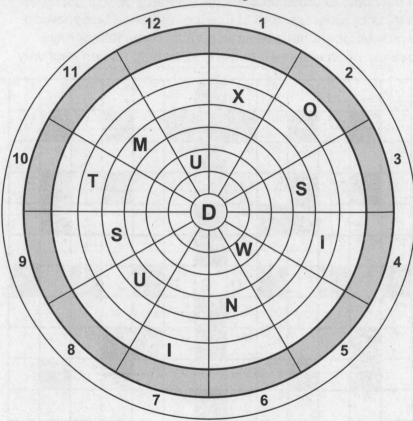

1 Word blindness

2 Entrance-opening device

3 Capital of Syria

4 Time limit

5 Main business or commercial area of a city

6 Most powerful

7 Refuse responsibility for

8 Rum and lime juice cocktail

9 Separation into parts

10 Beaten in a contest

11 Explosive compound

12 Inebriated person

The twelve-letter word is: _____

JIGSAW SUDOKU

Fit the numbers 1, 2, 3, 4, 5 and 6 into the grid in such a way that each horizontal row, each vertical column and each of the heavily outlined sections of six squares each contains a different number. Some numbers are already in place.

	4				
	2				
	6	2			
	1				
3		1	6		

WHAT DOES IT MEAN?

Which of the following is the correct definition of the word:

INCALESCENT

1 Becoming hot or warm; increasing in temperature

2 In an initial or early stage; beginning to develop

3 Of the moon: showing an increase in the extent of the portion illuminated

SPIDOKU

In the spider's web below, each of the eight segments should be filled with a different number from 1 to 8, in such a way that every ring also contains a different number from 1 to 8.

The segments run from the outside of the spider's web to the middle, and the rings run all the way around. So that you can see the rings more clearly, we've shaded them grey and white.

Some numbers are already in place. Can you fill in the rest?

CUBE ROUTES

Fill the words into the grid (one letter is ready in place), changing route where necessary, as with this example:

ASPECT   ENDURE   SPED

CARE   REASON   WRITHE

CASE   ROE

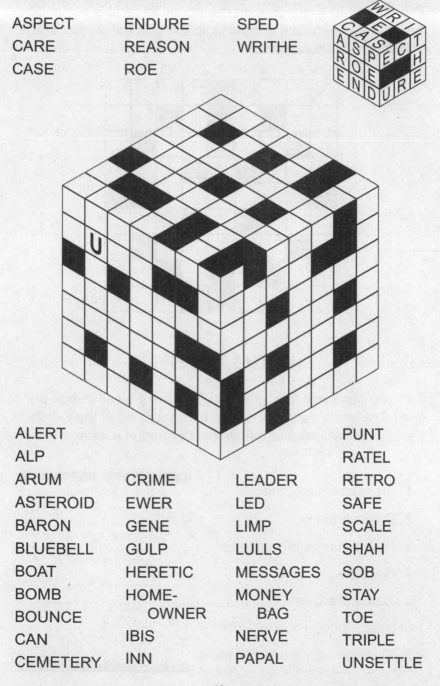

ALERT			PUNT
ALP			RATEL
ARUM	CRIME	LEADER	RETRO
ASTEROID	EWER	LED	SAFE
BARON	GENE	LIMP	SCALE
BLUEBELL	GULP	LULLS	SHAH
BOAT	HERETIC	MESSAGES	SOB
BOMB	HOME-	MONEY	STAY
BOUNCE	OWNER	BAG	TOE
CAN	IBIS	NERVE	TRIPLE
CEMETERY	INN	PAPAL	UNSETTLE

NUMBER CRUNCHER CROSSWORD

A little mathematical crossword, where a little knowledge of mathematics will come in very handy!

The answer to every clue on the opposite page is a number, the digits of which are entered into the grid below, just like a standard crossword puzzle.

EGG TIMER

Can you complete this puzzle in the time it takes to boil an egg? The answers to the clues are anagrams of the words immediately above and below, plus or minus a letter.

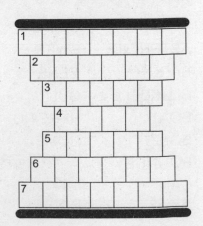

1 Branch of mathematics

2 Cultivatable

3 Harsh trumpeting sound

4 Genuine

5 Transparent

6 Baby's bed

7 Crept on hands and knees

NUMBER CRUNCHER CROSSWORD

Across

1 21 Across multiplied by 84 (4)

4 One ninth of 14 Across (4)

7 One sixth of 12 Across (2)

8 7 Across plus one tenth of 7 Across (2)

9 14 Across plus 15 Down minus 88 (5)

12 13 Across plus 20 Down minus 21 Across (3)

13 Degrees in a circle (3)

14 10 Down plus nine (5)

15 5 Down multiplied by eight (3)

16 One third of 24 Across (3)

18 270 squared plus 117 (5)

21 Four squared (2)

23 Ten per cent of 12 Across (2)

24 50 squared minus 21 Across (4)

25 4 Across minus 1671 (4)

Down

1 6 Down plus five (4)

2 Days in September (2)

3 2 Down plus 19 Down plus 20 Down minus 23 Down (3)

4 12 Across plus 20 Down plus three (3)

5 Square root of 2401 (2)

6 15 Across multiplied by five (4)

9 266 squared minus 29 (5)

10 13 Across multiplied by 20 Down (5)

11 184 squared plus 131 (5)

15 16 Across multiplied by four (4)

17 Minutes in six days (4)

19 Square root of 92416 (3)

20 14 squared (3)

22 21 Across multiplied by four (2)

23 Square root of 3249 (2)

Have regular hours for work and play; make each day both useful and pleasant, and prove that you understand the worth of time by employing it well. Then youth will be delightful, old age will bring few regrets, and life will become a beautiful success.

Louisa May Alcott

LINK WORDS

Fit eight different words into the grid, so that each one links up with the words on either side, eg table - lamp - shade.

When finished, read down the letters in the shaded squares to reveal another word, solving the clue.

DEATH					LIST
AFTER					WORM
BATH					SERVICE
TRUE					LETTER
MIDDLE					AFRICA
MARCHING					WAGON
CAST					CURTAIN
SUPER					SCOTIA

Clue: Country _____

BERMUDA TRIANGLE

Travel through the 'Bermuda Triangle', collecting a letter from each area. You can visit any area once only, and you must enter and exit through the holes in the walls between them. The starting letter may appear in any area.

When you've completed your tour, the 15 letters (in order) will spell out the name of an author.

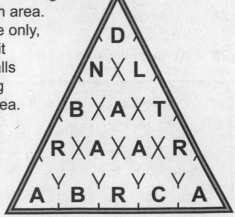

Author: _____

WORD LADDER

Change one letter at a time (but not the position of any letter) to make a new word — and move from the word at the top of the ladder to the word at the bottom using the exact number of rungs provided.

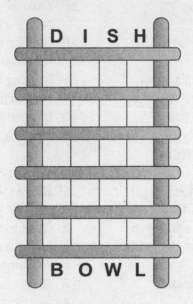

D I S H

B O W L

WORD WHEEL

How many words of three or more letters can you make from those in the wheel, without using plurals, abbreviations or proper nouns?

The central letter must appear once in every word and no letter in a section of the wheel may be used more than once.

There is at least one nine-letter word in the wheel.

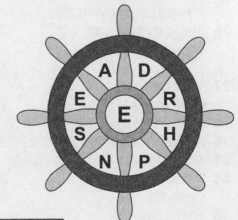

Nine-letter word(s):

_____

GENERAL KNOWLEDGE CROSSWORD

Across

1 Campaign period approaching an election (3-2)

8 Wish harm upon, curse (9)

9 Upstairs storage room (5)

10 One who looks after a sick relative (5)

11 Main part of the human body (5)

12 Third planet from the Sun (5)

13 Egyptian water lily (5)

14 Small tortilla topped with cheese and spices (5)

15 Mass of eggs deposited by frogs (5)

17 Public passenger vehicle (4)

18 Spirit traditionally imprisoned within a bottle or oil lamp (5)

20 Synthetic fabric (5)

22 Had existence (4)

23 Condensed but memorable saying (5)

25 Medium that was once supposed to fill all space (5)

27 Thin part of a wine glass (4)

29 Premature (5)

30 Aquatic mammal (5)

31 Scheme (4)

34 Temporary police force (5)

36 Remedies (5)

37 Dispense with, forgo (5)

38 Jolly ___, pirates' flag (5)

39 Daniel ___, English writer (1660–1731) (5)

40 Native of Baghdad, for example (5)

41 Musical composition to be performed slowly (5)

42 In small stages (9)

43 Accolade (5)

Down

1 Showing a response (8)

2 Device used to open walnuts, for example (10)

3 Small flute (7)

4 Short musical drama (8)

5 Causing sad feelings of gloom (10)

6 Disease transmitted by the mosquito (7)

7 Unbeliever, infidel (7)

16 Unspecified person (7)

17 Impart skills or knowledge to (5)

18 Nazi secret police force (7)

19 Central pillar of a circular staircase (5)

21 Agent used in fermenting beer (5)

24 Protective garment (5)

26 Manual printing machine (10)

GENERAL KNOWLEDGE CROSSWORD

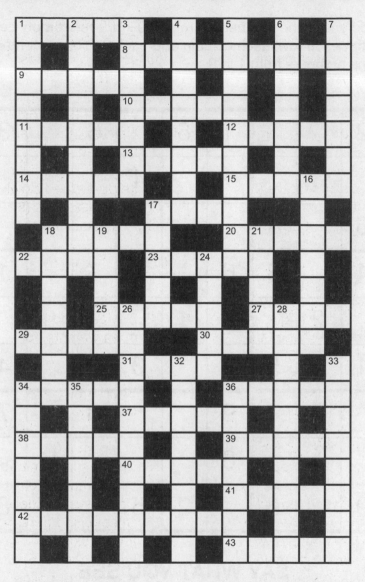

28 Solid ground (5,5)

32 Disturbed, charged up (8)

33 Minor celestial body composed of rock and metal (8)

34 Feasibly (7)

35 Sweetened (7)

36 Diacritical mark sometimes placed below the letter 'c' (7)

SUDOKU

Place one of the numbers from 1 to 9 into every empty cell so that each row, each column and each 3x3 block contains all the numbers from 1 to 9.

2			1	8		6		3
	3				4			
6		4			7		5	
4		8	6			7		1
	2			1			9	
1		5			3	2		4
	8		9			3		7
			8				6	
9		6		2	5			8

SAY WHAT YOU SEE

Tongue twisters can be an excellent way to practise speaking clearly, as every word needs to be carefully enunciated. Try these:

How can a clam cram in a clean cream can?

Tie twine to three tree twigs.

JIGWORD

A symmetrical crossword has been cut into pieces. Can you put it back together? Three pieces are already in position.

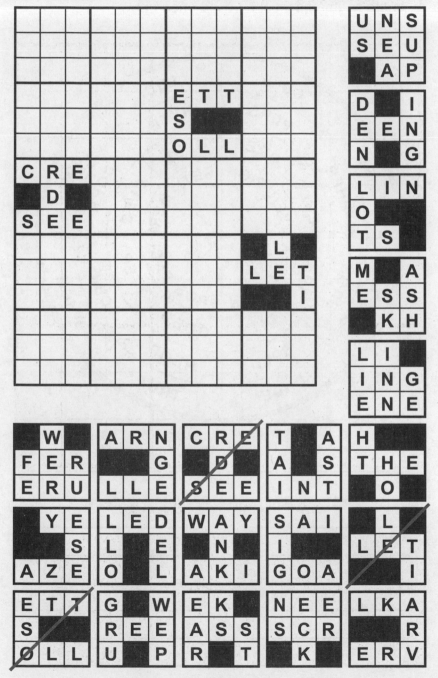

RING-WORDS

From the 32 segments below, find 16 eight-letter words by pairing one set of four letters with another.

All of the segments must be used once only.

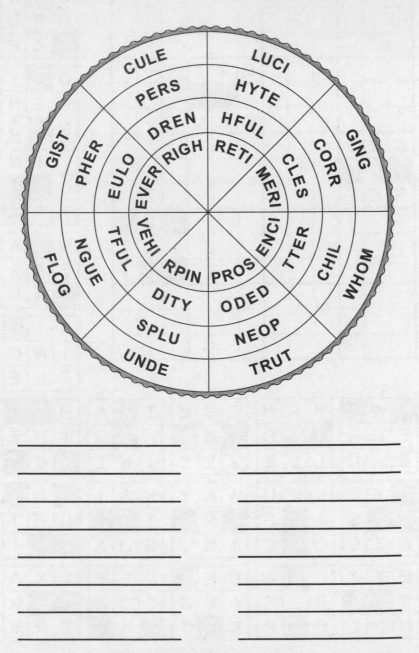

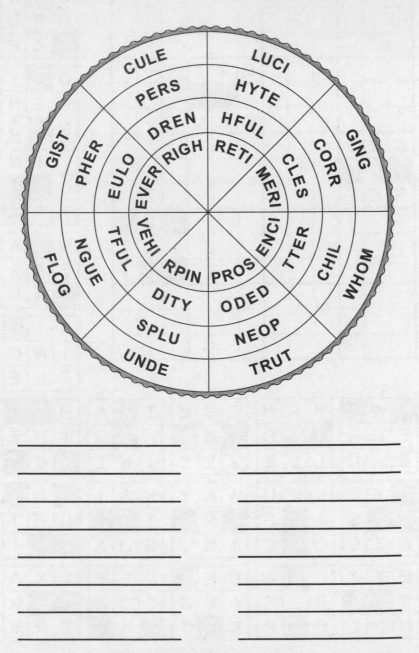

WELL SPOTTED

Some of the circles in this puzzle are already black. Fill in more white circles, so that the number of black circles totals the number inside the area they surround.

Every black circle surrounding an area with a number higher than '1' needs to be next to another black circle surrounding the same area.

When solving, it may help to put a small dot into any circle you know should not be filled.

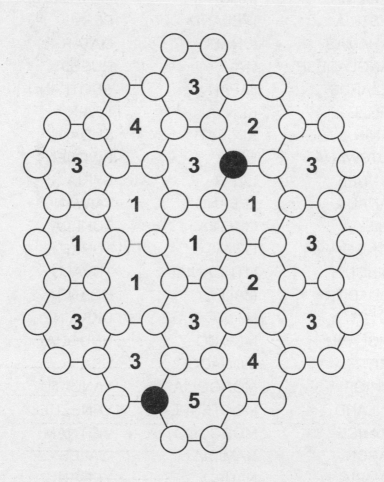

WORDSEARCH: COUNTRIES

Can you find all of the listed countries in the grid opposite?
Words run forwards or backwards, in either a horizontal,
vertical or diagonal direction.

ALBANIA	GUAM	NIGERIA
ALGERIA	HAITI	NORWAY
ANDORRA	ICELAND	OMAN
ANGOLA	IRAN	PANAMA
ARMENIA	IRAQ	PARAGUAY
AUSTRIA	IRELAND	PERU
BAHAMAS	ISRAEL	QATAR
BANGLADESH	ITALY	RUSSIA
BELARUS	JAPAN	SCOTLAND
BELIZE	KENYA	SPAIN
BENIN	KIRIBATI	SUDAN
BOTSWANA	LAOS	SWEDEN
BRUNEI	LATVIA	SYRIA
CANADA	LEBANON	TAIWAN
CHILE	LIBERIA	TUNISIA
CONGO	LIBYA	TURKEY
DJIBOUTI	LITHUANIA	TUVALU
ECUADOR	MALI	UGANDA
EGYPT	MALTA	UKRAINE
ENGLAND	MEXICO	URUGUAY
ERITREA	MONACO	USA
ETHIOPIA	MONGOLIA	VANUATU
FINLAND	MONTENEGRO	VENEZUELA
FRANCE	MOROCCO	VIETNAM
GABON	NAMIBIA	WALES
GAMBIA	NAURU	YEMEN
GEORGIA	NEPAL	ZAMBIA
GERMANY	NIGER	ZIMBABWE

WORDSEARCH: COUNTRIES

```
Y N A M R E G C A N A D A E T I P
M O N A C O N G O A K B K Z A Q A
E G S M A U G D K W A A Z I D N R
X U D B R U N E I I Y L L L J I A
I G R E O A K A R A R O J E I G G
C Q P U L T C T W T G I A B B E U
O X A E G W S R R N U D B I O R A
R M R T T U O W O M N R R A U I Y
G I A P A N A M A A D A K A T A S
E T Y N B R D Y G N N H N E I I S
N G V E N E Z U E L A O S D Y U C
E R I T R E A D N A L G N E R N O
T L W H S E D A L G N A B A F O T
N V I E T N A M A Y I E L B Z N L
O N P H P S R B A S F E L Y T A A
M O R O C C O I S X B I L U P B N
Z Z E F Q N N U C V B E V E X E D
A E E N I A R K U E A A N A G L J
M N T C U N R C R R L N E D E W S
B A D H U H Z I S U D A N I O F A
I M T O I A A I T A L Y N L R R M
A I T U R O D I M M A L I D G A A
L B V K N R P O T B V R A K I N H
A I H E M I A I R I A J M T A C A
N A B N J Y S M A R N B S E V E B
G L E Y I A E I A V U P W K N I E
O U N A A G P M A L A L G E R I A
L A I R Y S E A E I T G A M B I A
A I N A B L A R N N U A W A L E S
```

RED HERRING

Five of the words below must be entered in the grid, reading across, so as to create five more words reading down. Can you spot the red herring?

AVOID GLARE

DENSE MOIST

EDGED ROMAN

LETTER TRACKER

Starting at the top left corner and ending at the bottom right, track a path from letter to letter, in any direction except diagonally, in order to find 14 hidden countries. All of the letters must be used, but none more than once.

C	W	A	Y	P	Y	T	U	R	K
A	R	O	R	A	A	N	A	Y	E
N	A	N	A	G	U	D	L	S	P
A	D	Y	L	N	E	S	O	P	A
B	E	L	A	E	G	A	L	N	I
N	M	G	T	R	O	M	T	U	N
A	U	I	I	O	C	A	I	S	I
M	I	A	T	P	C	O	N	L	I
I	B	E	G	Y	O	M	G	O	A

DO IT YOURSELF!

In this crossword puzzle, the clues are in alphabetical order and there are no black squares in the grid. Black out the unwanted squares, to produce a symmetrically-patterned grid containing words that can be matched to the clues.

I	D	O	L	E	A	N	C	E	S	T	R	Y
A	R	M	E	T	W	O	O	V	M	A	U	E
M	A	I	N	T	A	I	N	E	A	R	I	D
A	M	T	I	N	Y	S	T	A	R	U	N	E
T	A	P	E	R	A	N	E	U	T	R	O	N
I	H	E	N	O	V	I	M	I	N	P	U	T
C	A	T	T	L	E	A	P	R	A	I	S	E
O	V	A	O	E	H	I	T	I	M	E	V	N
W	E	A	T	H	E	R	O	D	A	R	E	D
I	R	U	I	E	M	O	A	S	T	U	X	I
G	A	N	G	L	E	P	I	D	E	M	I	C
O	G	I	E	D	N	O	D	U	U	O	S	T
D	E	T	R	I	T	U	S	E	R	A	T	E

Acted presumptuously, without permission

Association of criminals

Atmospheric condition

Bovine animals

Catastrophic

Compliment

Conclusion

Debris

Departed

Elementary particle

Gives assistance

Graven image

Have actual being

Intense

Keep in a certain state

Lineage

Merciful

Narrow to a point

Nervous twitch

Non-professional

Open disrespect

Speed of progress

Standard

Striped cat

Theatrical entertainment

Very dry

Well turned-out

Widespread outbreak of disease

NUMBER CRUNCHER

Starting at the top left with the number provided, work
down from one box to another, applying the mathematical
instructions to your running total.

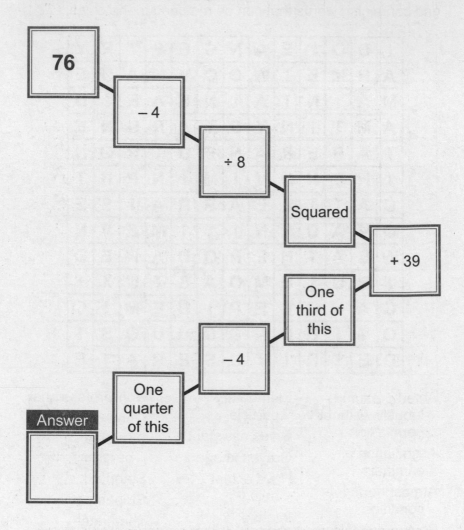

NAME THE DAY

What day is it if the day before yesterday was two days later
in the week than the day after Monday?

JIGSAW PUZZLE

Fit the jigsaw together to reveal eight animals.

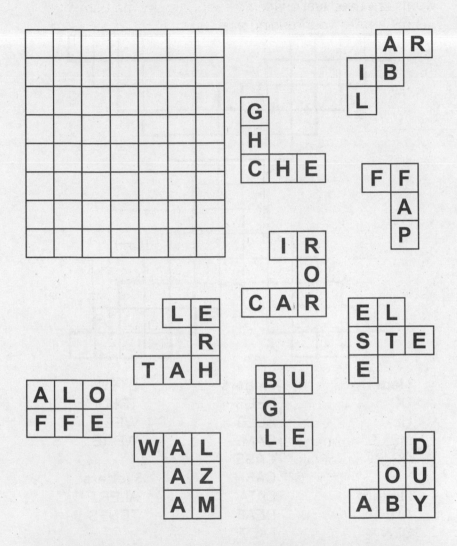

The great secret that all old people share is that you really haven't changed in seventy or eighty years. Your body changes, but you don't change at all. And that, of course, causes great confusion.

Doris Lessing

X MARKS THE SPOT

Fill the grid with the listed words, one letter per square. All words are used just once.

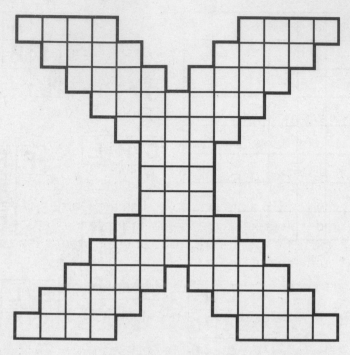

2 letters
DO
HE
ME
US

3 letters
ATE
DEN
LAP
LED
OAR
ONE
WIN

4 letters
BEES
BULB
CAME
CASE
CASH
DATA
DEAF
FACT
FATE
FIRE
HARD
KNOT
OILS
REED
SEED
SEEK

STEW
TOLD
WEED
WERE

5 letters
ALERT
TENTS

7 letters
FORGETS
MEANING
STOMACH

9 letters
CARPENTER
FOLLOWERS

GENERAL KNOWLEDGE QUIZ

Can you identify which one of the multiple-choice answers
(a, b, c or d) is correct for each of the questions below?

1   What is a jota?

    a   A bird   **b**   A Spanish dance

    c   A notepad   **d**   A punctuation mark

2   Of which country is Belmopan the capital?

    a   Honduras   **b**   Lesotho

    c   Belize   **d**   Namibia

3   In which US state would you find the Garden of the
Gods, an area of remarkable formations of eroded red
sandstone rocks resembling animals, gargoyles and
church spires?

    a   Utah   **b**   Arizona

    c   New Mexico   **d**   Colorado

4   Tabei Junko was the first woman to reach the summit
of Mount Everest. What is her nationality?

    a   Thai   **b**   Chinese

    c   Japanese   **d**   Taiwanese

5   Ganymede is the largest moon in the solar system. To
which planet does it belong?

    a   Jupiter   **b**   Uranus

    c   Saturn   **d**   Neptune

6   According to the Bible, Genesis chapter 7 verse 6,
how old was Noah when the flood of the waters was
upon the earth?

    a   969 years old   **b**   666 years old

    c   900 years old   **d**   600 years old

DOUBLE-CROSSER

Two crossword puzzles, but you have to decide which of the solutions to each clue fits into each grid. In both cases, one word has been entered to give you a start.

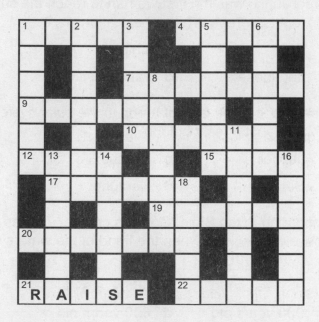

DOUBLE-CROSSER

Across

1 Arouses from slumber; Betting stake (5)

4 Shore of a sea; Tree branch (5)

7 Knaves; Use again after processing (7)

9 Bicycle for two; Boring quality (6)

10 Be in awe of; French form of the name Peter (6)

12 English flower; Give medicine to (4)

15 Drink often mixed with alcohol; Not any (4)

17 Scientific instrument that provides a flashing light; Strand of yarn (6)

19 Bedding material; Form of communication (6)

20 Cataract; Lubricated (7)

21 Advance; Away (5)

22 Notices on public display; Tall perennial grasses (5)

Down

1 Cold season; Desired (6)

2 Decorate; Most merciful (7)

3 Less common; Sweet sticky liquid (5)

5 Gas found in the atmosphere; Takes place (6)

6 Figured out; Of a brownish-yellow shade (6)

8 Diffusing warmth and friendliness; Green gem (7)

11 Decomposing; Habit (7)

13 Canadian capital; Egyptian god (6)

14 Mission; Puts up (6)

16 Faults; To the opposite side (6)

18 Actions; Duck valued for its soft down (5)

ROUND THE BLOCK

Each eight-letter word in the list is hidden in a square around a central letter that is not a part of the word itself, as shown by the example in the grid. The word may start anywhere within its 'square' and go either clockwise or anticlockwise. When all the listed words are found, the central letters spell out the name of a movie star.

```
A Q U A J N A I R E A S
K S M B R K J F I B R M
T E L B O R C K C A N C
C D O C S C R M P Y H Y
I A G K S B A D R O U B
T A M K B O T E D A L U
X T L C E O R P Y L D R
E L C A J T R I B I R A
C E D T P K T O Y L O N
O O B S T E H D A T I C
U R S N I U T T L U G L
E I N E C P A U G C S E
T L C A E D F R A L E T
A B U S C A L G N O S N
R T B B N U O N E P E A
```

ANTELOPE	FLOUNCED
BACKFIRE	INCUBATE
BIRTHDAY ✓	JACKBOOT
BUOYANCY	LADYBIRD
CROSSBAR	OBSTACLE
CULTURAL	PATHETIC
DOGMATIC	SQUABBLE

ROUND THE BEND

Instead of each word being hidden in a straight, continuous line, every word has one bend in it. This bend will not necessarily go off at a right angle; it may go in any direction at all! One word is given as an example.

```
I  T  U  O  H  S  C  W  F  R  W  B
S  N  V  E  M  E  V  O  N  E  M  D
R  P  G  I  A  B  R  O  D  S  O  C
T  L  O  A  R  E  E  N  Y  P  Y  D
W  T  D  E  N  E  E  R  E  H  E  A
L  A  N  V  E  S  T  R  A  T  O  R
X  H  O  A  D  B  I  R  A  B  E  D
R  I  S  R  C  A  P  C  C  E  U  G
O  N  R  B  L  I  Y  T  Y  H  R  R
S  D  E  E  L  S  H  D  V  E  D  A
G  E  P  P  O  M  A  O  S  N  N  N
R  R  P  M  I  Y  E  I  I  P  C  C
O  A  C  C  A  R  T  H  C  R  E  E
C  E  R  Y  K  I  W  L  E  A  S  W
T  M  R  E  W  O  L  F  I  L  U  O
```

APPLICANT	MOSAIC
BRAVEST	NOVEMBER
CAULIFLOWER	OPERATOR
DEBATED ✓	PERSONAL
FORENSIC	RHYTHMIC
GROCERY	SHOUTING
HINDRANCE	WEDNESDAY

WORDSEARCH: LET'S TALK

Can you find all of the listed words hidden in the grid below?
Words run forwards or backwards, in either a horizontal,
vertical or diagonal direction.

```
I G F C L K M I A L C O R P M
Q N Z B R O A C H X O M F R T
W U T N E P P P K N M O N E P
A M T E R L N X P E M G Q P M
J X C A R E T E N R U E U E H
E Z T N C V Q T E S N C T A T
L E F A H Y I L A I I I D T Q
B B U F U O A E P T C O I P E
M K N V N T O O W E A V S Y U
U Y A T E E T J R D T G C B G
M E E E Y M T E R D E A O V N
E L A T P Z P A R W C B U X A
L R D E R S W O B B Q B R X R
T A C R O L N W K E K L S N A
P P L X Q E U D R Q D E E I H
```

BROACH	INTERVIEW	RECITE
COMMUNICATE	JAW	RELATE
DEBATE	MENTION	REPEAT
DISCOURSE	MUMBLE	SPEAK
DRAWL	OPINE	TATTLE
DRONE	PARLEY	TELL
GABBLE	PRATE	UTTER
HARANGUE	PROCLAIM	VOICE

BREAK-TIME CROSSWORD

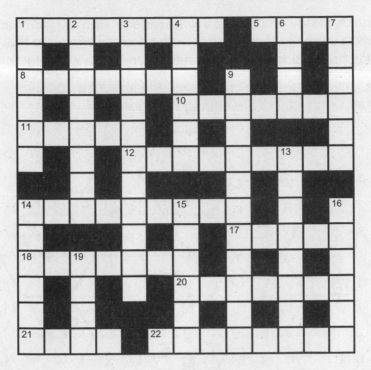

Across

1 Fastened together (8)

5 Be aware of a fact (4)

8 Perform surgery (7)

10 Imaginary sea nymph (7)

11 Jewish spiritual leader (5)

12 Filled to repletion (9)

14 Republic in Central America (5,4)

17 Smallest amount (5)

18 Fixing permanently in place (7)

20 Joyfulness (7)

21 Expressed in words (4)

22 Vigorously active (8)

Down

1 On a plane (6)

2 Shakes, shivers (8)

3 Possessing an extraordinary ability to attract (11)

4 Free from an obligation (6)

6 Star that ejects material (4)

7 Joined in matrimony (6)

9 Fortune-teller's globe (7,4)

13 Dreamer (8)

14 Universe (6)

15 Take up, as of knowledge (6)

16 Cultural (6)

19 Public passenger vehicle (4)

HEXAFIT

Place the listed words into the hexagons, one letter per cell, starting in any of those surrounding a black circle, so that words read clockwise. Some letters are already in place.

The letter is the same in any cell that shares a common border with a cell in a touching hexagon.

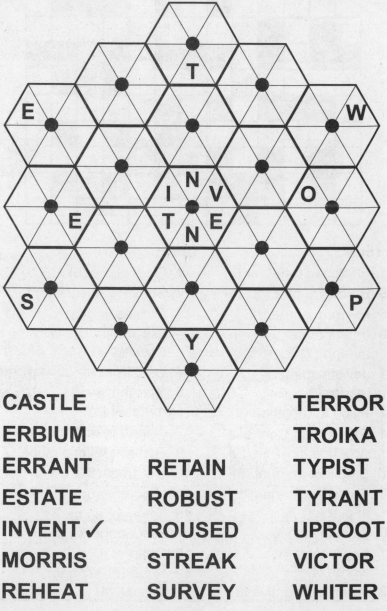

CASTLE

ERBIUM

ERRANT   RETAIN

ESTATE   ROBUST

INVENT ✓   ROUSED

MORRIS   STREAK

REHEAT   SURVEY

TERROR

TROIKA

TYPIST

TYRANT

UPROOT

VICTOR

WHITER

KAKURO

Fill the grid so that each block adds up to the total in the box above or to the left of it.

You can only use the digits 1-9, one per square, but the same digit must not be used twice in a block. The same digit may occur more than once in any row or column, but it must be in a separate block.

SUDOKU

Place one of the numbers from 1 to 9 into every empty cell so that each row, each column and each 3x3 block contains all the numbers from 1 to 9.

			8			4	2	5
2				6	4		3	
	7	9			2	1		
7	4			8		2		
		3	6		1	5		
		5		2			8	6
		4	7			8	9	
	6		5	1				4
3	8	7			9			

Some guy said to me: "Don't you think you're too old to sing rock 'n' roll?"

I said: "You'd better check with Mick Jagger."

Cher

46

DOMINO PLACEMENT

A standard set of twenty-eight dominoes has been laid out as shown below. Can you draw in the edges of them all? One is already in place.

It may be helpful to use the check-box to tick off the dominoes as they are found.

4	4	0	0	0	1	1	6
2	1	1	2	2	3	0	5
3	5	6	2	5	3	2	6
0	2	4	3	0	4	5	0
6	2	1	1	2	4	4	6
1	5	6	0	4	6	6	3
3	3	5	3	5	5	1	4

0-0	0-1	0-2	0-3	0-4	0-5	0-6	1-1

1-2	1-3	1-4	1-5	1-6	2-2	2-3	2-4	2-5	2-6
	✓								

3-3	3-4	3-5	3-6	4-4	4-5	4-6	5-5	5-6	6-6

ALPHAFILL

Place 25 different letters of the alphabet, one per circle, in order to spell out the listed words. Words are formed by moving between adjacent circles along the connecting lines, either horizontally, vertically or diagonally in any direction.

Begin by crossing out the letters already in place, together with the one letter which doesn't appear in any of the words.

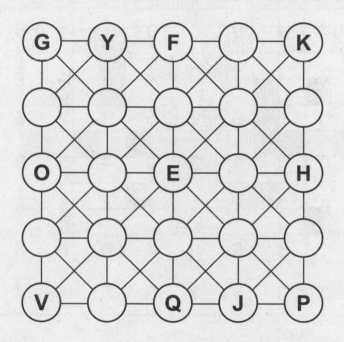

A B C D E F G H I J K L M
N O P Q R S T U V W X Y Z

AXLE	DRY	SORE
BANQUET	FRENETIC	TICK
CHUMP	JUNE	TWELFTH
DODGY	OXEN	VANE
DREW	SANE	WETLY

48

NUMBER FILLER

Can you fit all of the listed numbers into the grid? One is already in place, to get you off to a good start!

| | | | | | | | | | 8 | 5 | 8 | 3 |

2 digits	662	3146	8296	53648
48	732	3239	8400	68226
65	765	3241	8583	73457
79	904	3734	8601	79085
84 ✓	940	3765	9163	83754
	994	4587	9672	84662
		4881		93360
3 digits		5140	**5 digits**	
257	**4 digits**	5736	19442	**6 digits**
267	1217	6163	35881	513103
423	1583	6207	41278	557049
438	2099	6969	51999	845029
455	2479	7464	52987	954719
537	2715			

BREAK-TIME CROSSWORD

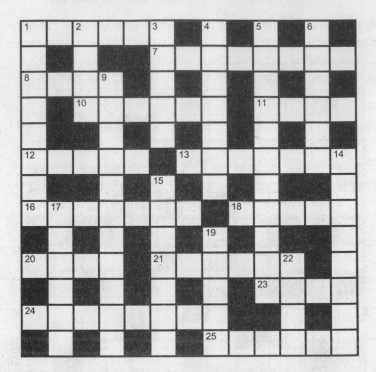

Across
1 Come into view (6)
7 Popular frozen dessert (3,5)
8 Coarse file (4)
10 Natural gift (6)
11 Second letter of the Greek alphabet (4)
12 List of contents of a book (5)
13 Destroy the peace of (7)
16 Sparkle (7)
18 Parts of a plant typically found under the ground (5)
20 Strong wind (4)
21 Swore (6)
23 Gown (4)
24 Send another way (8)
25 One of four playing-card suits (6)

Down
1 Concurring (8)
2 Former (4)
3 Large natural stream of water (5)
4 Positive (7)
5 Someone undergoing a trial period (11)
6 Person who serves at table (6)
9 Punctuation mark, bracket (11)
14 Commercial enterprise (8)
15 Educator (7)
17 Refrains from taking (6)
19 Thin meat soup (5)
22 Swinging or sliding barrier (4)

CODEWORD

Every letter in this puzzle has been replaced by a number, the number remaining the same for that letter wherever it occurs. Every letter of the alphabet has been used. Substitute numbers for letters to complete the codeword.

It may help to cross off the letters beneath the grid to keep a track of progress, and to use the reference box showing which numbers have been decoded. Three letters have already been entered into the grid, to help you on your way.

21	2	4	22	9		15	13	17	25 C	13 A	24 R	13
13		16		13		16		23		14		21
17	19	11	13	14	16	24		25	9	2	26	13
10		17		16		8	13	22		8		3
2	4	23	13		3	2	22		21	2	18	23
17			20	16	26	4	16	14	13		11	
9	23	24	16		2		26		14	11	26	20
	15		26	23	20	14	23	25	22			14
1	11	24	12		9	13	4		5	23	24	16
11		11		17	22	12		8		24		13
4	23	14	7	23		2	26	23	6	13	25	22
20		23		13		26		13		17		23
23	13	24	10	14	11	20		22	24	23	26	4

A B C D E F G H I J K L M

N O P Q R S T U V W X Y Z

1	2	3	4	5	6	7	8	9	10	11	12	13 A
14	15	16	17	18	19	20	21	22	23	24 R	25 C	26

ROUND DOZEN

First solve the clues. All of the solutions begin with the letter in the central circle, and some others are already in place. When the puzzle is complete, you can then go on to discover the twelve-letter word reading clockwise around the outermost ring of letters.

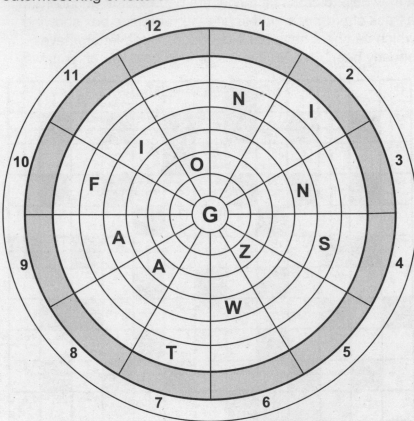

1 Leadership, counsel
2 Extremely large
3 Famous Apache chief
4 Male offspring of one's own child
5 Spanish vegetable soup, served cold
6 Beetle also known as the lightning bug or firefly

7 Mural scribbling or drawing
8 Pertaining to the Milky Way, for example
9 Athletics facilities
10 Flowing in movement
11 Earliest stage of development
12 Throughout the world

The twelve-letter word is: _____

JIGSAW SUDOKU

Fit the numbers 1, 2, 3, 4, 5 and 6 into the grid in such a way that each horizontal row, each vertical column and each of the heavily outlined sections of six squares each contains a different number. Some numbers are already in place.

		5		4	1
				5	2
1				6	
					6
6					

WHAT DOES IT MEAN?

Which of the following is the correct definition of the word:

CLAQUE

1 The fine cracking that occurs in the varnish or pigment of old paintings

2 A lively Polish dance, or the music for such a dance

3 A group of followers hired to applaud at a performance

SPIDOKU

In the spider's web below, each of the eight segments should be filled with a different number from 1 to 8, in such a way that every ring also contains a different number from 1 to 8.

The segments run from the outside of the spider's web to the middle, and the rings run all the way around. So that you can see the rings more clearly, we've shaded them grey and white.

Some numbers are already in place. Can you fill in the rest?

CUBE ROUTES

Fill the words into the grid (one letter is ready in place),
changing route where necessary, as with this example:

ASPECT   ENDURE   SPED

CARE   REASON   WRITHE

CASE   ROE

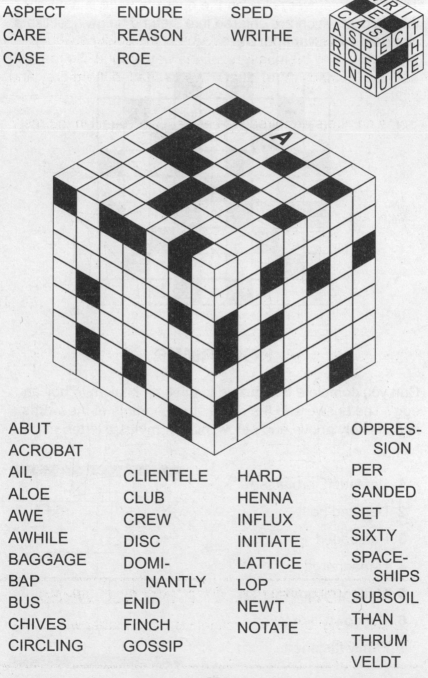

ABUT

ACROBAT

AIL   CLIENTELE   HARD

ALOE   CLUB   HENNA

AWE   CREW   INFLUX

AWHILE   DISC   INITIATE

BAGGAGE   DOMI-   LATTICE

BAP   NANTLY   LOP

BUS   ENID   NEWT

CHIVES   FINCH   NOTATE

CIRCLING   GOSSIP

OPPRES-
SION

PER

SANDED

SET

SIXTY

SPACE-
SHIPS

SUBSOIL

THAN

THRUM

VELDT

NUMBER CRUNCHER CROSSWORD

A little mathematical crossword, where a little knowledge of mathematics will come in very handy!

The answer to every clue on the opposite page is a number, the digits of which are entered into the grid below, just like a standard crossword puzzle.

EGG TIMER

Can you complete this puzzle in the time it takes to boil an egg? The answers to the clues are anagrams of the words immediately above and below, plus or minus a letter.

1 Defended, protected

2 Debated hotly

3 Persuaded

4 Ill-mannered

5 Made well again

6 Cut down

7 Firmly fastened

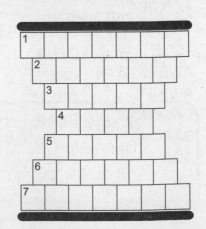

NUMBER CRUNCHER CROSSWORD

Across

1 Pounds in eight stone (3)

4 8 Down multiplied by three (3)

6 12 Down plus 17041 (5)

9 27 Down plus 42 (2)

11 28 Across plus 7 Down plus seven eighths of 12 Across (3)

12 22 Down multiplied by two (2)

13 4 Down plus 23 (2)

15 13 Across plus 44 (2)

16 28 Across multiplied by 13 (4)

17 24 Across plus 3 Down plus 145 (4)

18 9 Across plus 4 Down plus two (2)

20 Seven squared (2)

21 Feet in four yards (2)

22 4 Down squared plus 20 Across (3)

24 2 Down plus 4 Down (2)

26 10 Down plus 23 Down plus 1134 (5)

28 26 Down multiplied by 11 (3)

29 1 Down plus 2 Down plus 26 (3)

Down

1 26 Down multiplied by four (3)

2 Five squared (2)

3 8 Down multiplied by 21 Down (4)

4 22 Down minus ten (2)

5 1 Across multiplied by four (3)

7 Months in seven years (2)

8 23 Down minus 20 (2)

10 8 Down multiplied by 15 Down (5)

12 204 squared minus 23 (5)

14 One sixth of 3 Down (3)

15 14 Down plus 105 (3)

19 4 Across multiplied by 12 Across (4)

21 4 Across plus 23 Down minus 20 Across (3)

22 Square root of 576 (2)

23 12 Across plus ten (2)

25 14 Down plus 200 (3)

26 22 Down plus two-thirds of 21 Across (2)

27 One nineteenth of 14 Down (2)

He who is of a calm and happy nature will hardly feel the pressure of age, but to him who is of an opposite disposition, youth and age are equally a burden.

Plato

LINK WORDS

Fit eight different words into the grid, so that each one links up with the words on either side, eg table - lamp - shade.

When finished, read down the letters in the shaded squares to reveal another word, solving the clue.

SUMMER					FIRE
FAIL					GUARD
RIVER					BALANCE
UNDER					SOME
FALLEN					ENEMY
SPIDER					NEBULA
PAPER					ART
SWEET					FLAKES

Clue: Fruit _____

BERMUDA TRIANGLE

Travel through the 'Bermuda Triangle', collecting a letter from each area. You can visit any area once only, and you must enter and exit through the holes in the walls between them. The starting letter may appear in any area.

When you've completed your tour, the 15 letters (in order) will spell out the name of an author.

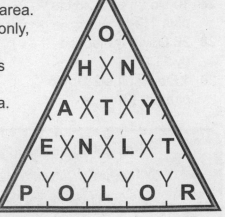

Author: _____

WORD LADDER

Change one letter at a time (but not the position of any letter) to make a new word – and move from the word at the top of the ladder to the word at the bottom using the exact number of rungs provided.

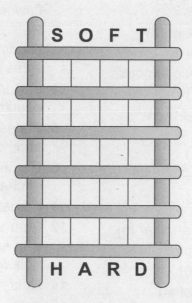

MEMORY TEST

Study the picture below for a few moments, then turn to page 95.

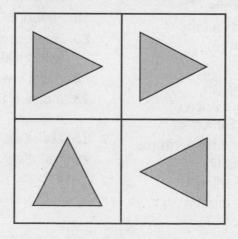

GENERAL KNOWLEDGE CROSSWORD

Across

4 Implement, tool (7)

7 Male graduate (7)

8 Most noticeable or important (7)

9 Written account (7)

10 Region of north-eastern France famous for its wines (6)

13 American city (3,4)

16 Efficient use of resources (7)

17 Characteristic mental attitude (7)

19 Message sent from one computer to another (5)

21 Meeting of spiritualists (6)

24 Bodyguard (6)

27 Subdivision of an act of a play (5)

28 Prisoner held as a form of insurance (7)

31 Fire-breathing monster in Greek mythology (7)

33 Sun umbrella (7)

34 Walks with a lofty, proud gait (6)

36 Study of living organisms (7)

38 Former province of northern Ethiopia (7)

39 Physician who performs operations (7)

40 Greek goddess of divine retribution and vengeance (7)

Down

1 In the process of losing hair (7)

2 Partially opened flowers (4)

3 Regions on diametrically opposite sides of the Earth (9)

4 Former communist country (inits) (4)

5 Plates covering the ends of the fingers (5)

6 Gamble, game of chance (7)

11 Female wild cat (7)

12 Pear-shaped fruit with green skin ripening to black (7)

14 Notify of danger (4)

15 John ___, English Romantic poet (1795–1821) (5)

17 Hebrew prophet and lawgiver, brother of Aaron (5)

18 Hideout (3)

20 Espresso coffee with milk (5)

22 Artist's workroom (7)

23 Inclined to show mercy (7)

25 Make an incision (3)

26 Relatively low in price (5)

GENERAL KNOWLEDGE CROSSWORD

29 Right side of a ship to someone facing the bow (9)

30 European mountain range (4)

31 Water tank (7)

32 Stripping (skin) (7)

35 Remove a knot (5)

36 Lowest adult male singing voice (4)

37 Follow instruction (4)

SUDOKU

Place one of the numbers from 1 to 9 into every empty cell so that each row, each column and each 3x3 block contains all the numbers from 1 to 9.

	9			1			4	
		7	2		8	1		
5		1	3		9	7		8
	1		8	5	6		3	
2		6				5		1
	3		7	2	1		8	
9		4	6		2	8		3
		2	1		5	4		
	7			8			2	

As you get older you must remember you have a second hand.

The first one is to help yourself. The second hand is to help others.

Audrey Hepburn

JIGWORD

A symmetrical crossword has been cut into pieces. Can you put it back together? Three pieces are already in position.

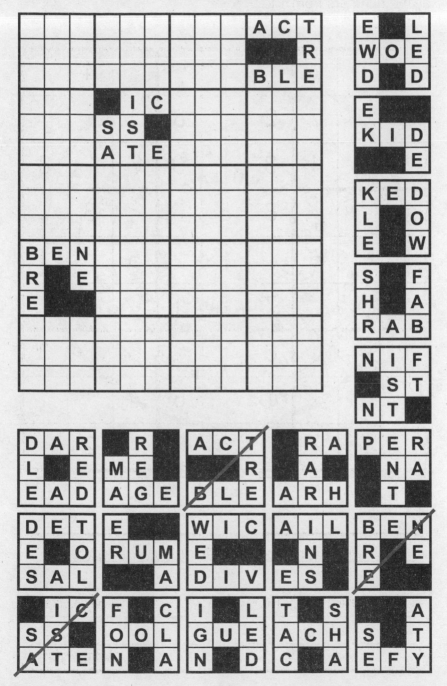

RING-WORDS

From the 32 segments below, find 16 eight-letter words by pairing one set of four letters with another.

All of the segments must be used once only.

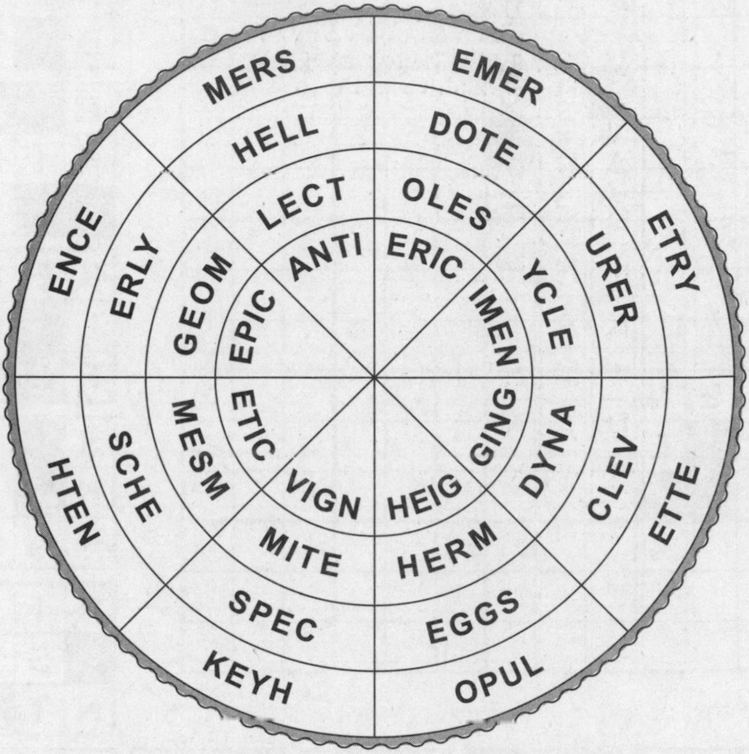

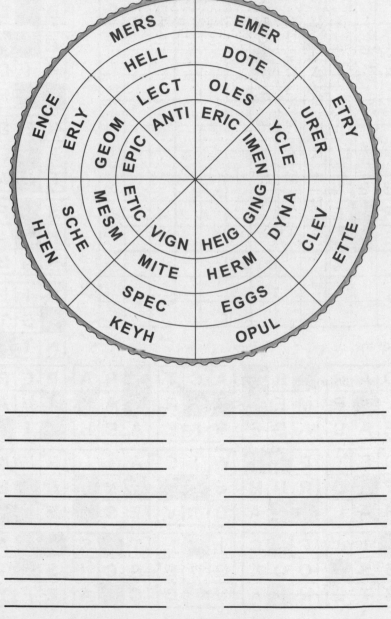

AROUND THE SQUARES

The answer to each clue is a four-letter word, to be entered in the four squares surrounding the corresponding number in the grid. The word can start in any of the four squares and read either clockwise or anticlockwise. The first has already been entered.

	R							
D	1 A	2		3		4		5	
	N							
	6		7		8		9		10
	11		12		13		14		15
	16		17		18		19		20
	21		22		23		24		25

1 South African currency unit
2 High
3 Prison room
4 Speed contest
5 Duo
6 River of Egypt
7 Wicked
8 Lazy, at rest
9 Scottish valley
10 Low-rank chess piece
11 Cultivated area of grass
12 Authorisation to enter a country
13 Passed away
14 Boundary
15 Feeble
16 Melt, defrost
17 Halt
18 Headland
19 Coin of the USA
20 Forearm bone
21 Loathe
22 Item of footwear
23 Native of Bangkok, for example
24 Agitate
25 Slither

WORDSEARCH: CAPITAL CITIES

Can you find all of the listed capital cities of the world in the grid opposite? They run forwards or backwards, in either a horizontal, vertical or diagonal direction.

ABUJA
ACCRA
AMMAN
ANDORRA LA
   VELLA
ANTANANARIVO
APIA
ASMARA
ASTANA
BAKU
BANDAR SERI
   BEGAWAN
BANGKOK
BANGUI
BANJUL
BEIRUT
BELFAST
BERNE
BISSAU
BOGOTA
BRATISLAVA
CAIRO
COLOMBO
DAKAR
DHAKA
DILI
DOHA
GABORONE
HANOI

HARARE
HAVANA
ISLAMABAD
KABUL
KIEV
KIGALI
LA PAZ
LIMA
LISBON
LOME
LUANDA
MADRID
MALABO
MALE
MANILA
MAPUTO
MASERU
MBABANE
MINSK
MORONI
MOSCOW
NAIROBI
NIAMEY
NUKU'ALOFA
OSLO
OTTAWA
PARIS
PRAGUE
PRAIA

QUITO
RABAT
RIGA
RIYADH
ROME
ROSEAU
SAINT JOHN'S
SAN JOSE
SANA'A
SANTO
   DOMINGO
SEOUL
SKOPJE
SOFIA
SUVA
TAIPEI
TARAWA ATOLL
THIMPHU
TIRANA
TOKYO
TUNIS
VADUZ
VALLETTA
VIENNA
VILNIUS
WARSAW
YAOUNDE
YAREN
YEREVAN

WORDSEARCH: CAPITAL CITIES

```
B A N G U I S L A M A B A D A M A
A N T A N A N A R I V O D E R B N
N S P A I U H A I F O S B O C A D
D I T N K R A A N N A C U O C B O
A E Z A P D O D N W T R L V A A R
R G B S N T U B A O A J O O A N R
S I I A U A B T I K I Q O M M E A
E S U R E A T V A Y P B V H E E L
R L I S B O N D A P E T A D N A A
I E O W A S R A W L I R O N P S V
B R A T I S L A V A L T E A J E E
E O H E G L Y I C A U E Z V I U L
G P G D U T H I M P H U T K A A L
A S K O P J E D A A G E A T K N A
W B E H T A Q M E U G A R P A A O
A S M A R A R U A R I Y A D H R S
N U F H A Z A I I L A H W N D I U
S A N J O S E M S T E B A Y N T I
P A U X S P I I A F O L A U K U N
R B N I L N C N O Y K O T T L W L
A K B T O M A S E R U L O K U T I
I H B R O Z I K M N N P L A B Y V
A Q O M A D R I D I B E L F A S T
V M A L A B O E A A C I P R K Q M
A I M W U I Q M N E N R E B I X O
D L E A M C E G I A S N V O G N S
U I F N N Y K V M N E R A R A H C
Z D Q E N O R O B A G A O S L J O
Z G Q K K A O B M O L O C H I Z W
```

RED HERRING

Five of the words below must be entered in the grid, reading across, so as to create five more words reading down. Can you spot the red herring?

ANISE   MAGMA

ARRAS   MANES

DEANS   MOSES

LETTER TRACKER

Starting at the top left corner and ending at the bottom right, track a path from letter to letter, in any direction except diagonally, in order to find 14 hidden musical instruments. All of the letters must be used, but none more than once.

T	R	U	B	A	T	E	H	A	R
O	R	M	T	S	U	A	C	I	M
M	T	P	E	S	L	S	I	N	O
B	T	E	N	O	F	A	T	N	O
O	R	P	I	O	N	R	I	A	B
N	A	T	R	A	L	C	P	N	A
E	H	U	B	A	I	O	N	J	O
A	T	I	U	G	D	O	C	E	R
R	A	C	C	O	R	R	D	E	R

DO IT YOURSELF!

In this crossword puzzle, the clues are in alphabetical order and there are no black squares in the grid. Black out the unwanted squares, to produce a symmetrically-patterned grid containing words that can be matched to the clues.

C	H	I	S	E	L	O	A	M	A	D	E	I
A	R	N	O	D	E	U	N	I	C	O	R	N
M	I	A	M	I	V	N	O	N	E	G	U	T
E	D	C	A	T	E	C	O	T	A	S	T	E
L	O	T	R	I	L	O	G	Y	L	O	U	R
L	E	I	S	O	O	N	A	E	F	L	O	E
I	V	V	A	N	O	S	E	D	M	I	S	S
F	E	E	D	I	M	C	A	R	A	T	O	T
E	L	A	M	B	R	I	G	A	D	E	A	R
L	A	S	S	O	L	O	S	C	A	R	E	H
E	L	I	N	G	A	U	E	U	S	A	G	E
S	U	C	C	E	S	S	L	L	E	T	U	A
S	T	K	E	Y	E	L	L	A	M	E	N	T

Able to read and
write
Army unit
Bram Stoker's
vampire
Canine creatures
Carpenter's tool
Employment
Feast upon
Flat mass of ice
floating at sea
Florida resort
Having a menthol
piquancy
Hawaiian garland
of flowers

Idle
Issue of a book
Lacking
excitement or
activity
Make warm
Noosed rope
Not in good
health
One-horned
beast of legend
One stroke over
par in golf
Pried
Reached a
destination

Sense of
concern or
curiosity
Sense of good
style
Set of three
related literary
or dramatic
works
Song or hymn of
mourning
Stunned,
knocked out
Victory
Young child

DICE SECTION

Printed onto every one of the six numbered dice are six letters (one per side), which can be rearranged to form the answer to each clue; however, some sides are invisible to you. Use the clues and write every answer into the grid. When correctly filled, the letters in the shaded squares, reading in the order 1 to 6, will spell out the name of a breed of dog.

1 Floor covering

2 Foaming

3 Nearly

4 Monetary plan

5 Arthurian magician

6 Hard-cased arthropod

JIGSAW PUZZLE

Fit the jigsaw together to reveal eight islands.

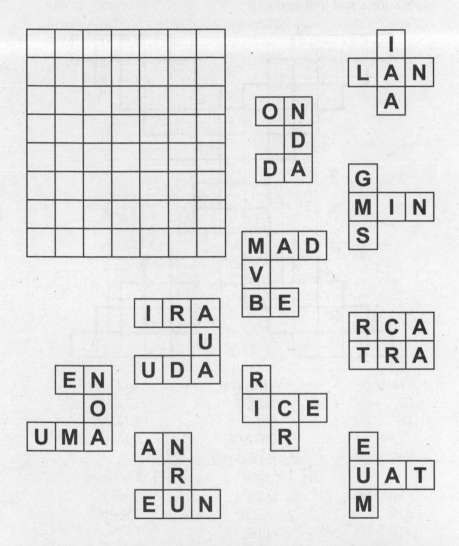

The game of life is a game of boomerangs. Our thoughts, deeds and words return to us sooner or later with astounding accuracy.

Florence Scovel Shinn

X MARKS THE SPOT

Fill the grid with the listed words, one letter per square. All words are used just once.

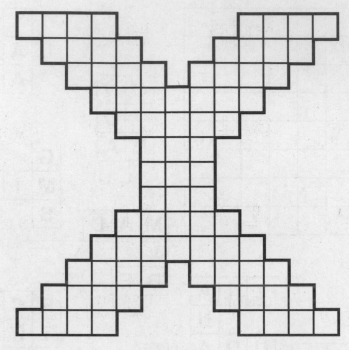

2 letters
IS
OF
SO
WE

3 letters
ALL
ARE
ILL
LAD
MAT
TEN
TOY

4 letters
BODY
DIAL
DRAG
EYED
LOAF
LOAN
LOOP
NINE
OILS
PONY
REAR
RIOT
SANG
SEAL
SEED
SELF

SLIT
SLOW
SNOW
WAIT

5 letters
DISCO
TREND

7 letters
NEAREST
PIONEER
PROTEIN

9 letters
FORMATION
SENTENCES

HALF AND HALF

Pair off these groups of three letters to name eight flowering plants, each comprising six letters.

VIA THR MAL ZIN

LET SAL CUS OSA

LOW LIA VIO DAH

CRO NIA MIM IFT

_____   _____

_____   _____

_____   _____

_____   _____

We shall not cease from exploration

And at the end of all our exploring

Will be to arrive where we started

And know the place for the first time.

T S Eliot

DOUBLE-CROSSER

Two crossword puzzles, but you have to decide which of the solutions to each clue fits into each grid. In both cases, one word has been entered to give you a start.

DOUBLE-CROSSER

Across

1 Organism that has undergone a genetic change;
Woven floor covering (6)

6 Capital of Cuba; Detesting (6)

8 Double-barrelled firearm; Make comprehensible (7)

9 Involuntary expulsion of air from the nose;
Without a sound (6)

10 Medium for communication; Object that has survived
from the past (5)

13 Fill with gas or air; Set apart from others (7)

16 Filled with a great quantity; Insect in the stage
between egg and pupa (5)

18 Break of day; Country, capital Belgrade (6)

20 Inhabitant of a town or community; Microchip
element (7)

21 Moved about secretively and furtively; Smaller in
amount (6)

22 Sweet; Without danger (6)

Down

1 Mean person; Unclouded (5)

2 Accomplish; Structure supporting the lower limbs (6)

3 In the way indicated; The thing here (4)

4 Became broader; Supplier of refreshments (7)

5 Consent; Religious belief (5)

7 Creature; Yearly (6)

11 Depart from the main subject; Room where books are
kept (7)

12 Direction; Place of work (6)

14 List of fixed charges; Removing (6)

15 In golf, a hole played in two strokes under par;
Song used to praise the deity (5)

17 Child's nurse; Make angry (5)

19 Affected manners intended to impress others;
Gives assistance (4)

ROUND THE BLOCK

Each eight-letter word in the list is hidden in a square around a central letter that is not a part of the word itself, as shown by the example in the grid. The word may start anywhere within its 'square' and go either clockwise or anticlockwise. When all the listed words are found, the central letters spell out the name of a comedy duo.

ACADEMIC   MINISTER

CONTINUE   NONSENSE

DEFENDER   PLANKTON

FLAGRANT   ROSEMARY ✓

GALACTIC   SEVERITY

GRANDSON   VACATION

MANAGING   ZEPPELIN

ROUND THE BEND

Instead of each word being hidden in a straight, continuous line, every word has one bend in it. This bend will not necessarily go off at a right angle; it may go in any direction at all! One word is given as an example.

```
I N R U F Q S O L B A D
T Y Y Z U L S I V E I D
U G S M P C K K N S A Q
R N D Y E D S C T G S R
E I P N R O I A S M U A
E R A P W T C O N A L L
Z E I H S E Y I L C E K
S P I A O E X D R A E I
S S T N A F N C S E N X
G L E X X J O P S P M G
X N U L G R   Y A E R U
D E I F D T T R V M U A
F C T H E Y A E Z D T G
B E B U T C R P N X T E
Z F F A H Y T S I G E R
```

ANECDOTE   PARACHUTE

CORDLESS   REGISTRATION ✓

DISTANCE   REPULSIVE

EVERYTHING   SINGULAR

FANTASTIC   SPITEFUL

FURNITURE   TURMERIC

LANGUAGE   WHISPERING

WORDSEARCH: TIME AND TIME AGAIN

Can you find all of the listed words relating to time hidden in the grid below? Words run forwards or backwards, in either a horizontal, vertical or diagonal direction.

```
D G L A U G N I N E V E L W E
L A N O O N R E T F A E B C T
Y T T I U Z M M L R C Y K E U
R T H E N F H N O N T Q Y R N
O E R G U R H K O N O O J M I
T W O S I A O E I O U O N U M
S O A S S N R M Y S E C S I E
I R O T E O T E D A R W F N T
H R E H Y T S R N E U E E N W
E O D V C T W A O S T X E E X
H M K Z E O P I C F U O L L K
T O Y R N A P S E O F T A L T
O T D E C A D E S E S T T I U
U A U E K F E N O G E I C M O
Y R U T N E C T X R E V E N H
```

AFTERNOON	HASTE	PACE
CENTURY	HISTORY	SEASON
DECADE	LATER	SECOND
EPOCH	MILLENNIUM	SOON
EVENING	MINUTE	TOMORROW
FORTNIGHT	MORNING	WEEK
FUTURE	NEVER	YESTERDAY
GONE	ONCE	YORE

BREAK-TIME CROSSWORD

Across

1 Put on clothes (7)
5 Alcoholic apple drink (5)
9 Plunge (into water) (4)
10 The longest typewriter key (5,3)
11 Distance downwards (5)
12 Competition (7)
14 Father or mother (6)
16 US coin worth one twentieth of a dollar (6)
18 Nearest planet to the Sun (7)
20 Largest artery of the body (5)
22 Rough guess (8)
24 Tortilla rolled around a filling (4)
25 Heavenly messenger (5)
26 Feeling guilt or remorse (7)

Down

2 Repeat again and again (9)
3 Enfold (7)
4 Compass point (4)
6 Dormant (5)
7 Historical period (3)
8 Body of water cut off by a reef of coral (6)
13 Visually striking display (9)
15 Plaid associated with Scotland (6)
17 Country, capital Zagreb (7)
19 Unlawful act (5)
21 Professional charges (4)
23 Male child (3)

HEXAFIT

Place the listed words into the hexagons, one letter per cell, starting in any of those surrounding a black circle, so that words read clockwise. Some letters are already in place.

The letter is the same in any cell that shares a common border with a cell in a touching hexagon.

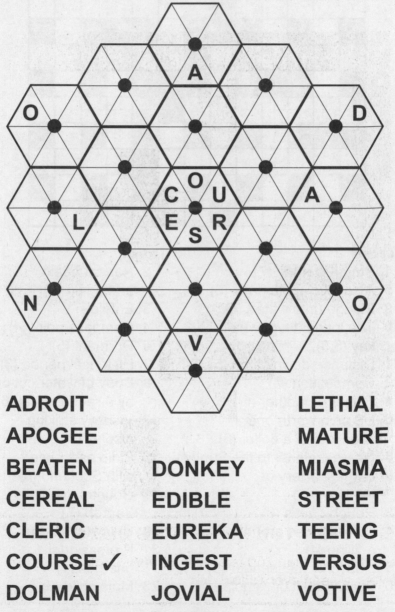

ADROIT		LETHAL
APOGEE		MATURE
BEATEN	DONKEY	MIASMA
CEREAL	EDIBLE	STREET
CLERIC	EUREKA	TEEING
COURSE ✓	INGEST	VERSUS
DOLMAN	JOVIAL	VOTIVE

80

KAKURO

Fill the grid so that each block adds up to the total in the box above or to the left of it.

You can only use the digits 1-9, one per square, but the same digit must not be used twice in a block. The same digit may occur more than once in any row or column, but it must be in a separate block.

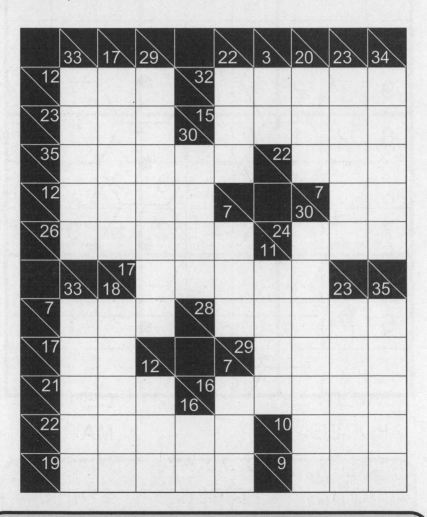

SUDOKU

Place one of the numbers from 1 to 9 into every empty cell so that each row, each column and each 3x3 block contains all the numbers from 1 to 9.

			3	8	1			
	6	3		7			4	5
9		2					7	
8	2	1	7					6
		4	1		3	2		
7					2	5	9	1
	4					9		2
6	7			2		3	1	
			5	3	4			

Twenty years of romance make a woman look like a ruin, but

twenty years of marriage make her something like a public building.

Oscar Wilde

DOMINO PLACEMENT

A standard set of twenty-eight dominoes has been laid out as shown below. Can you draw in the edges of them all? One is already in place.

It may be helpful to use the check-box to tick off the dominoes as they are found.

6	4	5	2	3	2	0	4
6	1	1	1	2	1	1	6
3	5	3	6	5	2	2	1
3	2	5	0	6	0	1	4
4	4	5	2	0	4	0	5
3	6	2	3	3	4	6	4
1	0	0	3	5	0	6	5

0 - 0	0 - 1	0 - 2	0 - 3	0 - 4	0 - 5	0 - 6	1 - 1

1 - 2	1 - 3	1 - 4	1 - 5	1 - 6	2 - 2	2 - 3	2 - 4	2 - 5	2 - 6

3 - 3	3 - 4	3 - 5	3 - 6	4 - 4	4 - 5	4 - 6	5 - 5	5 - 6	6 - 6
		✓							

ALPHAFILL

Place 25 different letters of the alphabet, one per circle, in order to spell out the listed words. Words are formed by moving between adjacent circles along the connecting lines, either horizontally, vertically or diagonally in any direction.

Begin by crossing out the letters already in place, together with the one letter which doesn't appear in any of the words.

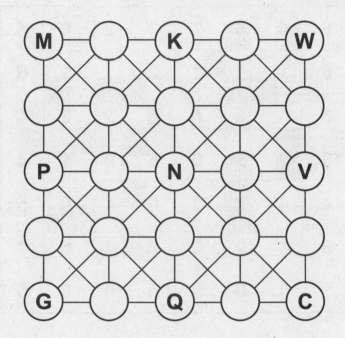

A   B   C   D   E   F   G   H   I   J   K   L   M

N   O   P   Q   R   S   T   U   V   W   X   Y   Z

APEX	GRANITE	OVINE
BRAN	GRUNT	SQUINT
CLUB	HEAR	THEME
DONATE	JAUNTY	TOKEN
FLINT	MENTION	WOKEN

NUMBER FILLER

Can you fit all of the listed numbers into the grid? One is already in place, to get you off to a good start!

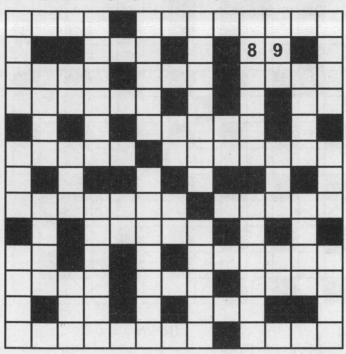

2 digits	3 digits	4 digits	5 digits	7 digits
15	135	2809	22057	1825711
32	200	3753	30683	6817792
48	285	4236	39152	7813186
51	450	4739	49252	8126494
54	499	4896	50913	
79	521	5053	63145	**8 digits**
80	547	6113		34761478
89 ✓	691	6610	**6 digits**	71535407
96	711	7760	189027	
97	942	7860	233435	
		8120	323776	
		8876	546023	
		9647	623541	
		9922	974558	

BREAK-TIME CROSSWORD

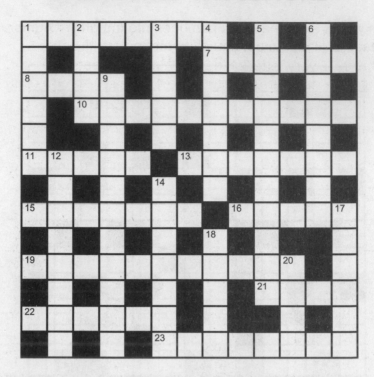

Across

1 US state in the Rocky Mountains (8)
7 Promise solemnly and formally (6)
8 Long narrative poem (4)
10 Become worse or disintegrate (11)
11 French composer (1875–1937) (5)
13 Throb (7)
15 Reflects (7)
16 Use jointly or in common (5)
19 In a foul mood (3-8)
21 Citrus fruit (4)
22 Turn into (6)
23 Unaffected by the passing years (8)

Down

1 Intelligent (6)
2 Produced an egg (4)
3 Monastery (5)
4 Best amount possible under given circumstances (7)
5 Rotating fairground ride (6,5)
6 Political troublemaker (8)
9 Occasion for festivities to mark a happy event (11)
12 Lively (8)
14 Valved brass instrument (7)
17 Quantity much larger than is needed (6)
18 Poison of snakes, etc (5)
20 Gaming cubes (4)

CODEWORD

Every letter in this puzzle has been replaced by a number, the number remaining the same for that letter wherever it occurs. Every letter of the alphabet has been used. Substitute numbers for letters to complete the codeword.

It may help to cross off the letters beneath the grid to keep a track of progress, and to use the reference box showing which numbers have been decoded. Three letters have already been entered into the grid, to help you on your way.

15	7	10	5	26	7		14	12	5	19	23	1
9		12			10	23	7		4			7
7	18	7	11		13		21	12	17	23		5
1		1	23	13	22	19	16		15	21	7	19
23			3		4		17			9	22	3
15 S	7 A	3 T	5	19		8	12	12	10	12	25	6
	25			19		1		3		12		23
17	7	11	7	1	12	20		2	22	7	11	3
23	26	23			12		7		19			7
10	23	7	1		11	23	18	22	25	23		15
26		1	11	23	24		3		23	7	15	3
5			22		7	25	23			21		23
21	10	22	4	15	6		11	22	15	9	23	1

A B C D E F G H I J K L M

N O P Q R S T U V W X Y Z

1	2	3 T	4	5	6	7 A	8	9	10	11	12	13
14	15 S	16	17	18	19	20	21	22	23	24	25	26

SUM TOTAL

Fill each empty square so that every row contains ten different numbers from 0 to 9. In columns, the numbers may be repeated. The black squares show the sum total of the numbers in each column.

Wherever one square touches another either vertically or diagonally, the numbers must be different. Some are already in place.

		7		0		8			2
1		0		3	2		7	8	9
5		6	2				0		
					9	5			
3	0				2		1	9	7
9	5	8	2	4		7	0		
27	25	32	26	14	25	37	23	32	29

DO IT DIFFERENTLY

Of course you know the alphabet: A, B, C, etc, but just how fast can you say it aloud, with the letters all in their correct alphabetical order? Time yourself.

And can you say it backwards? It's not as easy as you think, especially if you have been saying it forwards a few times!

You can also try counting back numbers from one hundred, first counting only the even numbers, then the odd numbers. Now count backwards from 99, only saying aloud those numbers that are divisible by three.

JIGSAW SUDOKU

Fit the numbers 1, 2, 3, 4, 5 and 6 into the grid in such a way that each horizontal row, each vertical column and each of the heavily outlined sections of six squares each contains a different number. Some numbers are already in place.

	2				
		2		1	
	4				
					3
				6	
5	1		3		

WHAT DOES IT MEAN?

Which of the following is the correct definition of the word:

PANDICULATION

1 The insertion of a cannula or tube into a hollow body organ
2 The act of stretching and yawning, especially on waking
3 The view or theory that the self is all that can be known to exist

SPIDOKU

In the spider's web below, each of the eight segments should be filled with a different number from 1 to 8, in such a way that every ring also contains a different number from 1 to 8.

The segments run from the outside of the spider's web to the middle, and the rings run all the way around. So that you can see the rings more clearly, we've shaded them grey and white.

Some numbers are already in place. Can you fill in the rest?

CUBE ROUTES

Fill the words into the grid (one letter is ready in place), changing route where necessary, as with this example:

ASPECT	ENDURE	SPED
CARE	REASON	WRITHE
CASE	ROE	

ANEW			
ANT			TAME
CAVERN			THUS
CORNET	GARDEN	POT	TIED
DANCE	HER	RENT	TILT
DIG	ICON	RETURN	TOR
DOTE	MOTHER	RIFLING	TWITTER
END	NINE	RIGID	URN
ENDURE	ONE	SCARLET	WELD
ERECT	ORE	SECONDED	WHIP
FOURTH	OVERDONE	TACT	WISE

91

NUMBER CRUNCHER CROSSWORD

A little mathematical crossword, where a little knowledge of mathematics will come in very handy!

The answer to every clue on the opposite page is a number, the digits of which are entered into the grid below, just like a standard crossword puzzle.

1	2		3		4		5	6
7							8	
		9		10		11		
12						13		
		14						
15						16		17
		18	19		20			
21	22						23	
24					25			

EGG TIMER

Can you complete this puzzle in the time it takes to boil an egg? The answers to the clues are anagrams of the words immediately above and below, plus or minus a letter.

1 Carrying

2 Get back

3 Ire

4 Toothed wheel

5 Tally

6 Treat, entertain

7 Comprehensive

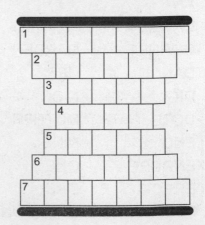

NUMBER CRUNCHER CROSSWORD

Across

1 15 Down plus 20 Down plus nine (4)

4 12 Across plus 13 Across plus 2 Down plus six (4)

7 5 Down plus half of 22 Down (2)

8 20 per cent of 240 (2)

9 9 Down minus 2815 (5)

12 One quarter of 6 Down (3)

13 One sixth of 6 Down (3)

14 310 squared plus 3 Down minus 60 (5)

15 8 Across plus 13 Across plus 20 Down minus five (3)

16 12 Across minus half of 23 Across (3)

18 247 squared plus six (5)

21 22 Down multiplied by two (2)

23 One twelfth of 3 Down (2)

24 16 Across multiplied by seven (4)

25 1 Across plus 12 Across plus 415 (4)

Down

1 15 Across plus 24 Across plus 19 Down plus 23 Down plus six (4)

2 One quarter of 20 Down (2)

3 Seconds in six minutes (3)

4 Square root of 21904 (3)

5 2 Down multiplied by two (2)

6 20 Down multiplied by 23 Down (4)

9 15 Down multiplied by six, plus 60 (5)

10 Seconds in four hours (5)

11 13 Across plus 10 Down plus 1047 (5)

15 17 Down minus 44 (4)

17 Minutes in five days (4)

19 4 Down plus one (3)

20 23 Down multiplied by three (3)

22 2 Down minus one (2)

23 Three quarters of 8 Across (2)

Adults are always so busy with the dull and dusty affairs of life which have nothing to do with grass, trees, and running streams.

Denys Watkins-Pitchford

BRICKWORK

Fill each empty square with a single-digit number from 1 to 8. No number may appear twice in any row or column.

In any set of two squares separated by dotted lines, one square contains an odd number and the other contains an even number.

7	6	2	1				
	4			5		3	1
6			3			2	
4			5		2	1	3
	8				6		
		5					6
	3			4	7		
		6	7			5	8

CHAIN LETTERS

Fill each empty circle with one of the letters A, B, C, D or E.

Every horizontal row, vertical column, set of five linked circles, and diagonal line of five circles should contain five different letters.

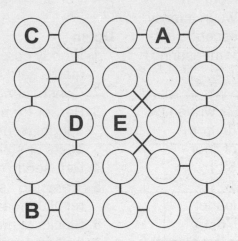

MEMORY TEST

Which of the following is a smaller version of the image on page 59? Make a choice, then turn back to page 59 to see if it is correct.

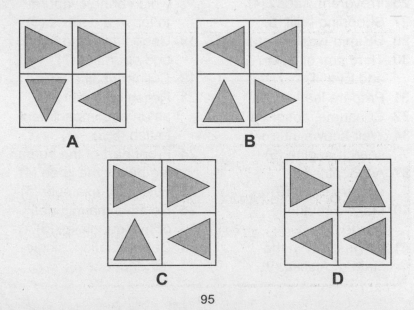

A   B

C   D

GENERAL KNOWLEDGE CROSSWORD

Across

1 Passed over (7)
8 Make more attractive (7)
9 Reminiscent of the past (fashion) (5)
10 Time between infancy and adolescence (9)
11 Device for measuring time (5)
12 Person to whom an envelope is written (9)
13 Food made from a dough of flour or meal (5)
16 Next to (6)
19 Chinese leader (1893–1976) (3)
20 Put things in order (4)
21 Notion (4)
22 Events enjoyed by bargain hunters (5)
23 Flip (a coin, for example) (4)
25 Irreverent, saucy (4)
27 Shopping mall (5)
28 US mid-western state (4)
30 Third son of Adam and Eve (4)
31 Prepare leather (3)
32 Consume, absorb (6)
34 Well-known internet search engine (5)
37 Advocates of country living (9)
40 Make a rhythmic sound (5)
41 Largest city in the state of Alaska (9)
42 Water-filled ditches surrounding castles (5)
43 Call together (for a meeting) (7)
44 Periods of ten years (7)

Down

1 Woody core of a maize ear (7)
2 Consequence (7)
3 Barrier formed from upright wooden posts or stakes (8)
4 Refused to obey (6)
5 Trembled as a result of fear (9)
6 Blocks of metal (6)
7 Embroidery resembling tapestry (11)
14 Powerful herbivore (abbr) (5)
15 Bottomless gulf (5)
17 Shallow depression in which brine evaporates to leave a deposit (7)
18 Unhealthy state of body or mind (7)
19 Culinary spice (4)
23 Relish often served as an accompaniment to fish (6,5)
24 Front part of the human leg below the knee (4)
25 Fusilli, for example (5)
26 Relative magnitudes of two quantities (5)
29 Determination, single-mindedness (9)

GENERAL KNOWLEDGE CROSSWORD

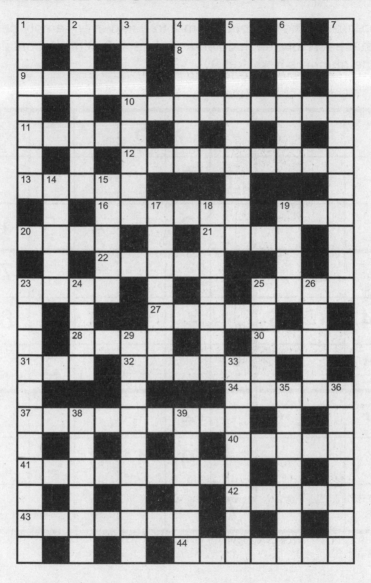

33 Affecting the body as a whole (8)

35 Oldest US university, founded in 1636 at Cambridge, Massachusetts (7)

36 Diffusion of liquid through a porous membrane (7)

38 Not long before the present (6)

39 Removed body hair (6)

SUDOKU

Place one of the numbers from 1 to 9 into every empty cell so that each row, each column and each 3x3 block contains all the numbers from 1 to 9.

		2			5			
		6	1	8				
		7		3		4	5	1
	2							7
4		5				9		8
1							3	
7	9	4		2		1		
				9	1	6		
			7			3		

We get up by the clock, eat and sleep by the clock,

get up again, go to work - and then we retire.

And what do they give us? A clock.

Dave Allen

JIGWORD

A symmetrical crossword has been cut into pieces. Can you put it back together? Three pieces are already in position.

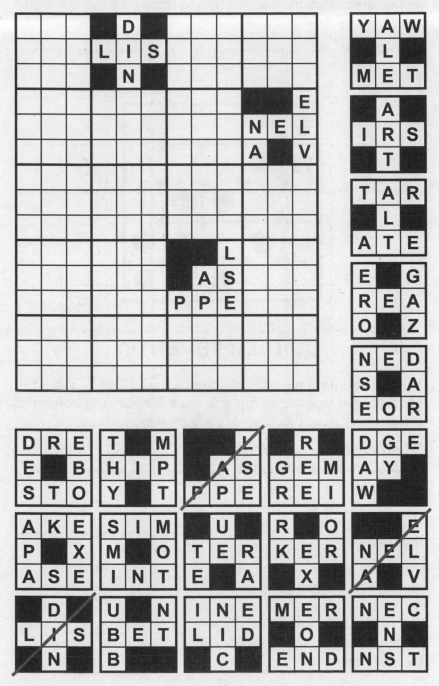

ISOLATE

Draw walls to partition the grid into areas (some walls are already drawn in for you). Each area must contain two circles, area sizes must match those shown by the numbers below and each '+' must be linked to at least two walls.

3   4   6   6   6

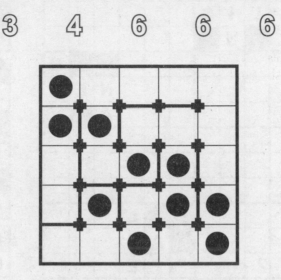

DO IT DIFFERENTLY

How do you normally button up your shirt, blouse, or coat? Most people start at the top and work towards the bottom of the garment, and this is an automatic action.

When you are next getting dressed, make a conscious effort to start at the bottom, and work up to the top, so that you'll actually being 'doing up' the garment!

It might sound easy, but it is surprising how difficult it can be, since it's not something you really think about, having dressed yourself successfully for so many years.

WELL SPOTTED

Some of the circles in this puzzle are already black. Fill in more white circles, so that the number of black circles totals the number inside the area they surround.

Every black circle surrounding an area with a number higher than '1' needs to be next to another black circle surrounding the same area.

When solving, it may help to put a small dot into any circle you know should not be filled.

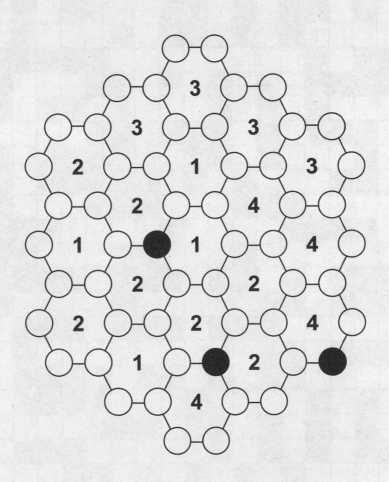

WORD FILLER

On the opposite page is a poem by Lewis Carroll that appears in his book *Alice's Adventures in Wonderland*. It is a parody of Robert Southey's poem *The Old Man's Comforts and How He Gained Them*, which wasn't half as humorous, as a result of which it is now largely forgotten.

All of the underlined words will fit into the grid below. One letter is already in place: complete the puzzle!

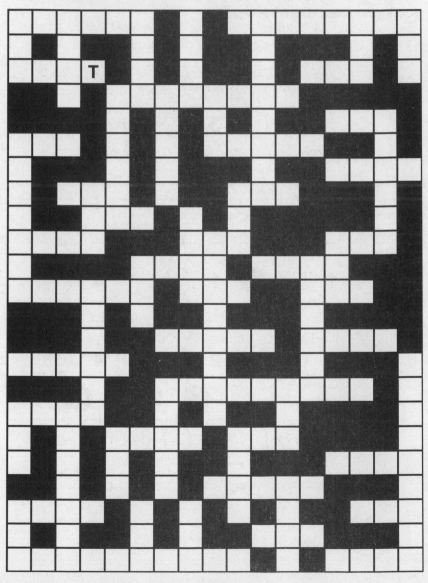

WORD FILLER

You Are Old, Father William

"You are old, Father William," the young man said,
"And your hair has become very white;
And yet you incessantly stand on your head,
Do you think, at your age, it is right?"

"In my youth," Father William replied to his son,
"I feared it might injure the brain;
But now that I'm perfectly sure I have none,
Why, I do it again and again."

"You are old," said the youth, "As I mentioned before,
And have grown most uncommonly fat;
Yet you turned a back-somersault in at the door,
Pray, what is the reason of that?"

"In my youth," said the sage, as he shook his grey locks,
"I kept all my limbs very supple
By the use of this ointment, one shilling the box,
Allow me to sell you a couple?"

"You are old," said the youth, "And your jaws are too weak
For anything tougher than suet;
Yet you finished the goose, with the bones and the beak,
Pray, how did you manage to do it?"

"In my youth," said his father, "I took to the law,
And argued each case with my wife;
And the muscular strength which it gave to my jaw,
Has lasted the rest of my life."

"You are old," said the youth, "one would hardly suppose
That your eye was as steady as ever;
Yet you balanced an eel on the end of your nose,
What made you so awfully clever?"

"I have answered three questions, and that is enough,"
Said his father; "don't give yourself airs!
Do you think I can listen all day to such stuff?
Be off, or I'll kick you down stairs!"

RED HERRING

Five of the words below must be entered in the grid, reading across, so as to create five more words reading down. Can you spot the red herring?

AROMA   NEVER

CALVE   PACTS

LILAC   TRESS

LETTER TRACKER

Starting at the top left corner and ending at the bottom right, track a path from letter to letter, in any direction except diagonally, in order to find 13 hidden flowering plants. All of the letters must be used, but none more than once.

T	U	L	G	E	N	I	S	M	I
A	I	I	L	R	A	U	A	E	N
L	N	P	I	D	O	M	J	I	R
A	U	D	A	O	R	C	Y	S	I
V	T	E	F	F	I	H	L	P	I
E	N	P	N	I	D	L	I	P	M
E	D	H	T	C	A	Y	H	E	R
R	I	M	S	E	R	I	L	E	N
P	R	R	O	M	A	G	O	L	D

DO IT YOURSELF!

In this crossword puzzle, the clues are in alphabetical order and there are no black squares in the grid. Black out the unwanted squares, to produce a symmetrically-patterned grid containing words that can be matched to the clues.

R	E	A	L	L	Y	E	F	R	A	N	C	E
A	X	L	E	C	A	L	L	A	L	E	H	E
I	N	S	O	M	N	I	A	C	T	O	E	S
N	O	O	P	A	G	E	M	E	A	S	S	P
B	R	O	A	D	S	R	E	F	R	E	S	H
O	V	E	R	E	G	U	N	S	T	A	R	E
W	O	N	D	E	R	M	C	A	C	T	U	S
E	P	O	C	H	E	R	O	L	O	U	D	U
B	A	R	R	I	E	R	I	B	O	G	U	S
B	L	O	O	D	T	A	G	E	K	E	S	P
B	O	L	D	O	I	N	I	T	I	A	T	E
I	N	S	E	W	N	O	R	E	N	S	U	N
B	E	L	O	N	G	E	L	E	G	E	N	D

Arc of light in the sky
Begin, start
Consume food
Digits of the foot
European country
Exhibition of cowboy skills
Fake, false
Female child
Fearless and daring
Give new strength to

Hang freely
Have a place
In fact
Marvel
Myth, fable
Neither
Object that impedes free movement
Popular board game
Preparing food by heating it
Prickly desert plant

Principle of Chinese philosophy; opposite of Yin
Sacred table in a church
Sign of welcome or recognition
Sleep disorder
Spanish style of dancing
Spotted wild cat
Wide
Unaccompanied

NUMBER CRUNCHER

Starting at the top left with the number provided, work down from one box to another, applying the mathematical instructions to your running total.

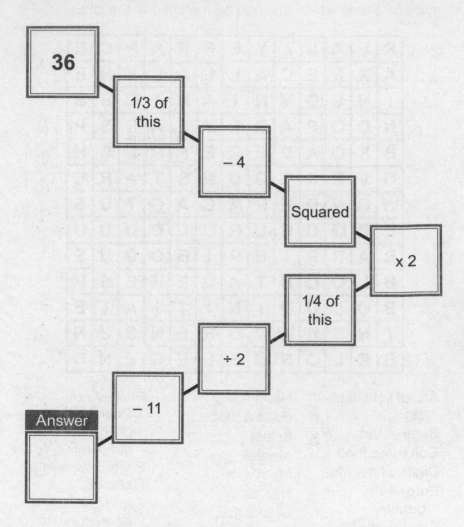

36

1/3 of this

− 4

Squared

x 2

1/4 of this

÷ 2

− 11

Answer

NAME THE DAY

What day immediately follows the day three days before the day immediately before the day two days after the day immediately before Thursday?

JIGSAW PUZZLE

Fit the jigsaw together to reveal eight fruits and nuts.

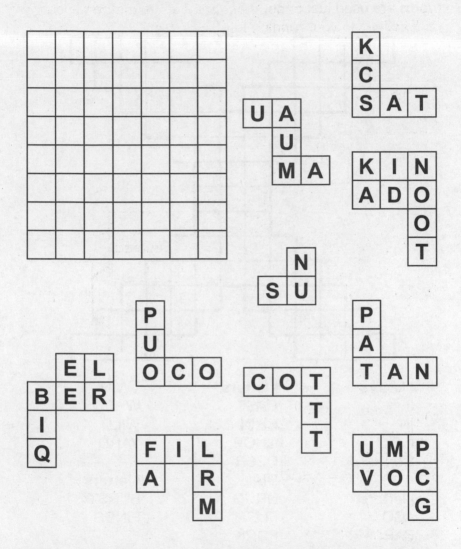

X MARKS THE SPOT

Fill the grid with the listed words, one letter per square. All words are used just once.

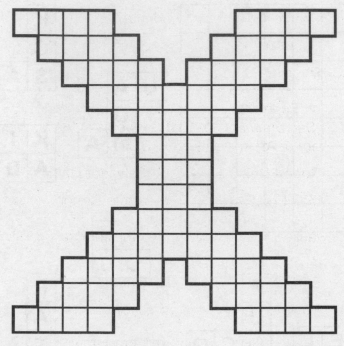

2 letters
IF
IN
ME
SO

3 letters
AGO
CAP
LIE
LOT
TON
WHO
WIN

4 letters
CAST
CHIN
CHOP
DEER
DIAL
DRUG
FLEW
FORK
HOOP
KNOB
RAIN
SHOW
SLIT
THIS
TRIM
TUNE

TWIN
WHEN
WILD
YARD

5 letters
BURST
FINDS

7 letters
CLOSELY
DRAGONS
GODDESS

9 letters
EDUCATION
RESPONDED

GENERAL KNOWLEDGE QUIZ

Can you identify which one of the multiple-choice answers (a, b, c or d) is correct for each of the questions below?

1   Who wrote the *Moonlight Sonata*?

   a Schubert   **b** Beethoven

   c Chopin   **d** Mozart

2   Which Spanish surrealist painter's 1955 work *The Sacrament of the Last Supper* is in the National Gallery of Art in Washington DC?

   a Robert Desnos   **b** Salvador Dali

   c Max Ernst   **d** Andre Breton

3   Milwaukee lies on which of North America's great lakes?

   a Erie   **b** Ontario

   c Superior   **d** Michigan

4   Ariel and Miranda are moons of which planet?

   a Saturn   **b** Uranus

   c Jupiter   **d** Neptune

5   Leon Bismark were the real first names of which jazz great?

   a Dizzy Gillespie   **b** Jelly Roll Morton

   c Bix Biederbecke   **d** Woody Herman

6   What was the name of the dog in the story *Three Men in a Boat?*

   a Montmorency   **b** Scamper

   c Peritas   **d** Boatswain

DOUBLE-CROSSER

Two crossword puzzles, but you have to decide which of the solutions to each clue fits into each grid. In both cases, one word has been entered to give you a start.

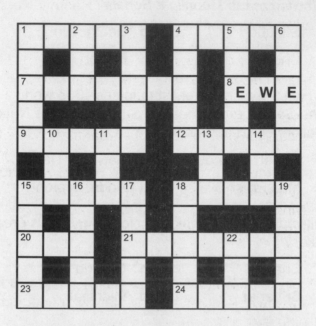

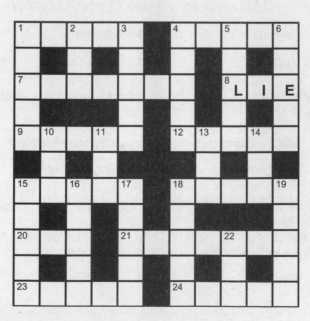

DOUBLE-CROSSER

Across

1 Fourth letter of the Greek alphabet; Thick sap from a tree (5)

4 Craftsman who works with stone; Hebrew prophet and lawgiver, brother of Aaron (5)

7 Burn bubble; Constructor (7)

8 Be in a horizontal position; Female sheep (3)

9 Dish of cold vegetables; Three-dimensional shape (5)

12 Fence made of shrubs; Overly eager speed (5)

15 Prevents, halts; Run off to marry (5)

18 Punctuation mark; Sturdy footwear that covers the lower legs (5)

20 Food wrapped in a pastry shell; Round vegetable (3)

21 Fruit resembling a small peach; Peculiar (7)

23 Having much foliage; Prepared for action (5)

24 Outmoded; Turn away from by persuasion (5)

Down

1 Financial obligations; Garments (5)

2 Hawaiian garland of flowers; Narrow runner used for gliding over snow (3)

3 Made a written record of; Summed up (5)

4 Low-lying wetland; Month of the year (5)

5 Exchanges for money; Rate of travel (5)

6 Daughter of a sibling; Subdivision of an act of a play (5)

10 Every one; Not at home (3)

11 Mischievous little fairy; Type of cobra (3)

13 Inflated feeling of personal worth; In the past (3)

14 Precious or semi-precious stone; Young child (3)

15 Fantastic; Send or drive out (5)

16 Largest city in Nebraska, USA; Last letter of the Greek alphabet (5)

17 Sheltered from light or heat; Short formal piece of writing (5)

18 Feeling weary and impatient; Healed (5)

19 Pay out; Stage-player (5)

22 Hard-shelled fruit of a tree; Make an incision (3)

ROUND THE BLOCK

Each eight-letter word in the list is hidden in a square around a central letter that is not a part of the word itself, as shown by the example in the grid. The word may start anywhere within its 'square' and go either clockwise or anticlockwise. When all the listed words are found, the central letters spell out the name of a movie star.

```
K A T Y R E D V U C E G
E B S L E R N P E V N X
N M I T D W O N N I I C
L A G E R H T E T O R H
Y N Y D I I R U I O T S
O R H L L L E T E M M U
O T T F H G L E C T X B
M B A U I P M O N G Q
E S T B N M O V P I A U
L E N A D E P G N T L I
A R D U J S O M E L N G
C R A S S A P O S V N E
P A C B G N D L H S I R
M O I C N N O E S T T B
S I F O S V I C C O T O
```

ABUNDANT ✓	MUSHROOM
BATHROOM	NAPOLEON
CALENDAR	PACIFISM
COMPLETE	QUILTING
DYNAMITE	SCOTTISH
INVENTOR	THRILLER
MISTAKEN	WONDERED

112

ROUND THE BEND

Instead of each word being hidden in a straight, continuous line, every word has one bend in it. This bend will not necessarily go off at a right angle; it may go in any direction at all! One word is given as an example.

```
L O D U C E S T C A R F
E A R E W A E I R R U H
F R U T D G G O C E R J
Y T M G N N L N T A M X
L L N V H I A A B X N R
L I L A T N I L N G M E
A D B A E A E J N D E N
U I B P R T G N C E S R
T S M P R U C M T E R L
O G R A C E D D A R G I
P R D R G C X T C G R D
M A B M L O I A U K N E
N Z R E D O I N D K I G
I B S A N Q S F E K F B
H S I L Y T F B G A Y S
```

ABSORBENT ✓   INTRODUCES

DISGRACED   LANDSLIDE

EDUCATION   LAUGHTER

FRACTIONAL   MAGNIFY

GREENLAND   NATURALLY

HABITUALLY   PARADOX

HURRICANE   UNSTYLISH

WORDSEARCH: PARTY

You're never too old to have fun! Can you find all of the listed words in the grid below? Words run forwards or backwards, in either a horizontal, vertical or diagonal direction.

```
T C A Y R A S R E V I N N A T
G G E T T O G E T H E R N H N
U A R L C E Y B A N Q U E T E
N B T J E T S G H L E T W Q M
O I R H R B M F L L E E Y V E
I R S A E M R E E F R J E F R
T T P O N R W A U A P I A U I
P H R E I E I E T V S W R N T
E D F V R R D N C I P T S C E
C A M A O H E R G N O G E T R
E Y F M K X M E A R A N V I Y
R B A R B E C U E G X D E O Y
N O I N U E R V A S V O L N Q
R A S W D Y E L F R O L I C D
S O C I A L A N O I S A C C O
```

ANNIVERSARY

BANQUET

BARBECUE

BIRTHDAY

CELEBRATION

DANCE

FAREWELL

FEAST

FETE

FROLIC

FUNCTION

GALA

GARDEN

GATHERING

GET-
 TOGETHER

NEW YEAR'S
 EVE

OCCASION

PARTY

RECEPTION

RETIREMENT

REUNION

REVEL

SOCIAL

SOIREE

SPREE

BREAK-TIME CROSSWORD

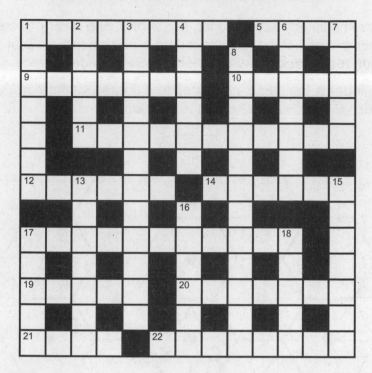

Across

1 Closet (8)
5 Corrosive compound (4)
9 Performance (7)
10 Proprietor (5)
11 Status of belonging to a particular country (11)
12 Escaped, as of liquid through a hole (6)
14 Not long before the present (6)
17 44th President of the USA (6,5)
19 In existence (5)
20 Copy (7)
21 Woodland plant (4)
22 Daughter of a king or queen (8)

Down

1 Exercising caution (7)
2 Smooth brown oval nut (5)
3 Fully extended, especially in length (12)
4 Put trust in, with confidence (4,2)
6 Tell a secret to (7)
7 Unclean (5)
8 Someone whose age is in the nineties (12)
13 Flight-operating company (7)
15 Pills (7)
16 Duplicator (6)
17 Wild animal (5)
18 Semi-precious stone (5)

HEXAFIT

Place the listed words into the hexagons, one letter per cell, starting in any of those surrounding a black circle, so that words read clockwise. Some letters are already in place.

The letter is the same in any cell that shares a common border with a cell in a touching hexagon.

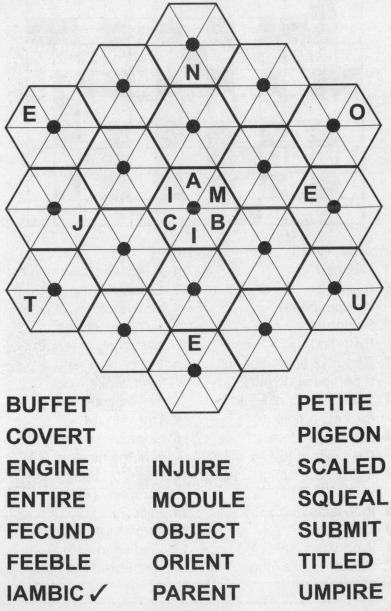

BUFFET		**PETITE**
COVERT		**PIGEON**
ENGINE	**INJURE**	**SCALED**
ENTIRE	**MODULE**	**SQUEAL**
FECUND	**OBJECT**	**SUBMIT**
FEEBLE	**ORIENT**	**TITLED**
IAMBIC ✓	**PARENT**	**UMPIRE**

116

KAKURO

Fill the grid so that each block adds up to the total in the box above or to the left of it.

You can only use the digits 1-9, one per square, but the same digit must not be used twice in a block. The same digit may occur more than once in any row or column, but it must be in a separate block.

SUDOKU

Place one of the numbers from 1 to 9 into every empty cell so that each row, each column and each 3x3 block contains all the numbers from 1 to 9.

				2				9
			6		4	3	1	
			8		1	2	5	
		9	5		7	6	3	
6								5
	3	7	4		2	9		
	6	1	2		3			
	7	8	9		6			
2				1				

DOMINO PLACEMENT

A standard set of twenty-eight dominoes has been laid out as shown below. Can you draw in the edges of them all? One is already in place.

It may be helpful to use the check-box to tick off the dominoes as they are found.

3	6	4	3	0	2	4	1
6	0	2	1	1	0	3	4
3	6	5	6	2	2	3	2
2	0	1	5	0	4	5	1
0	0	6	6	1	0	5	2
6	1	5	4	6	5	3	2
5	4	4	5	3	4	3	1

0-0	0-1	0-2	0-3	0-4	0-5	0-6	1-1

1-2	1-3	1-4	1-5	1-6	2-2	2-3	2-4	2-5	2-6

3-3	3-4	3-5	3-6	4-4	4-5	4-6	5-5	5-6	6-6
					✓				

ALPHAFILL

Place 25 different letters of the alphabet, one per circle, in order to spell out the listed words. Words are formed by moving between adjacent circles along the connecting lines, either horizontally, vertically or diagonally in any direction.

Begin by crossing out the letters already in place, together with the one letter which doesn't appear in any of the words.

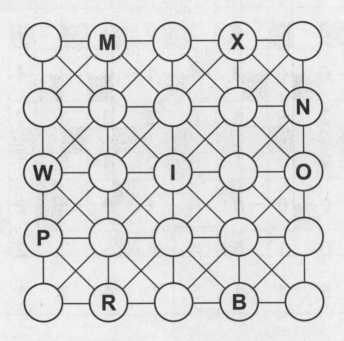

A B C D E F G H I J K L M

N O P Q R S T U V W X Y Z

CLOCK	JET	SILO
CONVEX	MUST	SQUID
FUTILE	QUITE	STICKY
GRAB	SHARP	TEXTILE
HARDBACK	SICKLE	WHISTLE

NUMBER FILLER

Can you fit all of the listed numbers into the grid? One is already in place, to get you off to a good start!

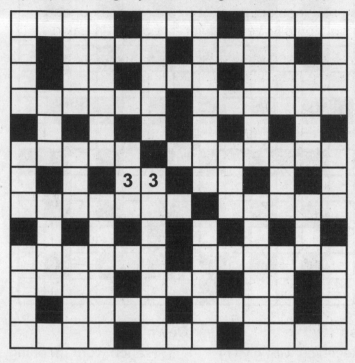

2 digits	632	3004	8854	380491
33 ✓	671	3559	9108	499326
63	693	4579		520821
75	763	4912	**5 digits**	806424
86	956	5091	55273	945341
	987	5679	67412	
3 digits		6406	76969	**7 digits**
101	**4 digits**	6784	93161	1027124
238	1453	7203		1958855
269	1625	7394	**6 digits**	3263108
425	2677	7702	178017	3564536
471	2803	8328	204674	
512	2847	8849	330602	

BREAK-TIME CROSSWORD

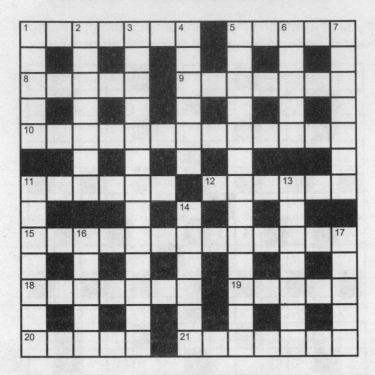

Across
1 Receives willingly (7)
5 Object (5)
8 Person who does no work (5)
9 Cheap purchase (7)
10 Lacking affectation (13)
11 Nebulous (6)
12 Interlaces (6)
15 Feeding on small invertebrate creatures (13)
18 Sordid dirtiness (7)
19 Female relative (5)
20 Country, capital Niamey (5)
21 One of several parallel layers of material (7)

Down
1 French word meaning farewell (5)
2 West Indian song (7)
3 Upright (13)
4 Wept convulsively (6)
5 Pass the difficult point and start to improve (4,3,6)
6 US state, capital Boise (5)
7 First book of the Bible (7)
11 Deep red (7)
13 Fierce (7)
14 Juicy fruit, such as lemon, orange, etc (6)
16 Thrown, hurled (5)
17 Water at boiling temperature diffused in the air (5)

CODEWORD

Every letter in this puzzle has been replaced by a number, the number remaining the same for that letter wherever it occurs. Every letter of the alphabet has been used. Substitute numbers for letters to complete the codeword.

It may help to cross off the letters beneath the grid to keep a track of progress, and to use the reference box showing which numbers have been decoded. Three letters have already been entered into the grid, to help you on your way.

11	2	9	14	25	■	6	23	17	3	7	23	15
24	■	26	■	14	17	17	■	5	■	17	■	14
18	23	2	20	16	■	24	■	9	17	5	15	7
5	■	14	■	5	■	5	8	16	■	4	■	22
17	14	20	14	18	23	■	5	9	6	24	25	16
■	10	■	24	13	14	16 T	■	14	■	23	■	■
12	5	9	16	17	3	■	22 H	5	15	18	17	24
■	16	■	23	■	7	10	24 E	19	■	■	14	■
21	24	16	16	17	24	■	10	24	1	24	25	16
14	■	10	■	14	15	21	■	9	■	12	■	24
25	22	5	15	16	■	15	■	23	15	14	23	15
21	■	14	■	22	■	24	17	11	■	25	■	23
9	14	15	25	24	10	24	■	24	15	16	24	10

A B C D E F G H I J K L M

N O P Q R S T U V W X Y Z

1	2	3	4	5	6	7	8	9	10	11	12	13
14	15	16 T	17	18	19	20	21	22 H	23	24 E	25	26

ROUND DOZEN

First solve the clues. All of the solutions begin with the letter in the central circle, and some others are already in place. When the puzzle is complete, you can then go on to discover the twelve-letter word reading clockwise around the outermost ring of letters.

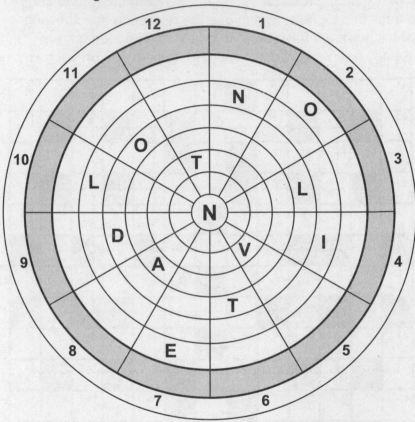

1 Annoyance, irritation
2 Mr Bonaparte
3 Story writer
4 Photographic image from which prints are made
5 Month of the year
6 Bedtime drink
7 Lesser in width

8 City, the target of the second atom bomb on 9 August 1945
9 In these times
10 Capital of India
11 Gas that forms most of the Earth's atmosphere
12 Marking or observing

The twelve-letter word is: _____

JIGSAW SUDOKU

Fit the numbers 1, 2, 3, 4, 5 and 6 into the grid in such a way that each horizontal row, each vertical column and each of the heavily outlined sections of six squares each contains a different number. Some numbers are already in place.

			5		
3		6			
	3				
5			4		
	1				5

WHAT DOES IT MEAN?

Which of the following is the correct definition of the word:

CONFLATE

1 To repeal or do away with (a law, a right, or a formal agreement)

2 To combine (eg two different versions of a text) into one

3 To engage in plots or intrigue; to scheme

SPIDOKU

In the spider's web below, each of the eight segments should be filled with a different number from 1 to 8, in such a way that every ring also contains a different number from 1 to 8.

The segments run from the outside of the spider's web to the middle, and the rings run all the way around. So that you can see the rings more clearly, we've shaded them grey and white.

Some numbers are already in place. Can you fill in the rest?

CUBE ROUTES

Fill the words into the grid (one letter is ready in place),
changing route where necessary, as with this example:

ASPECT ENDURE SPED

CARE   REASON WRITHE

CASE   ROE

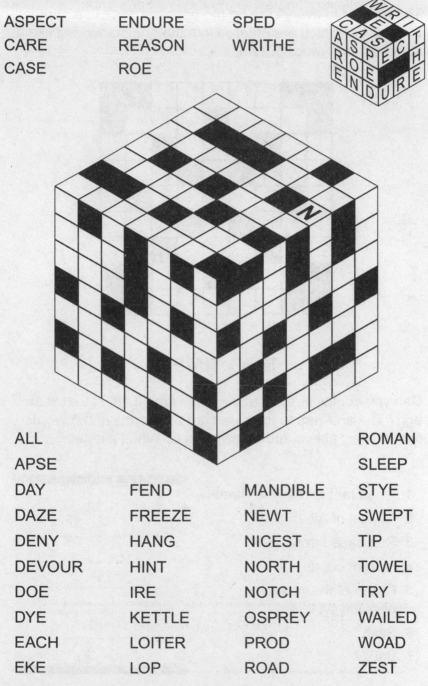

ALL			ROMAN
APSE			SLEEP
DAY	FEND	MANDIBLE	STYE
DAZE	FREEZE	NEWT	SWEPT
DENY	HANG	NICEST	TIP
DEVOUR	HINT	NORTH	TOWEL
DOE	IRE	NOTCH	TRY
DYE	KETTLE	OSPREY	WAILED
EACH	LOITER	PROD	WOAD
EKE	LOP	ROAD	ZEST

NUMBER CRUNCHER CROSSWORD

A little mathematical crossword, where a little knowledge of mathematics will come in very handy!

The answer to every clue on the opposite page is a number, the digits of which are entered into the grid below, just like a standard crossword puzzle.

EGG TIMER

Can you complete this puzzle in the time it takes to boil an egg? The answers to the clues are anagrams of the words immediately above and below, plus or minus a letter.

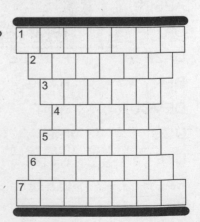

1 Inhabitant of the Red Planet?

2 Capital of Albania

3 Rail-based transport

4 Muslim country

5 Organ of the central nervous system

6 Sash

7 Bandit

NUMBER CRUNCHER CROSSWORD

Across

1 5 Across multiplied by 22 Across (5)

5 17 Across plus 19 (3)

6 21 Across multiplied by nine (3)

8 One fifteenth of 23 Down (2)

9 17 Across plus 21 Across (3)

11 One fifth of 17 Across (2)

13 16 squared (3)

15 Square root of 12544 (3)

16 3 Down multiplied by 22 Down (5)

17 Seconds in four minutes (3)

19 Seconds in nine minutes (3)

21 Square root of 625 (2)

22 13 Across minus ten (3)

24 One third of 17 Across (2)

25 14 squared (3)

27 22 Across multiplied by two (3)

29 1 Across plus 19036 (5)

Down

1 28 Down minus 21 Across (2)

2 25 Across multiplied by two (3)

3 21 Across multiplied by five (3)

4 8 Across minus one (2)

5 6 Across plus ten (3)

7 19 Across plus one (3)

8 206 squared plus 13 Across plus one third of 28 Down (5)

10 1 Across plus 24 Across (5)

12 29 Across minus 50 (5)

14 15 Down multiplied by six (3)

15 21 Across plus 24 Across (3)

18 7 Down minus 28 Down (3)

20 21 Across plus 18 Down plus six (3)

22 15 Across plus 21 Across plus 3 Down (3)

23 15 Across plus 27 Across plus 4 Down minus one (3)

26 One quarter of 2 Down (2)

28 One seventh of 14 Down (2)

LINK WORDS

Fit eight different words into the grid, so that each one links up with the words on either side, eg table - lamp - shade.

When finished, read down the letters in the shaded squares to reveal another word, solving the clue.

BLIND					LINE
GOLD					HOUR
ALARM					TOWER
CITRIC					TEST
SAILING					SHAPE
SMOKE					SHELL
FOR					GREEN
MOVIE					BOARD

Clue: Musical instrument _____

BERMUDA TRIANGLE

Travel through the 'Bermuda Triangle', collecting a letter from each area. You can visit any area once only, and you must enter and exit through the holes in the walls between them. The starting letter may appear in any area.

When you've completed your tour, the 15 letters (in order) will spell out the name of an author.

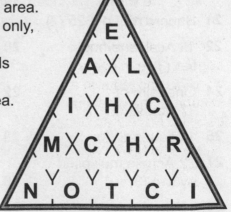

Author: _____

WORD LADDER

Change one letter at a time (but not the position of any letter) to make a new word — and move from the word at the top of the ladder to the word at the bottom using the exact number of rungs provided.

WORD WHEEL

How many words of three or more letters can you make from those in the wheel, without using plurals, abbreviations or proper nouns?

The central letter must appear once in every word and no letter in a section of the wheel may be used more than once.

There is at least one nine-letter word in the wheel.

Nine-letter word(s):

GENERAL KNOWLEDGE CROSSWORD

Across

1 Dairy product (5)
8 Onyx marble (9)
9 Detector used to locate distant objects (5)
10 Short, curved sword (7)
11 Fail to detonate (7)
12 Durable aromatic wood (5)
13 Greek mythological man who fell in love with his own reflection (9)
17 Woodworking tool (4)
20 Islamic fast (7)
21 City in Tuscany with a famous tower (4)
22 The smallest quantity (4)
23 One who journeys to a sacred place (7)
24 US space-flight agency (inits) (4)
25 Prayer-ending word (4)
26 Person serving a prison sentence (7)
27 Give up, relinquish (4)
30 Famous person (9)
34 Sycophant (5)
35 State of being behind in payments (7)
36 One who works in a coal mine (7)
37 Sugar frosting (5)
38 Hard brittle greyish-white metallic element (9)
39 Take (an examination) again (5)

Down

1 Formal event performed on a special occasion (8)
2 Ultimate client for which a thing is intended (3,4)
3 Cocktail of vermouth and gin (7)
4 Packages (7)
5 Plans for attaining a particular goal (7)
6 Marooned (8)
7 Maintain in unaltered condition (8)
14 Turtle's shell (8)
15 Likeness (9)
16 Destroy property or hinder normal operations (9)
17 Technician who produces moving cartoons (8)
18 Musical instrument with strings stretch over a flat sounding box (6)
19 Buccaneer (6)
27 Underground cemetery (8)
28 Point in time at which something must be completed (8)

GENERAL KNOWLEDGE CROSSWORD

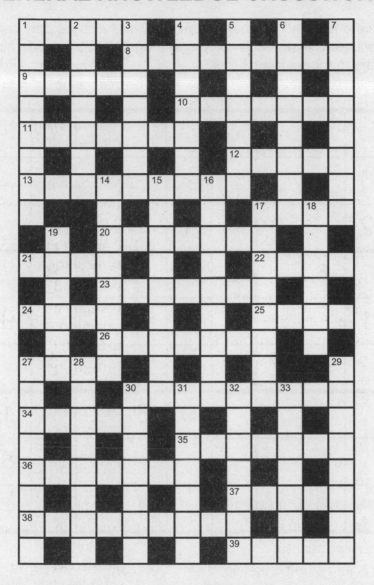

29 Vision (8)

30 Believing the worst of human nature and motives (7)

31 Acquired knowledge (7)

32 Object that impedes free movement (7)

33 Slanted letters (7)

SUDOKU

Place one of the numbers from 1 to 9 into every empty cell so that each row, each column and each 3x3 block contains all the numbers from 1 to 9.

			6				7	
3								
2		8	4	1				
	6		5			7	8	
1				8				9
	8	2			7		3	
				9	8	2		1
								8
	5				4			

JIGWORD

A symmetrical crossword has been cut into pieces. Can you put it back together? Three pieces are already in position.

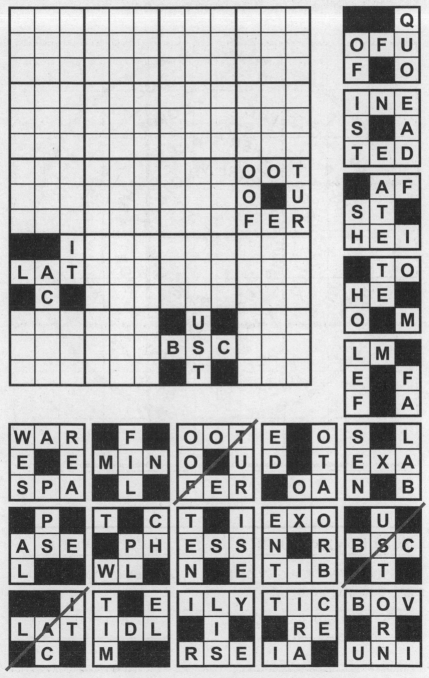

RING-WORDS

From the 32 segments below, find 16 eight-letter words by pairing one set of four letters with another.

All of the segments must be used once only.

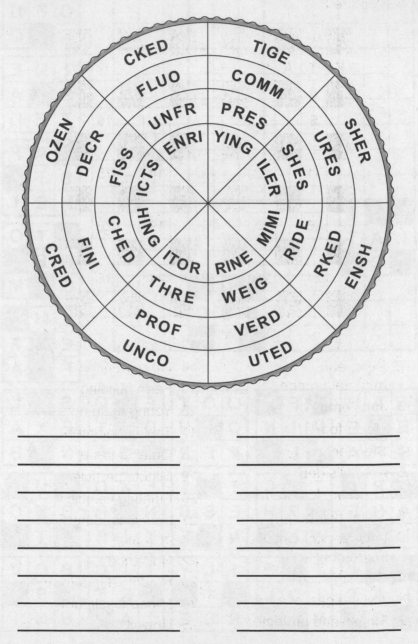

AROUND THE SQUARES

The answer to each clue is a four-letter word, to be entered in the four squares surrounding the corresponding number in the grid. The word can start in any of the four squares and read either clockwise or anticlockwise. The first has already been entered.

	W						
K	1	A	2		3		4		5	
	L						
	6		7		8		9		10	
	11		12		13		14		15	
	16		17		18		19		20	
	21		22		23		24		25	

1 Go on foot
2 European mountain range
3 Junk email
4 Haze, fog
5 Slender
6 Animal's den
7 The Sun, for example
8 Sister of a parent
9 Lowest-pitch brass instrument
10 Country road
11 Twelfth part of a foot
12 Finger-end protector
13 Pleasant, agreeable
14 Grizzly animal
15 Farm building
16 Young male horse
17 Table condiment
18 Quiet, serene
19 Minute particle
20 Fighting vehicle
21 Landlocked body of water
22 Nuisance
23 Hindmost in a race
24 Mined fossil fuel
25 Unwell

WORDSEARCH: GIRLS' NAMES

Can you find all of the listed girls' names in the grid opposite? They run forwards or backwards, in either a horizontal, vertical or diagonal direction.

ABIGAIL	FLEUR	MOLLY
AGNES	GABRIELLE	MORAG
AILSA	GAYLE	MYRTLE
ALEXIS	GAYNOR	NAOMI
AMBER	GEMMA	NERYS
ANITA	GEORGINA	NORMA
ANNABEL	GWENDOLINE	OCTAVIA
ANNIE	HOLLY	ODETTE
ANTOINETTE	INGRID	OLIVE
AURIEL	IRENE	OLIVIA
AVRIL	ISABEL	PEARL
BELLA	JANET	RACHEL
BERYL	JASMINE	REBECCA
BRENDA	JENNY	ROBERTA
CATHERINE	JOAN	ROMA
CHLOE	JUNE	RUBY
CLARA	KAREN	SUKIE
CLEMENTINE	KIMBERLEY	SYLVIA
CONSTANCE	LAVINIA	TESSA
DAPHNE	LEILA	TRACEY
DAWN	LESLEY	VERA
DORA	LIBBY	WANDA
DULCIE	LINDA	XENIA
EDITH	LYDIA	YVETTE
EMILY	MABEL	ZARA
ERICA	MADGE	ZELDA
ESTHER	MANDY	ZENA
FAITH	MARY	ZOE

WORDSEARCH: GIRLS' NAMES

```
G A R N D O E N I L O D N E W G A
E O Z O D V S U A M G R U Y S I O
M D R E H D G D L E I L A L V E C
M A T T N A N E R Y S M S L L L Q
A T I S Y A B E T T E V Y O E T E
E D R N W A D L E B A S I M G R N
E C O P N L U C I A T T E Q I Y H
V R M N E B L Y D I A N R J L M P
I N A O M I C F A I T H H E I D A
L N L V C U I H L I J V V B B Y D
O H G B R T E Y N D G T D B B O L
C L A R A I A E G E O B E U Y D R
O I Y Q I V L V T G E O R G I N A
N X L I N D A T I D A X Y E F A E
S R E H T S E J O A N L J M N H P
T E B N G N J A S M I N E C A D C
A B A O I N B H N M S I X E L A A
N M M O R A G Y E L R E B M I K E
C A T H E R I N E A D Z C U G I H
E N E R M V H S O S N E R A K K O
A D S Q A A E W K L T P R U I L L
L Y S A Y C E R A I X R S U I Y L
L Y A N N I E C A A R A U V E E Y
Y A R J T R C Y S G T E I H H L R
F N V E Z E R E E I K A N C B S F
M Z N I B E N W N B A O A E E E I
E A K E N U L A G A B R I E L L E
J R R D J I R D A U R I E L L W D
O A T Y J C A L A M R O N L A Q V
```

RED HERRING

Five of the words below must be entered in the grid, reading across, so as to create five more words reading down. Can you spot the red herring?

ALPHA   SOLOS

ERASE   SPACE

RESET   TIERS

LETTER TRACKER

Starting at the top left corner and ending at the bottom right, track a path from letter to letter, in any direction except diagonally, in order to find 14 hidden European capital cities. All of the letters must be used, but none more than once.

H	E	D	A	P	E	M	A	D	R
S	L	U	B	A	S	T	R	A	I
I	N	K	I	N	W	A	S	W	D
L	I	V	L	A	T	O	N	O	P
N	O	N	I	R	I	M	A	C	R
I	D	N	S	B	O	N	U	G	A
U	S	O	L	S	A	P	E	S	E
K	S	E	V	I	R	A	B	S	L
O	P	J	I	E	N	N	R	U	S

DO IT YOURSELF!

In this crossword puzzle, the clues are in alphabetical order and there are no black squares in the grid. Black out the unwanted squares, to produce a symmetrically-patterned grid containing words that can be matched to the clues.

A	V	A	I	L	I	P	A	R	A	S	O	L
N	O	N	E	O	R	E	V	E	N	O	R	A
T	R	A	C	T	O	R	U	N	O	R	T	H
I	A	C	O	U	N	I	C	E	V	E	G	O
C	R	O	S	S	Y	O	S	W	A	T	E	R
S	E	N	T	E	A	D	H	E	S	I	V	E
M	A	D	A	M	R	E	A	D	I	M	A	N
R	E	A	S	O	N	E	D	O	G	M	O	W
E	N	D	T	N	E	D	Y	C	H	O	K	E
W	E	P	E	S	K	I	L	O	T	B	E	I
A	D	A	P	T	A	B	A	C	K	I	N	G
R	O	S	E	E	P	L	Y	O	U	L	E	H
D	E	S	E	R	V	E	R	A	L	E	R	T

Bedtime beverage

Be worthy of

Bonding substance

Came to a conclusion

City in north-east Pakistan

Compass point at 0 or 360 degrees

Conform

Egyptian water lily

Emblem of Christianity

Farm vehicle

Frozen water

Glide over snow

Heaviness

Huge South American snake

Incapable of being shifted

Inhuman person

Ludicrous acts done for fun

Painful

Portion of time

Recompense

Restored, freshened

Sponsorship

Struggle for breath

Succeed in an examination

Suitable for eating

Sun umbrella

Use to one's advantage

Warn of danger

DICE SECTION

Printed onto every one of the six numbered dice are six letters (one per side), which can be rearranged to form the answer to each clue; however, some sides are invisible to you. Use the clues and write every answer into the grid. When correctly filled, the letters in the shaded squares, reading in the order 1 to 6, will spell out the name of a fruit.

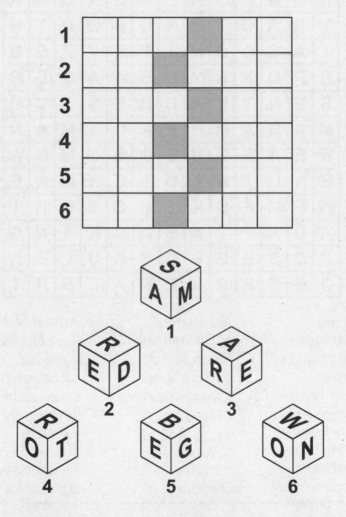

1 Lucky charm
2 Resist separation
3 Come into view

4 Ice cream container
5 Capital of Croatia
6 No matter what

JIGSAW PUZZLE

Fit the jigsaw together to reveal eight geographical features.

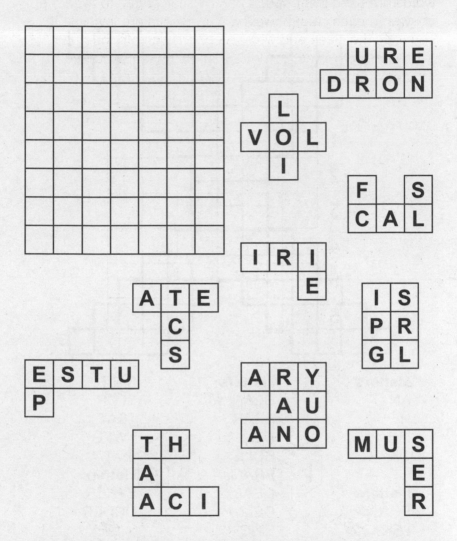

X MARKS THE SPOT

Fill the grid with the listed words, one letter per square. All words are used just once.

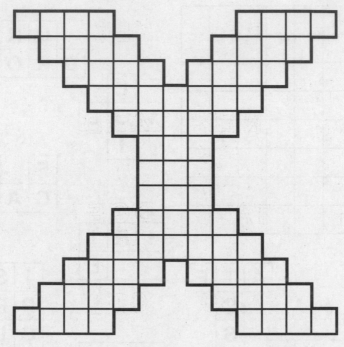

2 letters	4 letters	SALT
AN	BEAN	SLOP
HE	BEAR	TEAT
ME	BELL	TWEE
OK	BOLE	
	BRAG	**5 letters**
3 letters	DEAL	ETHER
ERA	DELL	ORDER
LEK	EPIC	
PAN	GELT	**7 letters**
RAT	HELL	CENTRAL
RET	KEPT	DRESSES
TEA	KIWI	THREADS
TEE	ORAL	
	PEEK	**9 letters**
	POEM	GREATNESS
	REAP	INTERPRET

HALF AND HALF

Pair off these groups of three letters to name eight nautical terms, each comprising six letters.

LEY BRI KLE HOR

ANC NEL ARD VES

DIN TAC DGE GAL

FUN ABO SEL GHY

_____   _____

_____   _____

_____   _____

_____   _____

YOU KNOW YOU'RE GETTING OLD WHEN …

You wake up with that morning-after feeling, and then you remember that you didn't do anything the night before.

You look forward to a nice, quiet evening.

You spend an hour hunting around for your glasses, only to find that they were on your head all the time.

DOUBLE-CROSSER

Two crossword puzzles, but you have to decide which of the solutions to each clue fits into each grid. In both cases, one word has been entered to give you a start.

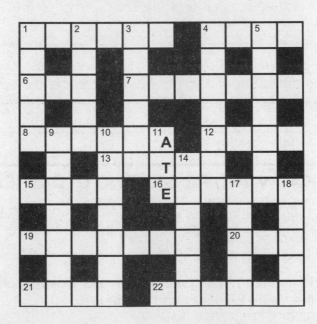

DOUBLE-CROSSER

Across

1 Force used in pushing; Unsullied, pure (6)
4 Deliver a blow with the foot; Item of footwear (4)
6 Flexible container with a single opening; Item of equipment used in baseball (3)
7 Appealing to many; Everlasting (7)
8 Satellite of Jupiter; Word famously uttered by Archimedes (6)
12 Approximation of quantity, degree or worth; Toy flown in the wind (4)
13 Implement passed between runners in a relay race; ___ Reed, Oscar-winning movie director of the musical *Oliver!* (1968) (5)
15 Behaves in a particular way; Bother (4)
16 Deep ditch; Greek god of darkness who dwelt in the underworld (6)
19 Country, capital Beirut; Occurring among members of a family usually by heredity (7)
20 Chest bone; Fish eggs (3)
21 Festival, celebration; One of the Seven Deadly Sins (4)
22 Conquer; Grass producing an edible grain (6)

Down

1 Electrical conductor connecting telephones, for example; Set of data arranged in rows and columns (5)
2 Fury; Revolving blade (5)
3 Capital of the US state of Kansas; Inhabitant of the Tibetan Himalayas (6)
4 Joint of a finger when the fist is closed; Small fish (7)
5 Disordered; French castle (7)
9 Dirty; Small guitar with four strings (7)
10 Designed to incite to indecency; Overwhelming happiness or joyful excitement (7)
11 Had a meal; Painting, sculpture, etc (3)
14 Citrus fruit; Prophet (6)
17 Care for sick people; Push one's way (5)
18 Custom; Fragrance (5)

ROUND THE BLOCK

Each eight-letter word in the list is hidden in a square around a central letter that is not a part of the word itself, as shown by the example in the grid. The word may start anywhere within its 'square' and go either clockwise or anticlockwise. When all the listed words are found, the central letters spell out the name of a movie star.

APPLAUSE	JUVENILE
BILBERRY	OCCASION
CAMPAIGN ✓	QUADRANT
DISSOLVE	ROADSIDE
FALTERED	SPLENDID
GRADUATE	TRACTION
INSOLENT	ULTIMATE

ROUND THE BEND

Instead of each word being hidden in a straight, continuous line, every word has one bend in it. This bend will not necessarily go off at a right angle; it may go in any direction at all! One word is given as an example.

```
R E X D I S T A K G U O
E N P T O N A M N U A R
V C O R Q Z O B H C P P
O C U R E A H I H B E P
G I I L R S N A T T R A
N N B T N H I G I C F D
D A S J T N E D E C E M
E M X S F I H Q N R G V
S R Y A U O F A P P L E
O M F R A C C Y E S R I
L R E Q E T N O C N H J
V C M D R U R N M R I D
Y M N T F R Z I L E O P
C O F E U E S Y V O H Q
W J G S L T L I V E T C
```

APPROACH	MANICURE
CHEMIST	MYSTIFY
CONTRIVE	PERFECTION
DISTANCE	PINEAPPLE ✓
ENCLOSED	PRESIDENT
FRACTURE	STRANGER
GOVERNOR	WONDERFUL

149

WORDSEARCH: IN THE PAST

Can you find all of the listed words relating to the past hidden in the grid below? Words run forwards or backwards, in either a horizontal, vertical or diagonal direction.

```
T N E I C N A H T I W R E V O
I O P A W H I L E A G O Y D K
D G R O D A Y S O F O L D E Z
Y A E S Z Y Y T P R I O R T O
K S C Y F R Z B C I A H C R A
Z R E L E O N N A M O P P A O
Y A D R E T S E Y C R S O P U
B E I E E S E K E E K U B E T
R Y N M T I L L V B T W Y D W
E V G R T H L I O O S X H C O
T H H O N M O R F S H A F E R
T L B F N U E D A A B F H X N
A W A Q S E A K B E F O R E E
L O L D I T S S E M I T D L O
O A N T E D I L U V I A N J V
```

A WHILE AGO	EARLIER	OUTWORN
ANCIENT	FORMERLY	OVER WITH
ANTEDILUVIAN	HAS-BEEN	PRECEDING
ARCHAIC	HISTORY	PREVIOUS
BEFORE	LATTER	PRIOR TO
BYGONE	OBSOLETE	WAY BACK WHEN
DAYS OF OLD	OLD TIMES	YEARS AGO
DEPARTED	OUT-OF-DATE	YESTERDAY

BREAK-TIME CROSSWORD

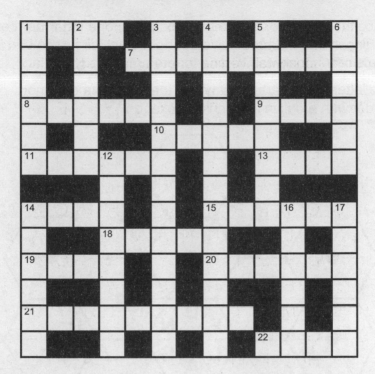

Across
1 Mislaid (4)
7 Dwelling place (9)
8 Design marked onto the skin (6)
9 Lubricates (4)
10 Projection at the end of a piece of wood (5)
11 Wade in shallow water (6)
13 Metallic element, symbol Fe (4)
14 Supports for a table (4)
15 Stay (6)
18 Gasps for breath (5)
19 Distribute playing cards (4)
20 Steal something (6)
21 Relaxed and informal in attitude or standards (4-5)
22 Naked (4)

Down
1 Portable computer (6)
2 Declared as a fact (6)
3 Device that is used to work a machine from a distance (6,7)
4 Interpret in the wrong way (13)
5 Lifestyle devoted to pleasure-seeking (8)
6 Human being (6)
12 Exhibits to view (8)
14 Tenant (6)
16 List of items for discussion (6)
17 Sewing tool (6)

HEXAFIT

Place the listed words into the hexagons, one letter per cell, starting in any of those surrounding a black circle, so that words read clockwise. Some letters are already in place.

The letter is the same in any cell that shares a common border with a cell in a touching hexagon.

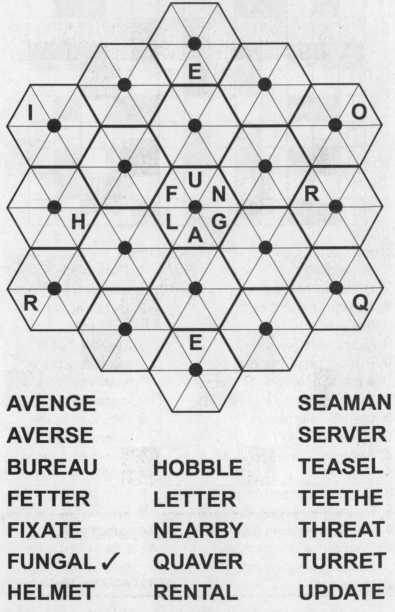

AVENGE

AVERSE

BUREAU   HOBBLE   TEASEL

FETTER   LETTER   TEETHE

FIXATE   NEARBY   THREAT

FUNGAL ✓   QUAVER   TURRET

HELMET   RENTAL   UPDATE

SEAMAN

SERVER

KAKURO

Fill the grid so that each block adds up to the total in the box above or to the left of it.

You can only use the digits 1-9, one per square, but the same digit must not be used twice in a block. The same digit may occur more than once in any row or column, but it must be in a separate block.

She has discovered the secret of perpetual middle age.

Oscar Levant about Zsa Zsa Gabor

SUDOKU

Place one of the numbers from 1 to 9 into every empty cell so that each row, each column and each 3x3 block contains all the numbers from 1 to 9.

5				7				1
8	2		5		1		7	4
			9	8	4			
	6						3	
1								5
	7						2	
			3	6	7			
7	9		2		5		4	6
3				9				2

What I've noticed is that almost no one who was a big star in high school is also a big star later in life.

For us overlooked kids, it's so wonderfully fair.

Mindy Kaling

DOMINO PLACEMENT

A standard set of twenty-eight dominoes has been laid out as shown below. Can you draw in the edges of them all? One is already in place.

It may be helpful to use the check-box to tick off the dominoes as they are found.

1	2	4	0	0	4	3	6
3	6	6	4	3	0	5	0
1	1	5	4	4	0	2	0
2	3	5	5	3	2	1	1
6	3	2	2	1	5	4	4
6	4	5	3	2	6	2	0
1	1	6	5	6	3	5	0

0-0	0-1	0-2	0-3	0-4	0-5	0-6	1-1

1-2	1-3	1-4	1-5	1-6	2-2	2-3	2-4	2-5	2-6
			✓						

3-3	3-4	3-5	3-6	4-4	4-5	4-6	5-5	5-6	6-6

ALPHAFILL

Place 25 different letters of the alphabet, one per circle, in order to spell out the listed words. Words are formed by moving between adjacent circles along the connecting lines, either horizontally, vertically or diagonally in any direction.

Begin by crossing out the letters already in place, together with the one letter which doesn't appear in any of the words.

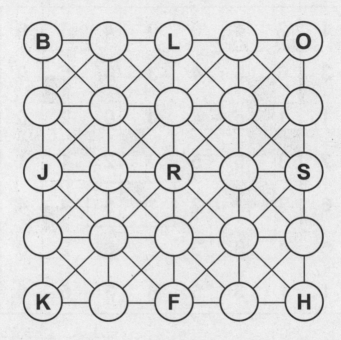

A B C D E F G H I J K L M

N O P Q R S T U V W X Y Z

BAUD	JURY	RINK
COVER	MYSTIQUE	SCOWL
DUPLEX	NIGH	STEP
JAB	PERVERT	VERIFY
JAPE	REVEL	VOWEL

NUMBER FILLER

Can you fit all of the listed numbers into the grid? One is already in place, to get you off to a good start!

2 digits	501	2618	7687	32732
17	563	3126	8181	47992
37 ✓	594	3624	8559	48378
49	844	3776	8695	53397
86	922	4245	8948	60458
	952	4544	9763	63170
3 digits		4886		92341
153	**4 digits**	5057	**5 digits**	
328	1360	5931	11313	**6 digits**
385	1537	6130	11576	267982
420	1906	6864	12533	710990
429	2270	6979	24769	751482
433	2455	7101	25358	805795

BREAK-TIME CROSSWORD

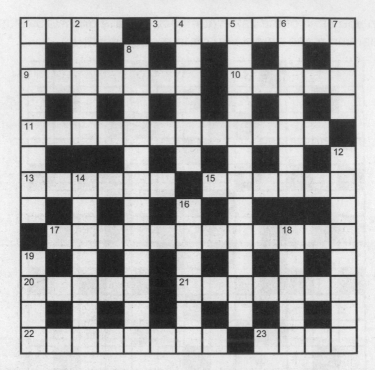

Across
1 Remedy (4)
3 Something that causes annoyance (8)
9 Ruled over (7)
10 Confusion, disarray (5)
11 Establish or decide in advance (12)
13 Replicated (6)
15 Consortium of companies formed to limit competition (6)
17 Expression of strong disapproval (12)
20 Develop fully (5)
21 Discharge (7)
22 Criminal who commits homicide (8)
23 Optical organs (4)

Down
1 Turtle's shell (8)
2 Bring up (5)
4 Blush, as if with shame (6)
5 Lacking in similar features (12)
6 Versus, opposed to (7)
7 Chore (4)
8 Freedom from control (12)
12 Steals goods, pillages (8)
14 Thrive, do well (7)
16 Come into view (6)
18 Country, capital Rome (5)
19 Percussion instrument (4)

CODEWORD

Every letter in this puzzle has been replaced by a number, the number remaining the same for that letter wherever it occurs. Every letter of the alphabet has been used. Substitute numbers for letters to complete the codeword.

It may help to cross off the letters beneath the grid to keep a track of progress, and to use the reference box showing which numbers have been decoded. Three letters have already been entered into the grid, to help you on your way.

8	18	25	25	9	9		3	8	1	23	2	9
3		3		17			3		22		14
10	15	6	6	9	10		8	10	3	4	11	9
6		11			18		10			15		10
18	10	9		12	18	7	9	10		8 C	18 O	5 G
22		4	9	3	25		7	9	10	9		9
			22				11					
8		13	15	23	1		14	3	24	19		4
9	14	15		8	3	11	16	26		23	8	9
11		23			22		1			21		3
11	18	2	23	22	5		19	3	20	3	10	4
3		9		23				5		8		11
10	3	10	9	11	16		4	18	22	17	9	16

A B C D E F G H I J K L M

N O P Q R S T U V W X Y Z

1	2	3	4	5 G	6	7	8 C	9	10	11	12	13
14	15	16	17	18 O	19	20	21	22	23	24	25	26

159

ROUND DOZEN

First solve the clues. All of the solutions begin with the letter in the central circle, and some others are already in place. When the puzzle is complete, you can then go on to discover the twelve-letter word reading clockwise around the outermost ring of letters.

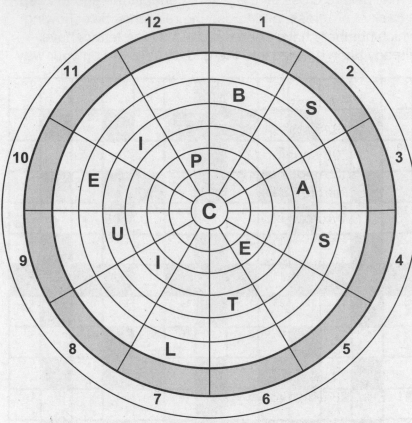

1 Barb-firing weapon
2 Infantile
3 Australian crested parrot
4 Merry-go-round
5 Animate being
6 Monument commemorating people who died in a war
7 Hymn-like song
8 Roman Emperor who succeeded Tiberius
9 Round
10 Shape of a new moon
11 Persuade by evidence
12 Storage place

The twelve-letter word is: _____

JIGSAW SUDOKU

Fit the numbers 1, 2, 3, 4, 5 and 6 into the grid in such a way that each horizontal row, each vertical column and each of the heavily outlined sections of six squares each contains a different number. Some numbers are already in place.

		1			
	3	5			
			2	1	
	5				
	6				4

WHAT DOES IT MEAN?

Which of the following is the correct definition of the word:

DISPARATE

1 To cause someone to lose their sense of direction

2 Showing extreme courage; especially of actions heroically undertaken as a last resort

3 Essentially different in kind; not able to be compared

SPIDOKU

In the spider's web below, each of the eight segments should be filled with a different number from 1 to 8, in such a way that every ring also contains a different number from 1 to 8.

The segments run from the outside of the spider's web to the middle, and the rings run all the way around. So that you can see the rings more clearly, we've shaded them grey and white.

Some numbers are already in place. Can you fill in the rest?

CUBE ROUTES

Fill the words into the grid (one letter is ready in place), changing route where necessary, as with this example:

ASPECT   ENDURE   SPED

CARE   REASON   WRITHE

CASE   ROE

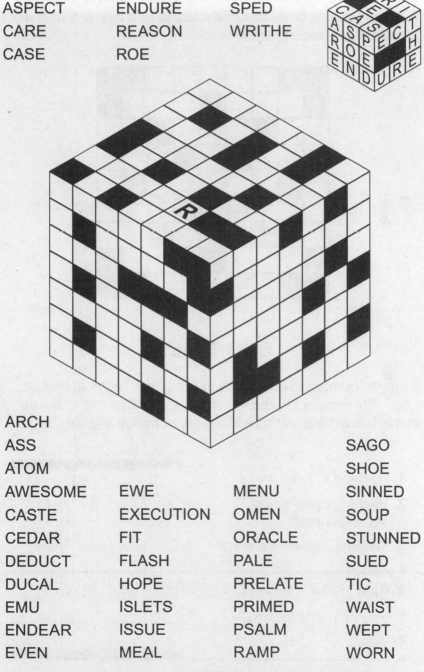

ARCH			
ASS			SAGO
ATOM			SHOE
AWESOME	EWE	MENU	SINNED
CASTE	EXECUTION	OMEN	SOUP
CEDAR	FIT	ORACLE	STUNNED
DEDUCT	FLASH	PALE	SUED
DUCAL	HOPE	PRELATE	TIC
EMU	ISLETS	PRIMED	WAIST
ENDEAR	ISSUE	PSALM	WEPT
EVEN	MEAL	RAMP	WORN

163

NUMBER CRUNCHER CROSSWORD

A little mathematical crossword, where a little knowledge of mathematics will come in very handy!

The answer to every clue on the opposite page is a number, the digits of which are entered into the grid below, just like a standard crossword puzzle.

EGG TIMER

Can you complete this puzzle in the time it takes to boil an egg? The answers to the clues are anagrams of the words immediately above and below, plus or minus a letter.

1 Relating to heat

2 Shakespearean play, set in Denmark

3 Material derived from ore

4 Squad

5 Bred

6 Bicycle made for two

7 Wild

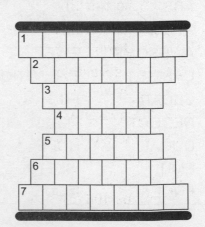

NUMBER CRUNCHER CROSSWORD

Across

1 203 squared plus 260 (5)

5 8 Across multiplied by four (3)

6 5 Across plus 14 Down plus nine (3)

8 One thirteenth of 7 Down (2)

9 Ounces in seven pounds (3)

11 One fifteenth of 15 Across (2)

13 22 Across multiplied by five (3)

15 27 Across minus one eleventh of 25 Across (3)

16 226 squared plus 292 (5)

17 21 Across plus 3 Down minus four (3)

19 Inches in 12 feet (3)

21 One thirteenth of 13 Across (2)

22 25 Across plus 28 Down (3)

24 One seventh of 14 Down (2)

25 11 squared (3)

27 13 Across plus 4 Down (3)

29 166 squared minus 108 (5)

Down

1 Two score (2)

2 19 Across minus three (3)

3 9 Across multiplied by six (3)

4 28 Down multiplied by two (2)

5 11 Across plus 2 Down plus one eleventh of 25 Across (3)

7 4 Down plus 14 Down plus 14 (3)

8 242 squared minus 88 (5)

10 106 squared plus 12 squared plus 4 squared (5)

12 22 Across multiplied by 25 Across (5)

14 17 Across minus seconds in three minutes (3)

15 13 Across plus 1 Down plus 4 Down (3)

18 5 Down plus 22 Down plus half of 1 Down (3)

20 Minutes in two hours plus 18 Down (3)

22 22 Across minus 52 (3)

23 1 Down plus 15 Down minus 27 (3)

26 Square root of 484 (2)

28 Months in four years (2)

LINK WORDS

Fit eight different words into the grid, so that each one links up with the words on either side, eg table - lamp - shade.

When finished, read down the letters in the shaded squares to reveal another word, solving the clue.

PLASTER					OFF
FOOT					LADDER
PENCIL					PIPE
GRAND					OPERATOR
LEAP					MARCH
EXTRA					PIECE
TAIL					DRIER
BUBBLE					TOWEL

Clue: Marine creature _____

BERMUDA TRIANGLE

Travel through the 'Bermuda Triangle', collecting a letter from each area. You can visit any area once only, and you must enter and exit through the holes in the walls between them. The starting letter may appear in any area.

When you've completed your tour, the 15 letters (in order) will spell out will spell out the name of an author (8,7).

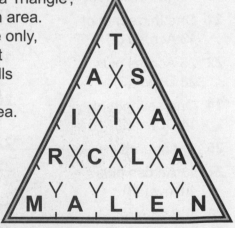

Author: _____

WORD LADDER

Change one letter at a time (but not the position of any letter) to make a new word – and move from the word at the top of the ladder to the word at the bottom using the exact number of rungs provided.

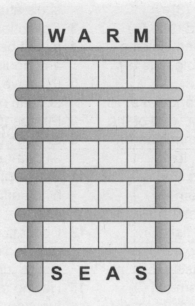

MEMORY TEST

Study the picture below for a few moments, then turn to page 203.

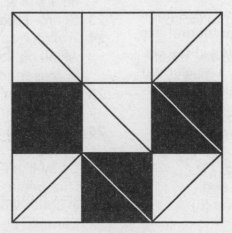

GENERAL KNOWLEDGE CROSSWORD

Across

1 Prejudiced (6)
7 Device that enables divers to breath under water (8)
8 Long noosed rope (6)
10 Australian tree yielding globular edible nuts (9)
13 Sag (5)
14 Angular distance of a place east or west of the Greenwich meridian (9)
17 Web-footed, long-necked birds (5)
20 Most free from danger or risk (8)
21 Salmon-like fish (5)
22 Put back into service after processing (5)
24 Pouched mammal (9)
26 Swamped with water (5)
27 Haemorrhage (5)
29 Property of being stiff and resisting bending (8)
30 From the Orient (5)
33 Pupa (9)
35 Belonging to those people (5)
36 Dish of stewed meat served in a thick white sauce (9)
40 Commend (6)
41 Clear soup made with concentrated meat stock (8)
42 In a level and regular way (6)

Down

1 Canine symbol of Britain (7)
2 Outermost region of the sun's atmosphere (7)
3 Collection of facts (4)
4 Insect between larva and adult stage (4)
5 Primitive, mainly aquatic organism (4)
6 Pitiless (6)
9 Enough to satisfy all demands (5)
11 Series of stories written by Geoffrey Chaucer: *The* ___ (10,5)
12 Cocktail made with rum and lime or lemon juice (8)
15 Having a valuable function (6)
16 Regarded highly (8)
18 Sense organ for hearing (3)
19 Steam baths (6)
21 Relating to the stage, actors or acting (8)
23 Sharp-eyed birds (6)
24 Trough from which cattle or horses feed (6)
25 Former name of Zimbabwe (8)
28 Geological time period (3)
30 Daisy-like flower (5)
31 Of a peninsula in south-western Europe (7)

GENERAL KNOWLEDGE CROSSWORD

32 Child's room (7)

34 Jean ___ (1911–37), US actress who made several movies with Clark Gable (6)

37 Proceedings in a court of law (4)

38 Japanese form of wrestling, contested in a small ring (4)

39 Fencing sword (4)

SUDOKU

Place one of the numbers from 1 to 9 into every empty cell so that each row, each column and each 3x3 block contains all the numbers from 1 to 9.

4							6	
9	8			7				
					3	1		
		3			1		7	
7	5			4			1	6
	9		5			2		
		5	8					
				6			4	7
	2							9

SAY WHAT YOU SEE

JIGWORD

A symmetrical crossword has been cut into pieces. Can you put it back together? Three pieces are already in position.

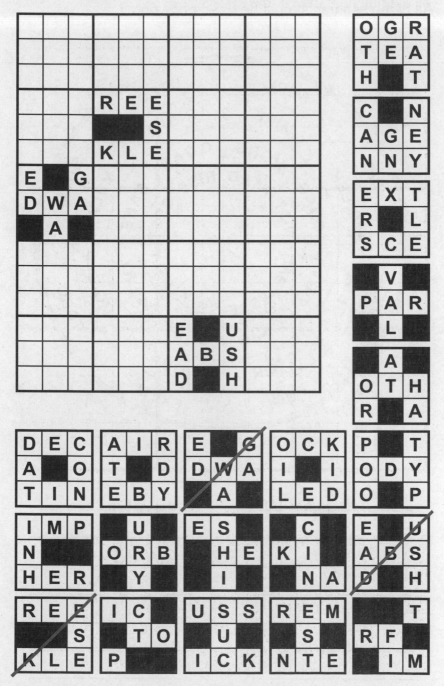

RING-WORDS

From the 32 segments below, find 16 eight-letter words by pairing one set of four letters with another.

All of the segments must be used once only.

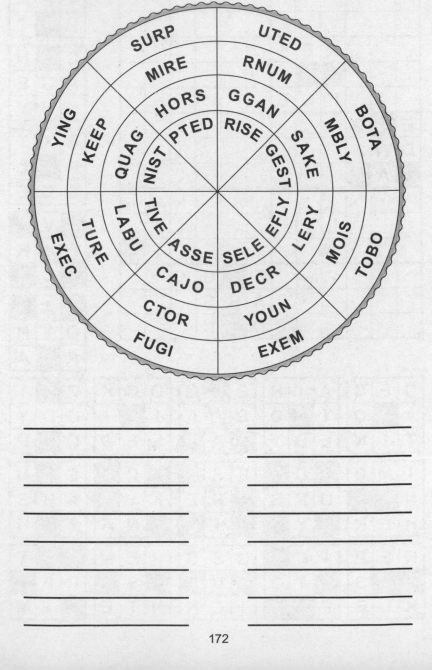

WELL SPOTTED

Some of the circles in this puzzle are already black. Fill in more white circles, so that the number of black circles totals the number inside the area they surround.

Every black circle surrounding an area with a number higher than '1' needs to be next to another black circle surrounding the same area.

When solving, it may help to put a small dot into any circle you know should not be filled.

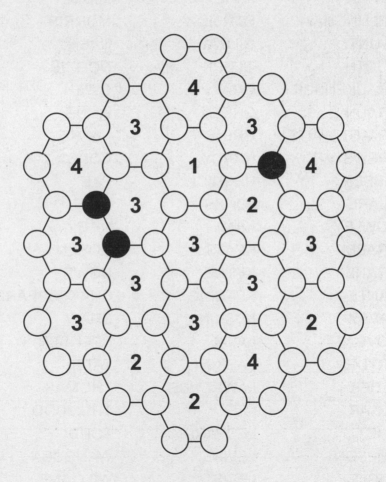

WORDSEARCH: POETS

Can you find all of the listed poets in the grid opposite?
Words run forwards or backwards, in either a horizontal,
vertical or diagonal direction.

ARMITAGE	ESHLEMAN	MAHON
BAKER	ESPADA	MANN
BARBOUR	EUSDEN	MARTIN
BEER	EVERSON	MCCUAIG
BEHAN	FAHEY	MILNE
BELLINGHAM	FORBES	MORRIS
BLUNT	GILRAY	NASH
BOOTH	GLUCK	NORTJE
BRACKENBURY	GRAY	OWEN
BRAUN	GREEN	PAINE
BRAUTHWAITE	GREY	PEAKE
BREWSTER	HARDY	POPE
CIBBER	HERRICK	PYE
CLARE	JONES	RICH
COWLEY	KANT	RILEY
CRABBE	KEATS	ROSEN
CRANE	KEENE	ROWE
DANTE	KEESING	SHAKESPEARE
DAVEY	KUSKIN	SHAW
DOVE	LAMB	SPENSER
DRYDEN	LARKIN	TATE
ELDER	LAWRENCE	THOMAS
ELGAR	LEE	THUMBOO
ELIOT	LEOPARDI	TODD
EMPSON	LEVINE	WANGUSA
ENGLE	LEVIS	WILLIAMS
ENRIGHT	LOGAN	WOLFE
ENSLIN	LONGFELLOW	WRIGHT

WORDSEARCH: POETS

```
L E O P A R D I R N T H G I R W T
H A R D Y E O X O Q I R I L I I J
C E M V B M T S W K I K L X L L I
P F T B R A C K E N B U R Y E L E
H O A A J J Q T L N A G A A Y I L
B R A U T H W A I T E D Y V L A G
C B A R B O U R O J H V A I V M N
L E K B L U N T T D C U Q P S S E
A S L B R E W S T E R L M V S Z D
R E G S A M O H T A K X D B U E S
E E N A G O L J M L J R E V O P U
N S I I O L F U O M Y O T C W O E
O H S I A B E N A D N D N X A P M
R L E P Q P G H E R E O A E H N P
T E E V E F G N H N K K D N S O S
J M K V E N M A C K A U A E Y H O
E A I L I R S O I D D R S E A A N
E N L L G N S E R G L U C K P M J
H O L D N Y E O R R Q L E Y I K E
W E S T A E K B N Q I S B E F N C
B N I L S N E K B B P S E O I H S
N Y G Q V Y N E C E Y E H A F T C
E E I B O W E N A I B N A S H O I
E V A Z A R A R A Q R R N G W O B
R A U L D K E N G M A R I L K B B
G D C E D O E D G G U R E P A S E
R Z C V O D V R L U N Y P H N K R
A R M I T A G E F E S M A R T I N
Y I B S E E C N E R W A L T P Y E
```

175

RED HERRING

Five of the words below must be entered in the grid, reading across, so as to create five more words reading down. Can you spot the red herring?

AGARS   **PASTA**

EASED   **ROLES**

KRONA   **SANDY**

LETTER TRACKER

Starting at the top left corner and ending at the bottom right, track a path from letter to letter, in any direction except diagonally, in order to find 15 hidden creepy-crawlies. All of the letters must be used, but none more than once.

G	R	A	A	I	L	S	I	F	I	S	M	L
B	D	S	T	G	N	I	L	R	M	H	R	O
U	E	S	H	O	P	R	V	E	E	W	O	C
G	B	R	E	F	P	P	S	O	A	L	S	U
M	I	H	A	F	E	V	I	T	I	U	T	T
L	L	C	Y	L	R	E	L	O	S	Q	R	H
I	P	K	C	F	W	E	H	M	G	I	I	P
D	E	C	O	R	E	V	O	N	E	W	L	F
E	I	C	H	N	E	U	M	O	A	R	E	A

DO IT YOURSELF!

In this crossword puzzle, the clues are in alphabetical order and there are no black squares in the grid. Black out the unwanted squares, to produce a symmetrically-patterned grid containing words that can be matched to the clues.

C	A	P	I	T	A	L	S	C	A	B	I	N
R	O	U	H	H	O	O	T	O	U	R	Y	E
A	I	R	E	R	E	A	D	A	M	A	N	T
M	U	G	L	E	A	D	I	X	A	V	I	D
P	R	E	P	A	R	E	D	I	D	O	D	O
U	O	M	I	T	E	D	A	N	C	E	I	T
B	A	S	K	E	T	O	S	A	L	U	T	E
A	D	O	A	N	U	T	S	U	C	H	T	L
T	S	A	R	A	P	R	O	T	O	C	O	L
O	P	O	P	W	A	I	L	I	T	L	P	I
W	A	R	S	H	I	P	E	C	H	A	I	N
I	N	T	O	I	T	O	P	A	Z	S	E	E
G	R	A	S	P	E	D	O	L	P	H	I	N

Clench, clutch tightly

Cloth woven from flax

Clothes drier

Collide

Combat vessel

Diplomatic etiquette

Extinct bird of Mauritius

Flog

Got ready

Intransigent

Main artery

Maritime

Mesh

Military greeting

Muscular spasm

Present a danger to

Primed with ammunition

Range of mountains

Rid of impurities

Routes

Russian monarch

Same again

Shopping bag

Sea mammal

Small house in the woods

Synthetic hairpiece

Three-legged support

Upper-case letter

Well done!

Wheedle

CALCUDOKU

Each row and column should contain the numbers 1-6. The numbers placed in a heavily outlined set of squares may be repeated, but must produce the calculation in the top left corner, using the mathematical symbol provided. So, for example, when multiplied, the numbers 3 and 4 total 12:

x12	
4	**3**

Any block of one square will contain the number in the top left corner.

−3		/4		+10	−2
/3		x180			
x6	+11		/2		+6
			+15	x6	
/2	+8				
			+14		

JIGSAW PUZZLE

Fit the jigsaw together to reveal eight sports and games.

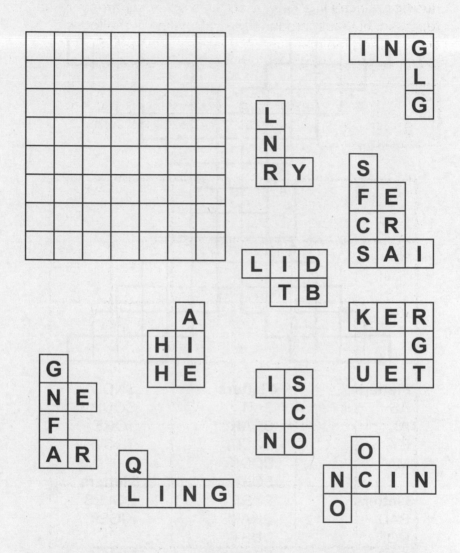

Like all young men, I set out to be a genius,

but mercifully laughter intervened.

Lawrence Durrell

X MARKS THE SPOT

Fill the grid with the listed words, one letter per square. All words are used just once.

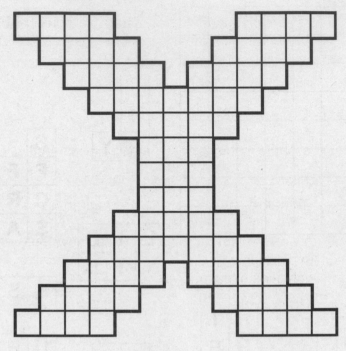

2 letters
AS
AT
BY
MA

3 letters
BAD
CON
GAS
LOT
OLD
SET
THE

4 letters
BAIT
BOAR
BOLT
BOOK
BORN
CYST
DRAM
DUST
EDAM
EURO
GUST
LORD
PALE
PORK
QUIT
SAND

SNOB
SOUP
TORE
TROW

5 letters
DOLES
KIOSK

7 letters
ORATION
QUADRAT
TOEHOLD

9 letters
LISTENERS
WAISTCOAT

GENERAL KNOWLEDGE QUIZ

Can you identify which one of the multiple-choice answers (a, b, c or d) is correct for each of the questions below?

1   The single-headed Middle Eastern darabuka and the double-headed Japanese tsuzumi are types of which musical instrument?

    a Tuba   **b** Drum

    c Organ   **d** Horn

2   Love Apple is the original name of which fruit?

    a Fig   **b** Pineapple

    c Tomato   **d** Pomegranate

3   Who was the first tennis player to achieve the Grand Slam of holding the Wimbledon, US, Australian and French titles simultaneously?

    a Rod Laver   **b** Fred Perry

    c Don Budge   **d** Bill Tilden

4   What was the first name of Spain's General Franco?

    a Juan   **b** Francisco

    c Frederico   **d** Pedro

5   The Camp David Agreement of 1978 was a Peace Treaty between which two nations?

    a India and Pakistan   **b** Iran and Iraq

    c USA and Russia   **d** Egypt and Israel

6   How many eyes does a bee have?

    a Two   **b** Three

    c Four   **d** Five

DOUBLE-CROSSER

Two crossword puzzles, but you have to decide which of the solutions to each clue fits into each grid. In both cases, one word has been entered to give you a start.

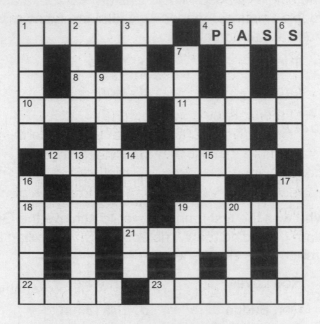

DOUBLE-CROSSER

Across

1 Concerned with religion; ___ Pepys, famous diarist (1633–1703) (6)

4 Overtake; Set of two (4)

8 On no occasion; Vivien ___, English film actress (1913–67) (5)

10 In an unfortunate manner; Totted up (5)

11 Fully developed person; Nimble (5)

12 Scurrilous, abusive; Unable to be heard (9)

18 Chief monk; Excuse for failure (5)

19 ___ Island, New York Bay area; Mixture containing two or more metallic elements (5)

21 Cone-shaped tent; State indirectly (5)

22 Speech defect; Wide way leading from one place to another (4)

23 Entry; One who transmits a message (6)

Down

1 Cold vegetable dish; Spicy sauce to accompany Mexican food (5)

2 Chilly; Intellect (4)

3 ___ Blyton, author; Feeling of desire (4)

5 Every twelve months; Something done (6)

6 Course; Less dangerous (5)

7 Native of Basra, for example; Recite with musical intonation (5)

9 Napoleon's exile island; Slippery fishes (4)

13 Immense cloud of gas and dust in space; Sounds (6)

14 Combine; Up to a time that (5)

15 Hollow metal device that rings when struck; Inactive (4)

16 Capital of Afghanistan; Capital of Senegal (5)

17 Consumers; ___ Cup, golf tournament played every two years (5)

19 Heroic; Recess in a church (4)

20 Ancient Greek harp; Let have for a limited time (4)

ROUND THE BLOCK

Each eight-letter word in the list is hidden in a square around a central letter that is not a part of the word itself, as shown by the example in the grid. The word may start anywhere within its 'square' and go either clockwise or anticlockwise. When all the listed words are found, the central letters spell out the name of a movie star.

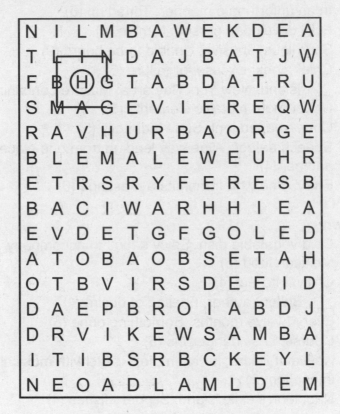

N	I	L	M	B	A	W	E	K	D	E	A
T	L	I	N	D	A	J	B	A	T	J	W
F	B	H	G	T	A	B	D	A	T	R	U
S	M	A	G	E	V	I	E	R	E	Q	W
R	A	V	H	U	R	B	A	O	R	G	E
B	L	E	M	A	L	E	W	E	U	H	R
E	T	R	S	R	Y	F	E	R	E	S	B
B	A	C	I	W	A	R	H	H	I	E	A
E	V	D	E	T	G	F	G	O	L	E	D
A	T	O	B	A	O	B	S	E	T	A	H
O	T	B	V	I	R	S	D	E	E	I	D
D	A	E	P	B	R	O	I	A	B	D	J
D	R	V	I	K	E	W	S	A	M	B	A
I	T	I	B	S	R	B	C	K	E	Y	L
N	E	O	A	D	L	A	M	L	D	E	M

ABSEILED   FEBRUARY

ADDITIVE   GAMBLING ✓

BATTERED   OBVIATED

DIABETES   SKEWBALD

EMBALMED   VERTEBRA

ROUND THE BEND

Instead of each word being hidden in a straight, continuous line, every word has one bend in it. This bend will not necessarily go off at a right angle; it may go in any direction at all! One word is given as an example.

ADJACENT	INSTRUCTIONS
BARRICADE	LEAKAGE ✓
CHARACTER	TELEPHONED
CONCENTRATE	HELICOPTER
DECEMBER	MAGICAL
DISPLAYING	NAPOLEONIC
HAPPINESS	REVERSAL

WORDSEARCH: HOBBIES AND PASTIMES

Can you find all of the listed hobbies and pastimes hidden in the grid below? Words run forwards or backwards, in either a horizontal, vertical or diagonal direction.

```
H H R G G N I T A K S J Y R G
V I R A N T W O I G U G A X N
C K M X F I O H N V O O A E S
J I I U H F F I A S D Y S T T
G N I W E S I R T U U Q R E G
W G X W O K N A U I J A H M A
G G H I S I M R W S D C W B R
U N Z N S P V I W O O K E R C
O I I H S R U D D R R E A O H
R G I L K G B I C J N K V I E
I N Q C W D A N C I N G I D R
G I K F H O L G L G S N N E Y
A S I I I E B T B A G U G R M
M P O Y X U S T I J U J M Y Z
I L Y R T E K S A B S G C T I
```

ARCHERY	HIKING	SINGING
BASKETRY	JUDO	SKATING
BOWLING	JU-JITSU	SKIING
CHESS	MUSIC	STAMPS
CROCHET	ORIGAMI	SURFING
DANCING	RAFFIA WORK	VARNISHING
DARTS	RIDING	WEAVING
EMBROIDERY	SEWING	YOGA

BREAK-TIME CROSSWORD

Across

1 Type of embroidery (5-6)
9 African venomous snake (5)
10 Less clouded (7)
11 Move forward (7)
12 Carved pole associated with native North Americans (5)
13 Act of returning a person to consciousness (13)
16 Spanish title of respect for a man (5)
18 Cry out (7)
20 Book of the New Testament written in the form of a letter (7)
21 Nimble, spry (5)
22 Claimed back (11)

Down

2 Takes away (7)
3 European country (5)
4 Trait of keeping things to oneself (13)
5 Popular chilled beverage (4,3)
6 Unit of weight for precious stones (5)
7 Caused to feel ashamed (11)
8 Integer that has no other factors but itself and one (5,6)
14 Musical passage in quicker time (7)
15 Fancy, suppose (7)
17 Ingenuous (5)
19 Talons (5)

HEXAFIT

Place the listed words into the hexagons, one letter per cell, starting in any of those surrounding a black circle, so that words read clockwise. Some letters are already in place.

The letter is the same in any cell that shares a common border with a cell in a touching hexagon.

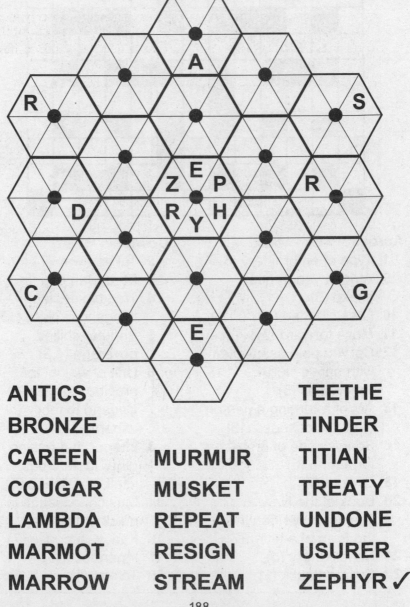

ANTICS   TEETHE

BRONZE   TINDER

CAREEN   MURMUR   TITIAN

COUGAR   MUSKET   TREATY

LAMBDA   REPEAT   UNDONE

MARMOT   RESIGN   USURER

MARROW   STREAM   ZEPHYR ✓

KAKURO

Fill the grid so that each block adds up to the total in the box above or to the left of it.

You can only use the digits 1-9, one per square, but the same digit must not be used twice in a block. The same digit may occur more than once in any row or column, but it must be in a separate block.

SUDOKU

Place one of the numbers from 1 to 9 into every empty cell so that each row, each column and each 3x3 block contains all the numbers from 1 to 9.

		9				1		
	1		8		7		2	
4			1		5			6
		7	5	8	3	6		
	5						8	
		6	7	1	9	3		
8			4		6			3
	9		3		1		7	
		4				2		

You can live to be a hundred if you give up all the
things that make you want to live to be a hundred.

Woody Allen

DOMINO PLACEMENT

A standard set of twenty-eight dominoes has been laid out as shown below. Can you draw in the edges of them all? One is already in place.

It may be helpful to use the check-box to tick off the dominoes as they are found.

6	5	3	1	6	2	4	5
4	1	0	0	1	3	1	2
3	6	6	6	1	3	2	0
4	1	4	6	1	4	5	5
4	2	4	5	6	2	5	5
5	3	3	2	2	6	3	3
0	2	0	1	4	0	0	0

0 - 0	0 - 1	0 - 2	0 - 3	0 - 4	0 - 5	0 - 6	1 - 1

1 - 2	1 - 3	1 - 4	1 - 5	1 - 6	2 - 2	2 - 3	2 - 4	2 - 5	2 - 6
								✓	

3 - 3	3 - 4	3 - 5	3 - 6	4 - 4	4 - 5	4 - 6	5 - 5	5 - 6	6 - 6

ALPHAFILL

Place 25 different letters of the alphabet, one per circle, in order to spell out the listed words. Words are formed by moving between adjacent circles along the connecting lines, either horizontally, vertically or diagonally in any direction.

Begin by crossing out the letters already in place, together with the one letter which doesn't appear in any of the words.

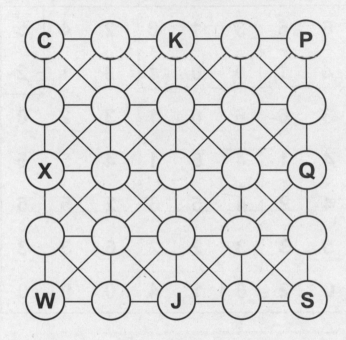

A B C D E F G H I J K L M

N O P Q R S T U V W X Y Z

BULK	FONT	PUNY
CHIN	JONQUIL	SOYA
CREAMY	LUNGS	WATER
CREDIT	MATING	WAVER
EXAM	NOTED	YETI

NUMBER FILLER

Can you fit all of the listed numbers into the grid? One is already in place, to get you off to a good start!

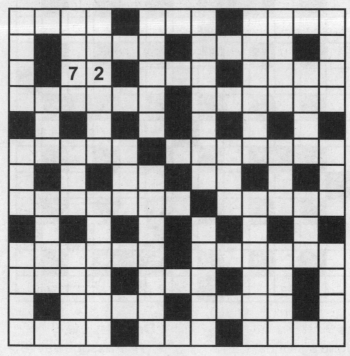

2 digits	739	6119	5 digits	7 digits
31	832	6147	12145	1007299
58	945	6573	16978	5023613
72 ✓	981	6657	37934	9583005
86		6698	72586	9814203
	4 digits	7279		
3 digits	1526	7421	**6 digits**	
189	1657	7570	137507	
231	2352	8038	264679	
283	2609	8547	322740	
304	4421	9921	332537	
387	4721		495669	
476	4735		648213	
598	5146		714834	
649	5846		849588	

BREAK-TIME CROSSWORD

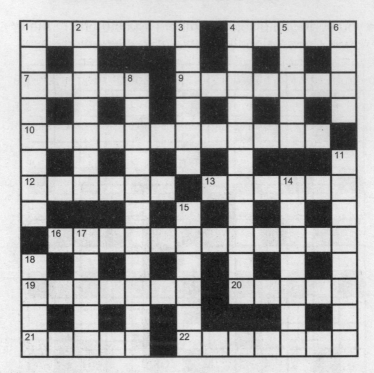

Across

1 World's swiftest mammal (7)
4 Drainage channel (5)
7 Circular (5)
9 Form again or differently (7)
10 Quirk (12)
12 Device for removing the tops of bottles, cans, etc (6)
13 Plot, plan (6)
16 Not fanciful or imaginative (6-2-4)
19 Bill (7)
20 Deviating from the truth (5)
21 Mark (~) placed over the letter 'n' in Spanish (5)
22 Castle cellar (7)

Down

1 Passageway (8)
2 Hard to catch (7)
3 Renting out (6)
4 Shockingly unacceptable (11)
5 Groups forming sides in a sport (5)
6 Pay close attention to (4)
8 Drink usually served with the final course of a meal (7,4)
11 Five-sided shape (8)
14 Consider in detail (7)
15 Pal, chum (6)
17 Blacksmith's block (5)
18 Cut back on certain foods (4)

CODEWORD

Every letter in this puzzle has been replaced by a number, the number remaining the same for that letter wherever it occurs. Every letter of the alphabet has been used. Substitute numbers for letters to complete the codeword.

It may help to cross off the letters beneath the grid to keep a track of progress, and to use the reference box showing which numbers have been decoded. Three letters have already been entered into the grid, to help you on your way.

24	14	25	5	5		23	14	6	15	10	5	6
5		12		25		13		2		17		1
25	12	23	6	12	11	6		21	14	26	7	6
12		6		6			13	15	22			2
16	13	14	26	12	25	16		14	6	16	15	9
13		20				13		4		26		23
	3	6	12	23	14	25	5	26	19	17	22	
11		16		14		6				12		9
6	1	23	14	15		24	5	17	11	23	6	14
12			26	9	23			12		10		15
11	13	15	10	6		24	15	16	23	26	14	22
26		24		18		25		17		8		6
14	6	23	14	6	15	23		23	6	12	26	14

Grid hints: cell (col7,row11) = 24 F; cell (col7,row12) = 25 I; cell (col7,row13) = 23 T

A B C D E F G H I J K L M

N O P Q R S T U V W X Y Z

1	2	3	4	5	6	7	8	9	10	11	12	13
14	15	16	17	18	19	20	21	22	23	24	25	26
									T	F	I	

SUM TOTAL

Fill each empty square so that every row contains ten different numbers from 0 to 9. In columns, the numbers may be repeated. The black squares show the sum total of the numbers in each column.

Wherever one square touches another either vertically or diagonally, the numbers must be different. Some are already in place.

	2							0	
6				5	3	0			7
	0	3			8	1	4	9	2
8		7	9	2	6	3	0		
	0				7				
	2	9		6		0	8		1
30	**6**	**36**	**42**	**27**	**37**	**6**	**29**	**32**	**25**

DO IT DIFFERENTLY

Do you always go for a walk following the same route? Maybe you always shop at the same store, or drive to work along the same roads? Take an alternative route, or shop at a different store.

Rearrange your kitchen, putting things in different cupboards or on different shelves. Who knows what you might come across while sorting things out!

Got a preferred armchair? Sit in another for the rest of the day and enjoy a different view of your room.

JIGSAW SUDOKU

Fit the numbers 1, 2, 3, 4, 5 and 6 into the grid in such a way that each horizontal row, each vertical column and each of the heavily outlined sections of six squares each contains a different number. Some numbers are already in place.

			1	5	
					4
		6			5
6	3			2	

WHAT DOES IT MEAN?

Which of the following is the correct definition of the word:

MELIORISM

1 The biological condition of having dark fur, scales, skin, plumage, etc
2 The belief that the world can be made significantly better by human effort
3 A ludicrous misuse of words, especially in mistaking a word for another resembling it

SPIDOKU

In the spider's web below, each of the eight segments should be filled with a different number from 1 to 8, in such a way that every ring also contains a different number from 1 to 8.

The segments run from the outside of the spider's web to the centre, and the rings run all the way around. So that you can see the rings more clearly, we've shaded them grey and white.

Some numbers are already in place. Can you fill in the rest?

CUBE ROUTES

Fill the words into the grid (one letter is ready in place), changing route where necessary, as with this example:

ASPECT	ENDURE	SPED
CARE	REASON	WRITHE
CASE	ROE	

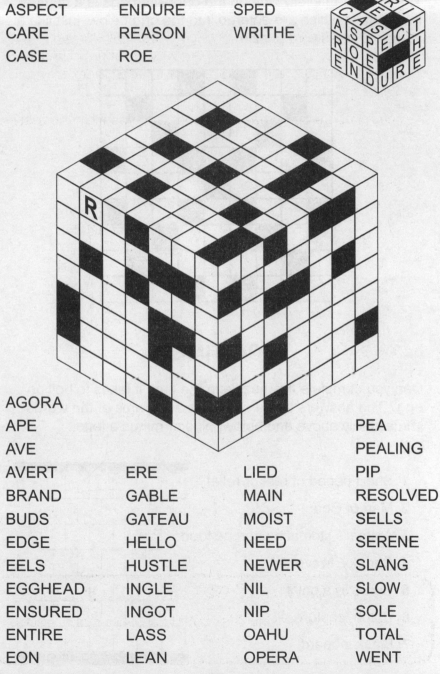

AGORA			PEA
APE			PEALING
AVE			PIP
AVERT	ERE	LIED	PIP
BRAND	GABLE	MAIN	RESOLVED
BUDS	GATEAU	MOIST	SELLS
EDGE	HELLO	NEED	SERENE
EELS	HUSTLE	NEWER	SLANG
EGGHEAD	INGLE	NIL	SLOW
ENSURED	INGOT	NIP	SOLE
ENTIRE	LASS	OAHU	TOTAL
EON	LEAN	OPERA	WENT

NUMBER CRUNCHER CROSSWORD

A little mathematical crossword, where a little knowledge of mathematics will come in very handy!

The answer to every clue on the opposite page is a number, the digits of which are entered into the grid below, just like a standard crossword puzzle.

EGG TIMER

Can you complete this puzzle in the time it takes to boil an egg? The answers to the clues are anagrams of the words immediately above and below, plus or minus a letter.

1 Short period of rest or relief

2 Man of God

3 Animal's stomach used as food

4 Cheeky, irreverent

5 Come to a point

6 Catch, capture

7 Black leopard

NUMBER CRUNCHER CROSSWORD

Across

1 One eighteenth of 26 Across (3)

4 14 Down minus 15 (3)

6 19 Down plus 3025 (5)

9 12 Across plus 15 Across plus 21 Across (2)

11 1 Across minus 27 Down (3)

12 Five ninths of 15 Across (2)

13 One eighteenth of 28 Across (2)

15 24 Across multiplied by two (2)

16 5 Down multiplied by nine (4)

17 28 Across multiplied by five (4)

18 2 Down minus 7 Down (2)

20 27 Down minus 7 Down (2)

21 One third of 12 Across (2)

22 One third of 28 Across (3)

24 One twelfth of 28 Across (2)

26 22 Across multiplied by 21 Down (5)

28 Inches in nine yards (3)

29 9 Across plus 11 Across plus two (3)

Down

1 5 Down plus 27 Down (3)

2 One quarter of 28 Across (2)

3 20 cubed (4)

4 2 Down plus two (2)

5 9 cubed plus 11 squared (3)

7 One third of 23 Down (2)

8 12 Across plus 27 Down (2)

10 5 Down multiplied by 27 Down (5)

12 185 squared minus square root of 169 (5)

14 12 Across plus 22 Across plus 25 Down (3)

15 24 squared minus 26 Down (3)

19 9 Across squared plus 212 (4)

21 12 Across plus 22 Across plus five (3)

22 30 per cent of 50 (2)

23 8 Down plus one third of 22 Down (2)

25 21 Down multiplied by five (3)

26 Days in a fortnight (2)

27 Seven squared (2)

BRICKWORK

Fill each empty square with a single-digit number from 1 to 8. No number may appear twice in any row or column.

In any set of two squares separated by dotted lines, one square contains an odd number and the other contains an even number.

	8		2	4			1
	4			7		8	
	2	4			8	3	
1	6		3		5		
		5		3			2
		6	7				4
		8					3
6		2		1	4		7

CHAIN LETTERS

Fill each empty circle with one of the letters A, B, C, D or E.

Every horizontal row, vertical column, set of five linked circles, and diagonal line of five circles should contain five different letters.

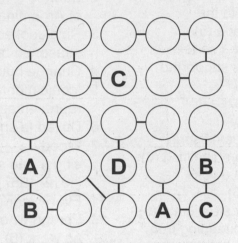

MEMORY TEST

Which of the following is a smaller version of the image on page 167? Make a choice, then turn back to page 167 to see if it is correct.

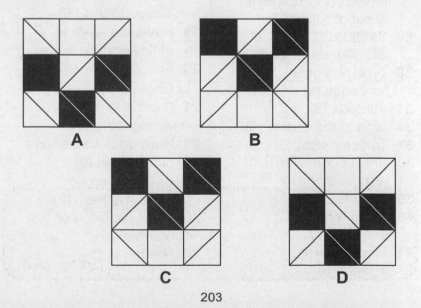

GENERAL KNOWLEDGE CROSSWORD

Across

1 Chafe at the bit, like a horse (5)
4 Letter carrier's shoulder pouch (7)
8 Relating to the countryside (5)
9 Bridge of a series of arches supported by piers (7)
10 Chimpanzee, for example (3)
12 Thick creamy soup made from shellfish (6)
14 One who owes money (6)
15 Domesticated llama (6)
17 Corset extending from waist to thigh (6)
20 Fear of spiders (13)
22 Small river (6)
23 Immature insects (6)
24 Predacious insect that rests with forelimbs raised as if in supplication (7,6)
28 Small solid extraterrestrial body (6)
30 Type of monkey, macaque (6)
31 Vitreous (6)
33 Sign of the zodiac (6)
37 To stretch out (3)
38 Short poem with a witty ending (7)
39 Particle of sand (5)
40 Tenth month of the year (7)
41 Flock of geese in flight (5)

Down

1 Tree with edible pods used as a chocolate substitute (5)
2 Buenos ___, capital of Argentina (5)
3 Rice cooked in well-seasoned broth (5)
4 Change position (4)
5 Iconic mental representation (5)
6 Dulled (a sharp edge) (7)
7 Woody ___, US folk singer and songwriter (1912–1967) (7)
11 Every year (3,5)
13 Person who does no work (5)
14 Excavate (3,2)
16 Thing that serves as a model or a basis for making copies (9)
18 River, the boundary between Mexico and Texas, USA (3,6)
19 Hawaiian garland of flowers (3)
20 Fabulist of Ancient Greece (5)
21 Assists in wrongdoing (5)
23 Humorous verse form of five lines (8)
25 Strong-scented perennial herb (3)
26 Easily agitated or alarmed (5)
27 Harden to (5)

GENERAL KNOWLEDGE CROSSWORD

28 Small dynamo with a
secondary winding (7)
29 Upholder of Russian
emperorship (7)
32 Bushy plant (5)
34 Kindly endorsement
and guidance (5)

35 Large wading bird (5)
36 Angry dispute (3-2)
37 Arabian ruler (4)

SUDOKU

Place one of the numbers from 1 to 9 into every empty cell so that each row, each column and each 3x3 block contains all the numbers from 1 to 9.

			1		9		6	4
			6		7		3	5
				5		2		
2			8		3		4	9
		9				3		
8	4		5		1			2
		5		6				
6	9		4		5			
7	8		9		2			

JIGWORD

A symmetrical crossword has been cut into pieces. Can you put it back together? Three pieces are already in position.

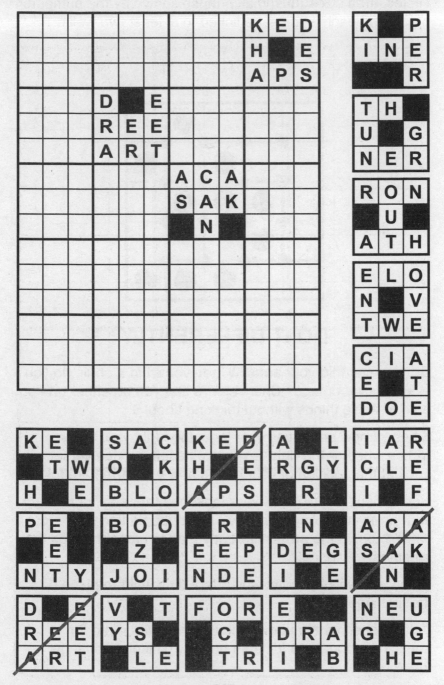

ISOLATE

Draw walls to partition the grid into areas (some walls are already drawn in for you). Each area must contain two circles, area sizes must match those shown by the numbers below and each '+' must be linked to at least two walls.

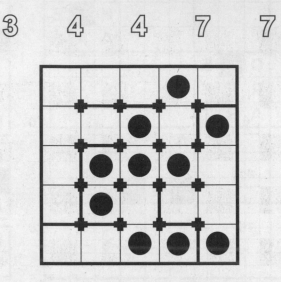

DO IT DIFFERENTLY

Do you ever fold your arms? When you sit in a chair, do you ever cross your legs? Chances are that you do either one or both of these things without thinking about it.

Sit down now and cross your legs, then fold your arms. Notice whether the right leg cross the left, or vice versa. Look at the position of your hands now your arms are folded.

How difficult is it to cross your legs the other way, or to fold your arms in the opposite way? Most people find it far more difficult to fold the arms differently than to cross the legs the other way.

When you walk upstairs, which foot do you lift to place on the first step?

Actions such as the above occur without the need for conscious thought, and it can be very difficult to change these habits.

AROUND THE SQUARES

The answer to each clue is a four-letter word, to be entered in the four squares surrounding the corresponding number in the grid. The word can start in any of the four squares and read either clockwise or anticlockwise. The first has already been entered.

	T					
T	1 E	2	3	4	5	
	N					
	6	7	8	9	10	
	11	12	13	14	15	
	16	17	18	19	20	
	21	22	23	24	25	

1 Canvas shelter
2 Person's title
3 Agricultural business
4 Self-satisfied
5 Group of criminals
6 Lacking sensation
7 Shaft of light
8 Capital of Latvia
9 Wrecked building
10 Ladder step
11 White lactic liquid
12 Weight-loss regime
13 Birthday present, for example
14 Piece of money
15 Common water bird
16 Place to swim
17 Poke
18 Idiot
19 Flat mass of ice floating at sea
20 Large brown seaweed, wrack
21 Magnifying camera lens
22 Ripped
23 Midday
24 Settee
25 Soft white bath powder

WORD FILLER

On the opposite page is a poem for those solvers who enjoy the style of nonsense verse propagated in the 19th century by Edward Lear. If you are sharp enough to work out the hidden meaning contained within the verses, you are best advised to keep it to yourself.

All of the underlined words will fit into the grid below. One letter is already in place: complete the puzzle!

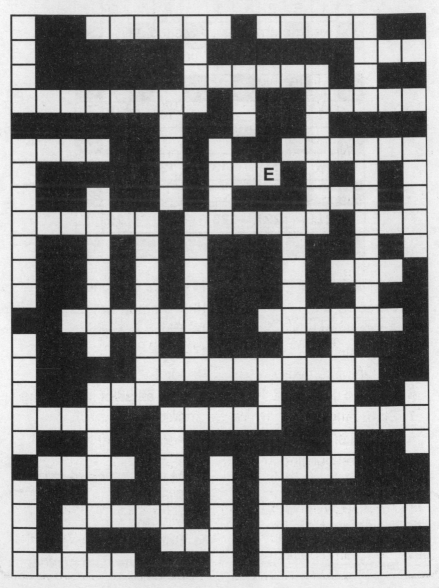

WORD FILLER

Medical Problem

The <u>medicine</u> <u>men</u> of the <u>Linctus</u> <u>tribe</u>
<u>Spend</u> a great <u>many</u> <u>hours</u> making potions
Together with tablets and <u>syrups</u> and <u>creams</u>
And a range of <u>superb</u> <u>suntan</u> lotions.

Ailing children <u>are</u> visited daily
<u>Medication</u> is <u>spooned</u> down <u>their</u> throats
<u>Made</u> <u>from</u> chickweed and apricot <u>essence</u>
And fresh <u>milk</u> from Peruvian <u>goats</u>.

No <u>illness</u> proves such a great <u>problem</u>
<u>That</u> they <u>cannot</u> (by using their <u>brains</u>)
Diagnose <u>all</u> the <u>symptoms</u> and <u>cure</u> them
So their <u>patient</u> <u>his</u> <u>health</u> <u>soon</u> <u>regains</u>.

<u>Every</u> <u>doctor</u> should truly consider, therefore
Utilizing <u>the</u> methods <u>and</u> wealth
Of knowledge <u>these</u> <u>people</u> can offer
For the <u>sake</u> of the <u>national</u> health!

<u>But</u> <u>there</u> is just the tiniest <u>setback</u>
(And <u>it's</u> <u>one</u> <u>which</u> we should <u>not</u> forgive)
Simply: <u>no-one</u> <u>can</u> ever consult <u>them</u>
For nobody knows where they <u>live</u>!

YOU KNOW YOU'RE GETTING OLD WHEN ...

The clothes that you put away until they came back in style have now come back in style, yet again.

RED HERRING

Five of the words below must be entered in the grid, reading across, so as to create five more words reading down. Can you spot the red herring?

AGREE   MESSY

IMAGE   PAPAW

LAIRD   SLAVE

LETTER TRACKER

Starting at the top left corner and ending at the bottom right, track a path from letter to letter, in any direction except diagonally, in order to find 18 hidden metals and alloys. All of the letters must be used, but none more than once.

P	L	A	T	I	H	O	N	G	E	C	R	T
Z	S	S	A	N	R	D	A	A	S	O	E	I
I	N	B	R	U	M	I	M	N	E	P	P	T
P	C	Y	C	R	M	U	E	Z	N	O	N	A
E	W	R	U	E	E	C	T	M	B	R	I	U
E	T	U	M	M	L	E	R	U	F	L	S	M
R	N	I	C	R	I	Z	M	A	R	O	T	E
C	I	N	O	O	N	A	D	N	G	W	L	E
K	E	L	I	R	L	E	T	U	S	T	E	N

DO IT YOURSELF!

In this crossword puzzle, the clues are in alphabetical order and there are no black squares in the grid. Black out the unwanted squares, to produce a symmetrically-patterned grid containing words that can be matched to the clues.

L	I	B	E	L	L	A	L	L	E	G	E	D
E	V	A	N	I	M	B	U	E	M	E	N	U
M	A	N	E	F	O	R	E	I	G	N	E	R
U	R	D	U	E	T	U	R	I	N	I	A	A
R	E	A	P	S	A	P	R	O	V	E	R	B
U	R	G	E	T	O	T	E	P	E	R	I	L
W	E	E	D	Y	E	A	R	P	A	D	R	E
I	D	E	A	L	S	C	A	R	Y	R	O	E
T	A	F	F	E	T	A	M	E	N	A	C	T
H	V	I	R	U	S	N	E	S	T	S	K	I
O	U	R	S	E	L	V	E	S	U	T	U	G
U	P	S	A	Y	S	A	L	E	T	I	C	H
T	O	T	T	E	R	S	A	D	U	C	A	T

Adult male person
Aladdin's spirit
Brandy measure
Claimed, but not proved
Close-fitting
Crushed, persecuted
Devoid of
Dressing for a wound
Forceful and extreme
Foremost

Gold coin formerly used in Europe
Hard-wearing
Harvests
Madagascan primate
Manner of existing
Military chaplain
Play out
Pull sharply
Of poor stature
Organ of sight

Ornamental garland
Road vehicle
Saying
Shiny silk-like fabric
Sudden
Type of strong cloth
Us
Visitor from another country
Walks unsteadily
Written defamation

DICE SECTION

Printed onto every one of the six numbered dice are six letters (one per side), which can be rearranged to form the answer to each clue; however, some sides are invisible to you. Use the clues and write every answer into the grid. When correctly filled, the letters in the shaded squares, reading in the order 1 to 6, will spell out the name of a composer.

1 Blossom, bloom
2 Beaded counting frame
3 Mythical fire-breather
4 Landing strip
5 Most uncommon
6 Orange root vegetable

JIGSAW PUZZLE

Fit the jigsaw together to reveal eight car manufacturers.

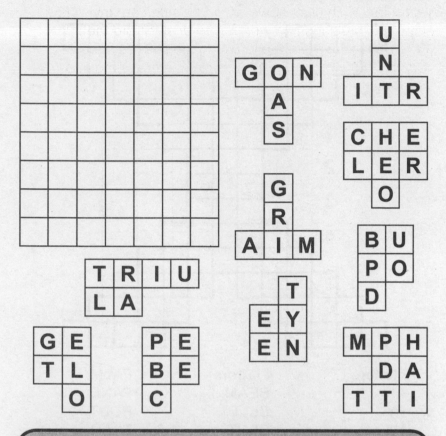

The trouble about reaching the age of 92, which I did last October, is that regrets for a misspent life are bound to creep in, and whenever you see me with a furrowed brow you can be sure that what is on my mind is the thought that if only I had taken up golf earlier and devoted my whole time to it, instead of fooling about writing stories, I might have got my handicap down to under 18. If only they had put a putter in my hands when I was four and taught me the use of the various clubs, who knows what heights I might not have reached?

P G Wodehouse

X MARKS THE SPOT

Fill the grid with the listed words, one letter per square. All words are used just once.

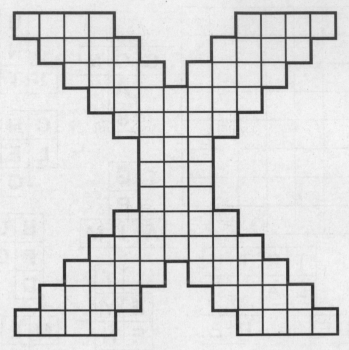

2 letters	4 letters	PALM
AN	BEAM	PANE
BY	BELT	POUT
ME	BENT	TSAR
WE	BLED	
	CRIB	**5 letters**
	DYED	BORIC
3 letters	EACH	FILLY
ANT	GONE	
COT	GORY	**7 letters**
LAY	HALF	CLIP ART
NIL	HASP	PERTURB
PER	LAWN	PLACARD
SPA	LOUD	
TAD	LYRE	**9 letters**
	MILL	PALLADIUM
	NOAH	RAINSTORM

HALF AND HALF

Pair off these groups of three letters to name eight weather-related words, each comprising six letters.

MER UDY GHT FRO

RMY CHI STY TOR

BRI RID CLO SQU

WAR ALL LLY STO

_____   _____

_____   _____

_____   _____

_____   _____

Stuff your eyes with wonder; live as if
you'd drop dead in ten seconds.

See the world. It's more fantastic than any
dream made or paid for in factories.

Ray Bradbury

DOUBLE-CROSSER

Two crossword puzzles, but you have to decide which of the solutions to each clue fits into each grid. In both cases, one word has been entered to give you a start.

DOUBLE-CROSSER

Across

1 Nick; Trick (5)

3 Discernment ;Jobs that must be done (5)

6 Police investigator; Refused to do business with (9)

10 Poke or thrust abruptly; Sign of something about to happen (4)

12 Form of address; Perceive by sight (3)

13 Close by; Dread (4)

15 Communist state in the Caribbean; Three-dimensional shape (4)

16 Fish eggs; Public transport vehicle (3)

17 Decorates with frosting; Lob, pitch (4)

20 Foundation garments; Unorthodox (9)

23 Flexible part of a whip; Projection on a fork (5)

24 Celestial path; Worth (5)

Down

1 Notorious Roman emperor; Prolonged periods of time (4)

2 Periodic rise and fall of sea level; Type of sousaphone (4)

3 As well; Twitch (3)

4 Posed for artistic purposes; Travel across snow (3)

5 Large northern sea duck; Remove the fleece from (5)

7 Lewd; Subjugate (7)

8 Arch of facial hair; Large deer (7)

9 Republic in north-western Africa; Shiny silk-like fabric (7)

11 Ballet skirt; List of dishes available (4)

14 Exclamation expressive of sorrow; Having the skills and qualifications to do well (4)

15 Compact mass, cluster; Hollywood actor, ____ Eastwood (5)

18 Examination conducted by word of mouth; Marine crustacean (4)

19 Condiment, sodium chloride; Identical (4)

21 Brazilian port, ____ de Janeiro; Two performers (3)

22 Piece of scrap material; Prevent from speaking out (3)

ROUND THE BLOCK

Each eight-letter word in the list is hidden in a square around a central letter that is not a part of the word itself, as shown by the example in the grid. The word may start anywhere within its 'square' and go either clockwise or anticlockwise. When all the listed words are found, the central letters spell out the name of a movie star.

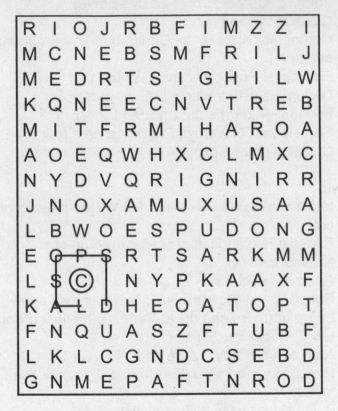

R	I	O	J	R	B	F	I	M	Z	Z	I
M	C	N	E	B	S	M	F	R	I	L	J
M	E	D	R	T	S	I	G	H	I	L	W
K	Q	N	E	E	C	N	V	T	R	E	B
M	I	T	F	R	M	I	H	A	R	O	A
A	O	E	Q	W	H	X	C	L	M	X	C
N	Y	D	V	Q	R	I	G	N	I	R	R
J	N	O	X	A	M	U	X	U	S	A	A
L	B	W	O	E	S	P	U	D	O	N	G
E	O	P	S	R	T	S	A	R	K	M	M
L	S	C		N	Y	P	K	A	A	X	F
K	A	L	D	H	E	O	A	T	O	P	T
F	N	Q	U	A	S	Z	F	T	U	B	F
L	K	L	C	G	N	D	C	S	E	B	D
G	N	M	E	P	A	F	T	N	R	O	D

CHARMING   REJOICED

DISPOSAL ✓   SAUCEPAN

DYNAMITE

     STUBBORN

GARRISON

KRAKATOA   THRILLER

MINISTER   UPSTREAM

ROUND THE BEND

Instead of each word being hidden in a straight, continuous line, every word has one bend in it. This bend will not necessarily go off at a right angle; it may go in any direction at all! One word is given as an example.

ASCERTAIN   RENDITION

CAPTAINCY   SHOPPING ✓

CHILLING   SUPERVISE

FESTIVAL   TOMORROW

GULLIBLE   TORRENTIAL

INVITED   VEHEMENT

MARGINAL   WALLABY

WORDSEARCH: MOUNTAIN RANGES

Can you find all of the listed mountain ranges hidden in the grid below? Words run forwards or backwards, in either a horizontal, vertical or diagonal direction.

```
A S B U E O C L M K I O K B C
T L H S A L T A S J L R G Q I
V A T A M A U K H R A N Y B P
V R W X L M S R O Z D V O S M
U U E N U T H O O J S O W I Y
P B S F A T A B S F H P U E L
N O T E T P R I A B A A S R O
H T E C I Q I N C X N D R R O
P Z R Q H M N S N J K V I A H
C A N W J I X O N D I S S N Z
J G G P N G T N J A N O F E D
R R H J W T A I W H F Q N V F
J O A G U L S G U F G Y D A N
M S T S J R T H T N A M A D A
E L S C H W A T K A K M Q A E
```

ADAMANT	HANKIN	SIERRA NEVADA
ALTAI	HARAZ	SUTTON
ATLAS	HOOSAC	TETON
BYNAR	JURA	TUSHAR
DOURO	OLYMPIC	TUXTLA
FANNIN	OZARK	URALS
FANSIPAN	ROBINSON	WESTERN GHATS
GYDAN	SCHWATKA	ZAGROS

BREAK-TIME CROSSWORD

Across

1 In attendance (7)
5 Slightly wet (5)
9 Bird, a symbol of peace (4)
10 Stand still, cease to flow (8)
12 Commence (5)
13 Unusually great in size (7)
15 Precious stones (6)
17 Misplacing (6)
19 Inhabitant of Rome, maybe (7)
21 Book of maps (5)
23 Fashionable seaside resort in Mexico (8)
25 Once ____ a time (4)
26 High body temperature (5)
27 Removed dirt (7)

Down

2 Former US president (9)
3 Germ-free (7)
4 Olfactory organ (4)
6 Unit of weight (5)
7 Took a chair (3)
8 Warm-blooded creature (6)
11 Biblical first woman (3)
14 Island south of the Malay Peninsula (9)
16 Slow-moving molluscs (6)
18 Citrus fruit (7)
19 Former Hollywood star, ____ Lupino (3)
20 Momentary failure (5)
22 Young horse (4)
24 Signal for action (3)

HEXAFIT

Place the listed words into the hexagons, one letter per cell, starting in any of those surrounding a black circle, so that words read clockwise. Some letters are already in place.

The letter is the same in any cell that shares a common border with a cell in a touching hexagon.

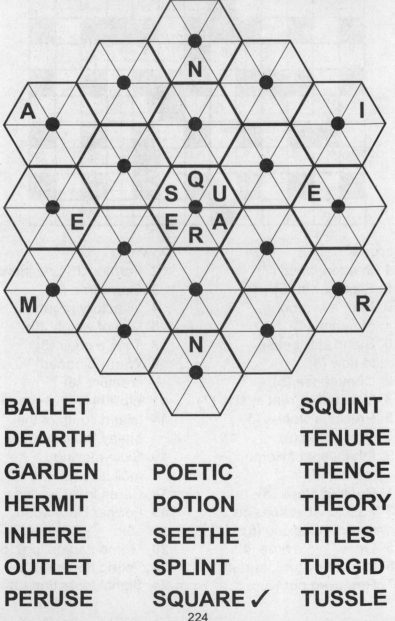

BALLET

DEARTH

GARDEN   POETIC

HERMIT   POTION

INHERE   SEETHE

OUTLET   SPLINT

PERUSE   SQUARE ✓

SQUINT

TENURE

THENCE

THEORY

TITLES

TURGID

TUSSLE

KAKURO

Fill the grid so that each block adds up to the total in the box above or to the left of it.

You can only use the digits 1-9, one per square, but the same digit must not be used twice in a block. The same digit may occur more than once in any row or column, but it must be in a separate block.

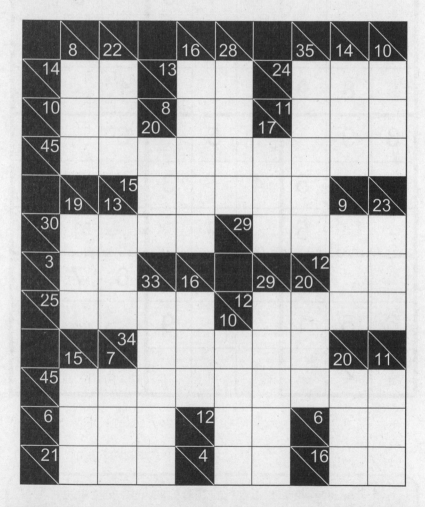

SUDOKU

Place one of the numbers from 1 to 9 into every empty cell so that each row, each column and each 3x3 block contains all the numbers from 1 to 9.

1				4	6		3	
			8			7	9	2
	8	9			7	1		
3	9			5		6		
		6	4		3	2		
		5		9			1	7
		4	5			8	7	
6	5	1			9			
	2		1	3				5

The love we have in our youth is superficial compared

to the love that an old man has for his old wife.

Will Durant

DOMINO PLACEMENT

A standard set of twenty-eight dominoes has been laid out as shown below. Can you draw in the edges of them all? One is already in place.

It may be helpful to use the check-box to tick off the dominoes as they are found.

3	3	3	6	6	0	3	0
1	4	2	3	1	1	2	1
5	1	4	6	2	4	5	6
4	4	3	5	1	6	0	2
0	4	5	0	6	5	2	1
3	2	0	2	2	4	4	6
5	6	3	5	5	0	0	1

0-0	0-1	0-2	0-3	0-4	0-5	0-6	1-1
				✓			

1-2	1-3	1-4	1-5	1-6	2-2	2-3	2-4	2-5	2-6

3-3	3-4	3-5	3-6	4-4	4-5	4-6	5-5	5-6	6-6

ALPHAFILL

Place 25 different letters of the alphabet, one per circle, in order to spell out the listed words. Words are formed by moving between adjacent circles along the connecting lines, either horizontally, vertically or diagonally in any direction.

Begin by crossing out the letters already in place, together with the one letter which doesn't appear in any of the words.

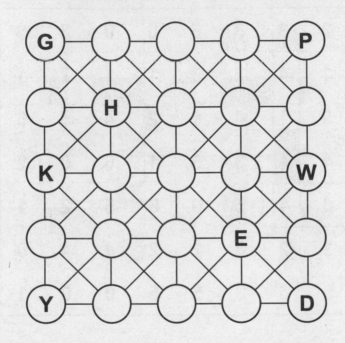

A B C D E F G H I J K L M

N O P Q R S T U V W X Y Z

AMAZE	FAME	SPOIL
AQUALUNG	JUNK	STILE
CHUNK	KALE	THUMBED
DELAY	NUMBER	WITH
EXIST	POWER	YAK

NUMBER FILLER

Can you fit all of the listed numbers into the grid? One is already in place, to get you off to a good start!

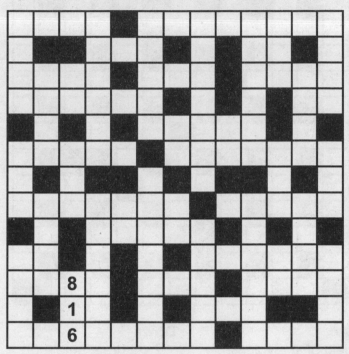

2 digits	3 digits	4 digits	5 digits	7 digits
15	136	1056	16810	1440142
32	137	1099	23690	2923378
35	329	2553	26484	7836695
44	400	3071	37782	7953648
54	515	4676	49642	
66	647	5410	52930	**8 digits**
71	703	5435		39709528
88	800	5577	**6 digits**	45699222
91	816 ✓	6082	231507	
92	825	6088	328259	
		7604	665348	
		7778	911476	
		8934	965311	
		9810	992203	

BREAK-TIME CROSSWORD

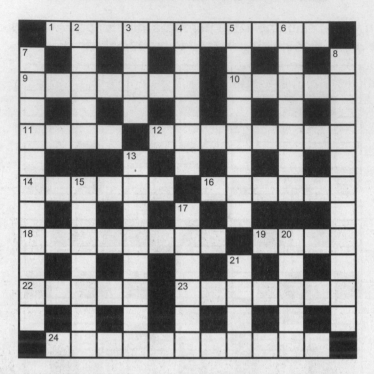

Across

1 Field of study dealing with numbers (11)
9 Male sibling (7)
10 Extremely angry (5)
11 Ballet dancer's skirt (4)
12 Penitent (8)
14 False (6)
16 Hard-cased arthropod (6)
18 Country, capital Bangkok (8)
19 Sound reflection (4)
22 Further from the middle (5)
23 As a rule (7)
24 Movement by successive stages (11)

Down

2 At great height (5)
3 Ditch used to divide lands without hiding a view (2-2)
4 Looking glass (6)
5 Number widely considered to be unlucky (8)
6 Two-wheeled, horse-drawn vehicle (7)
7 Blockage (11)
8 Be of one mind, think alike (3,3,2,3)
13 North American amphibian with a deep-pitched voice (8)
15 Disloyal person (7)
17 Put up with (6)
20 Musical instrument (5)
21 Hard fruits (4)

CODEWORD

Every letter in this puzzle has been replaced by a number, the number remaining the same for that letter wherever it occurs. Every letter of the alphabet has been used. Substitute numbers for letters to complete the codeword.

It may help to cross off the letters beneath the grid to keep a track of progress, and to use the reference box showing which numbers have been decoded. Three letters have already been entered into the grid, to help you on your way.

23	10	11	20	11	5	10		17	11	7	9	24
11		7		8		13		12		24		11
15	10	13	21	11		2	12	21	13	23	24	20
4		24		13		11		15		5		18
11	3	12	11	6 T	13 I	15 C		10	5	6	18	26
9				24		4			19		13	
24	14	17	5	7	26		6	20	11	19	24	18
	13		7			16		13				24
24	25	23	24	18		24	11	1	6	24	20	21
18		20		11		23		4		18		9
22	5	5	18	13	1	10		13	21	24	23	6
13		21		6		26		21		15		10
21	24	24	7	26		20	13	9	10	6	18	26

A B C D E F G H I J K L M

N O P Q R S T U V W X Y Z

1	2	3	4	5	6 T	7	8	9	10	11	12	13 I
14	15 C	16	17	18	19	20	21	22	23	24	25	26

ROUND DOZEN

First solve the clues. All of the solutions begin with the letter in the centre of the circle. When the puzzle is complete, you can then go on to discover the twelve-letter word reading clockwise around the outermost ring of letters.

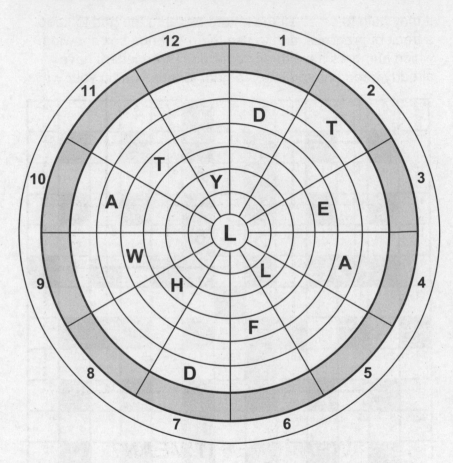

1 Retriever dog		**7** Da Vinci's forename
2 Set free		**8** Lack of energy
3 Reduced		**9** Tepid
4 Sparkling citrus drink		**10** Rip or tear
5 Sweet on a stick		**11** Extend
6 Rubbish burial		**12** Lazy person

The twelve-letter word is: _____

JIGSAW SUDOKU

Fit the numbers 1, 2, 3, 4, 5 and 6 into the grid in such a way that each horizontal row, each vertical column and each of the heavily outlined sections of six squares each contains a different number. Some numbers are already in place.

	4	6			
				4	
	1		5		
5			6		2
	2				

WHAT DOES IT MEAN?

Which of the following is the correct definition of the word:

INTEROSCULATE

1 To share certain characteristics; to form a connecting link, as between objects, genera, etc
2 To insert (misleading words or passages, for example) into a book, etc
3 To act as a mediator, especially in disputes between people who are related by marriage

SPIDOKU

In the spider's web below, each of the eight segments should be filled with a different number from 1 to 8, in such a way that every ring also contains a different number from 1 to 8.

The segments run from the outside of the spider's web to the centre, and the rings run all the way around. So that you can see the rings more clearly, we've shaded them grey and white.

Some numbers are already in place. Can you fill in the rest?

CUBE ROUTES

Fill the words into the grid (one letter is ready in place), changing route where necessary, as with this example:

ASPECT   ENDURE   SPED
CARE   REASON   WRITHE
CASE   ROE

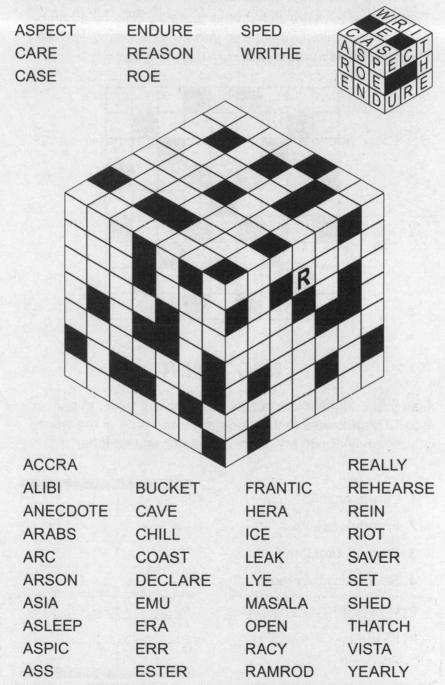

ACCRA			REALLY
ALIBI	BUCKET	FRANTIC	REHEARSE
ANECDOTE	CAVE	HERA	REIN
ARABS	CHILL	ICE	RIOT
ARC	COAST	LEAK	SAVER
ARSON	DECLARE	LYE	SET
ASIA	EMU	MASALA	SHED
ASLEEP	ERA	OPEN	THATCH
ASPIC	ERR	RACY	VISTA
ASS	ESTER	RAMROD	YEARLY

NUMBER CRUNCHER CROSSWORD

A little mathematical crossword, where a little knowledge of mathematics will come in very handy!

The answer to every clue on the opposite page is a number, the digits of which are entered into the grid below, just like a standard crossword puzzle.

1		2		3		4		5
		6	7		8			
9	10		11				12	
	13	14				15		
16					17			
	18			19		20		
21			22		23		24	25
		26					27	
28						29		

EGG TIMER

Can you complete this puzzle in the time it takes to boil an egg? The answers to the clues are anagrams of the words immediately above and below, plus or minus a letter.

1 Lured, cajoled

2 Fraudulence

3 Decree, proclamation

4 Secured with a rope

5 Lukewarm

6 Portray

7 Forecast

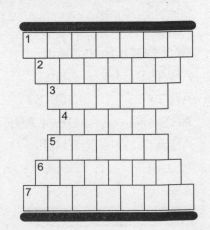

NUMBER CRUNCHER CROSSWORD

Across

1 One eleventh of
17 Across (3)

4 11 Across minus 87 (3)

6 205 squared plus
seven (5)

9 4 Down plus one sixth
of 12 Across (2)

11 8 Down multiplied
by six (3)

12 7 Down plus eight (2)

13 12 Across plus nine (2)

15 18 Across plus 8 Down
minus one (2)

16 8 Down plus 19 Down
plus 12 Across plus
18 Across (4)

17 16 Across plus
24 Across minus 292 (4)

18 4 Down plus 22 Down
plus two (2)

20 15 Across plus one (2)

21 Months in four years (2)

22 11 Across plus
21 Across (3)

24 One eighth of
28 Across (2)

26 311 squared plus half
of 28 Across (5)

28 2 Down multiplied
by four (3)

29 1 Across minus two (3)

Down

1 29 Across plus 22 Down
plus one (3)

2 Four cubed (2)

3 Ounces in
126 pounds (4)

4 Feet in four yards (2)

5 12 Across multiplied
by 24 Across (3)

7 One twelfth of
22 Across (2)

8 Six squared (2)

10 21 Down multiplied
by 179 (5)

12 188 squared
minus 81 (5)

14 5 Down plus 7 Down
minus two (3)

15 1 Down minus 134 (3)

19 Fathoms in 11 miles (4)

21 21 Across plus
22 Across plus 2 Down
plus 8 Down (3)

22 One ninth of
25 Down (2)

23 7 Down multiplied
by two (2)

25 13 Across multiplied
by six (3)

26 Months in eight years (2)

27 One tenth of
14 Down (2)

I have no regrets. I wouldn't have lived my life the way I did

if I was going to worry about what people were going to say.

Ingrid Bergman

LINK WORDS

Fit eight different words into the grid, so that each one links up with the words on either side, eg table - lamp - shade.

When finished, read down the letters in the shaded squares to reveal another word, solving the clue.

HILL					KNOX
BURNING					BABY
ATOMIC					MARKET
SWORD					POND
BENCH					TIME
ANKLE					MEAL
WEDDING					LEADER
MAGNETIC					MEASURE

Clue: Mountain _____

BERMUDA TRIANGLE

Travel through the 'Bermuda Triangle', collecting a letter from each area. You can visit any area once only, and you must enter and exit through the holes in the walls between them. The starting letter may appear in any area.

When you've completed your tour, the 15 letters (in order) will spell out the name of an author.

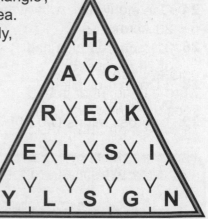

Author: _____

WORD LADDER

Change one letter at a time (but not the position of any letter) to make a new word – and move from the word at the top of the ladder to the word at the bottom using the exact number of rungs provided.

WORD WHEEL

How many words of three or more letters can you make from those in the wheel, without using plurals, abbreviations or proper nouns?

The central letter must appear once in every word and no letter in a section of the wheel may be used more than once.

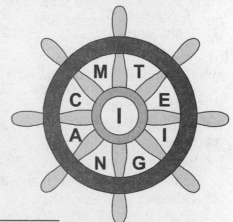

There is at least one nine-letter word in the wheel.

Nine-letter word(s):

_____

GENERAL KNOWLEDGE CROSSWORD

Across

4 Relating to swine (7)
7 Stipulated condition (7)
8 Go faster (5,2)
9 Reflective road stud (4-3)
10 Canine film star (6)
13 Instrument that measures the flow of electrical current (7)
16 Eight-limbed sea animal (7)
17 Sweet course of a meal (7)
19 Slow-moving arboreal mammal (5)
21 Former name of Chennai, India (6)
24 Small carnivore with short legs and an elongated body (6)
27 Convex strip of wood or plaster with a cross section of a quarter of a circle (5)
28 Childhood disease caused by a deficiency of vitamin D (7)
31 Light, open four-wheeled carriage (7)
33 Pungent gas compounded of nitrogen and hydrogen (7)
34 Peruser of text (6)
36 Transportation of people or goods by plane or helicopter (7)
38 Edmund ___, English poet (1552–99) (7)

39 Seasonal wind in southern Asia (7)
40 Globes, orbs (7)

Down

1 Surpassing what is common or expected (7)
2 Ditch around a castle (4)
3 Distance indicator at the side of a road (9)
4 Assume a stance, as for artistic purposes (4)
5 Popular board game (5)
6 Female ruler of many countries (7)
11 Professional entertainer (7)
12 Draws off liquid (7)
14 Celebration of the Eucharist (4)
15 Parts of a plant typically found under the ground (5)
17 Walt Disney's flying, cartoon elephant (5)
18 Form of address to a man (3)
20 Perforations (5)
22 Model representing a scene with three-dimensional figures (7)
23 Original disciple (7)
25 Boat built by Noah (3)
26 Central area of an ancient Roman amphitheatre (5)
29 Gluttonous seabird with a distensible pouch (9)

GENERAL KNOWLEDGE CROSSWORD

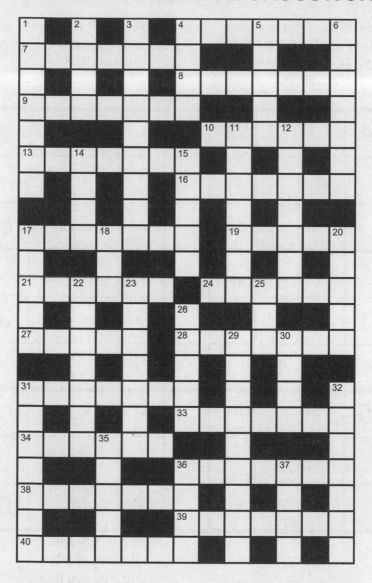

30 Garden of Adam and Eve (4)

31 Muscular weakness caused by nerve damage (7)

32 Boxes made of cardboard (7)

35 Classroom fool (5)

36 Official symbols of a family, state, etc (4)

37 Religious picture (4)

SUDOKU

Place one of the numbers from 1 to 9 into every empty cell so that each row, each column and each 3x3 block contains all the numbers from 1 to 9.

4			3			5	7	
	3			1			4	
			4					8
			8			7	2	
1								3
	2	6			5			
5					9			
	1			4			5	
	8	9			7			6

The man who views the world at fifty the same as he did at 20 has wasted 30 years of his life.

Muhammad Ali

JIGWORD

A symmetrical crossword has been cut into pieces. Can you put it back together? Three pieces are already in position.

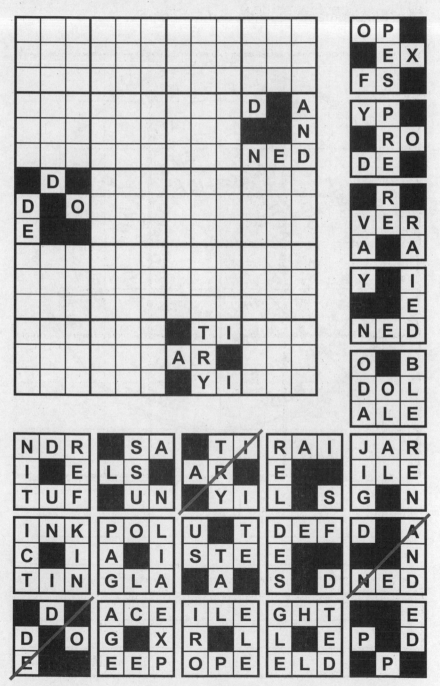

RING-WORDS

From the 32 segments below, find 16 eight-letter words by pairing one set of four letters with another.

All of the segments must be used once only.

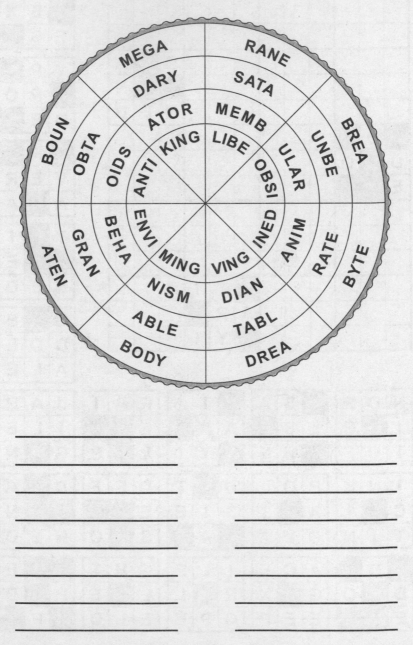

_____   _____

_____   _____

_____   _____

_____   _____

_____   _____

_____   _____

_____   _____

_____   _____

WELL SPOTTED

Some of the circles in this puzzle are already black. Fill in more white circles, so that the number of black circles totals the number inside the area they surround.

Every black circle surrounding an area with a number higher than '1' needs to be next to another black circle surrounding the same area.

When solving, it may help to put a small dot into any circle you know should not be filled.

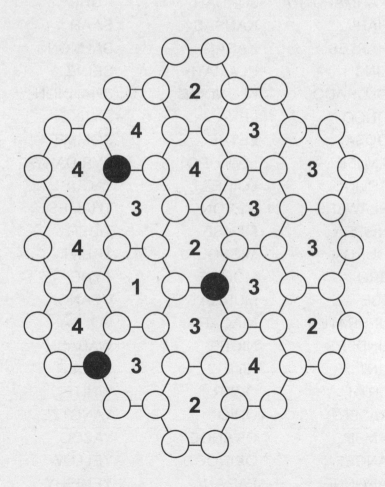

WORDSEARCH: RIVERS

Can you find all of the listed rivers in the grid opposite?
Words run forwards or backwards, in either a horizontal,
vertical or diagonal direction.

ANGARA	HUANG HO	RHINE
ARGUN	HUDSON	RHONE
AVON	INDUS	RHUR
BLACKWATER	IRTISH	ROTHER
BRAHMAPUTRA	JORDAN	RUHR
CHARI	KANSAS	SAAR
CHARLES	KASAI	SALMON
CLINCH	KLAMATH	SEINE
COLORADO	KLONDIKE	SHANNON
CONGO	LENA	SNAKE
COOSA	LETHE	SOMME
DANUBE	LIMPOPO	SYR DARYA
DARLING	LOIRE	TAGUS
DELAWARE	MEKONG	THAMES
DNEIPER	MEUSE	TIBER
DOURO	MISSOURI	TRENT
EBRO	MOBILE	TYNE
ELBE	MURRAY	UBANGI
EUPHRATES	NIAGARA	VOLGA
FLINDERS	NIGER	WABASH
FLINT	NILE	WESER
FORTH	ODER	WHITE
FRASER	OHIO	YANGTZE
GAMBIA	ORANGE	YAZOO
GANGES	ORINOCO	YELLOW
GARONNE	PARANA	YENISEY
GREEN	PLATTE	YUKON
HAVEL	PURUS	ZAMBEZI

WORDSEARCH: RIVERS

```
P A R A N A Z A M B E Z I M D O A
L E T H E G R A L W A E O E N H S
F F O C U E G A M B I A L K Y G O
D E N O H R C O L O R A D O A N O
N C L T C K G E O T W I R N N A C
E O O B W B K Z U A R U G G G U T
I R R A E I A P R T O E P L T H N
P B T A D Y A E I D S A G J Z U I
E E V N N M Q S M Y R U N I E D L
R L O O H G H F J A E M R N N S F
W L I A L T E C G L I S L U U O R
K H R B N G H N H S I Q I A P N A
P B I U O R A A S A L M O N I V S
G J G T R M B O M P R L P G E G E
I R V O E H U F M E Z L O O N Y R
A N E L F R I U O L S O E I P O R
S W N E I O R N E R I O L S R O C
A W O N N R R V E Y I R M E U S E
K A N S A S A T G G A N P M Y R W
L B N Y U H Z H H D I U O R E F E
A A A V O N T S C V S B D C A A S
M S H Z U I R E B U N A D R O C E
A H S C B E E J G E R N A P L N R
T Y N E D I N A O Y E G N I N E G
H E R N I T T S A R A I N O K U Y
W L I O I N D U S I D C R A D G I
K L L H B I E L N L H A N J K E C
F O J I P L A T T E G S N I K G R
J W Y O S E T A R H P U E F V V O
```

RED HERRING

Five of the words below must be entered in the grid, reading across, so as to create five more words reading down. Can you spot the red herring?

ASSET **ESTER**

BEAUS **ORLON**

CAPRI **RANGE**

LETTER TRACKER

Starting at the top left corner and ending at the bottom right, track a path from letter to letter, in any direction except diagonally, in order to find 15 hidden dogs. All of the letters must be used, but none more than once.

A	L	K	H	Z	O	I	P	O	H	O	D	L
L	E	N	O	R	O	L	D	O	G	U	N	U
S	I	A	U	T	B	E	S	T	A	H	C	R
A	T	D	N	E	P	H	C	V	E	E	R	R
E	S	W	H	I	P	I	R	E	I	R	T	E
S	E	N	I	K	E	H	U	A	M	A	A	B
H	E	E	Y	E	P	A	U	H	R	N	L	R
O	D	P	O	D	E	Y	U	N	E	B	D	A
G	S	A	M	G	R	H	O	D	D	O	O	R

DO IT YOURSELF!

In this crossword puzzle, the clues are in alphabetical order and there are no black squares in the grid. Black out the unwanted squares, to produce a symmetrically-patterned grid containing words that can be matched to the clues.

N	A	C	H	O	I	C	O	M	P	A	S	S
E	M	O	C	K	N	A	T	O	W	N	A	U
C	O	N	T	A	I	N	O	D	E	I	G	N
T	W	E	E	P	A	C	U	E	N	M	E	S
A	N	Y	T	I	M	E	R	S	T	A	G	E
R	A	C	E	R	A	R	E	T	S	T	E	T
A	C	E	A	S	E	A	T	Y	P	E	S	W
F	I	X	S	I	M	P	E	R	A	N	G	I
R	E	P	E	L	E	O	P	I	N	I	O	N
O	W	L	E	E	R	R	A	N	O	D	I	D
L	E	A	R	N	P	O	U	T	L	I	V	E
I	C	I	S	C	O	U	T	E	N	O	N	N
C	O	N	F	E	S	S	U	R	E	M	I	T

Able to absorb
   fluids
Admit one's guilt
Afternoon meal
At no particular
   moment
Billiards stick
Burrowing,
   rabbit-like
   animal
Bury
Caper, cavort
Close of day
Condescend
Fend off

Find out
Freedom from
   vanity
Giraffe-like
   creature
Give a reason
Give life to
Have within
Make a mistake
Malignant growth
Metal cooking
   vessel
Mode of
   expression

Navigational
   instrument
Peace and quiet
Platform
Point of view
Send (payment)
Stop
Survive longer
   than
Sweet plant fluid
Topped tortilla
   chip
To set in from a
   margin
Uses a keyboard

NUMBER CRUNCHER

Starting at the top left with the number provided, work down from one box to another, applying the mathematical instructions to your running total.

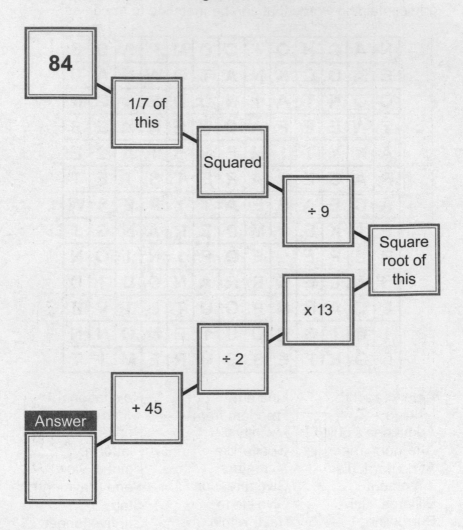

84

1/7 of this

Squared

÷ 9

Square root of this

x 13

÷ 2

+ 45

Answer

NAME THE DAY

What day comes two days after the day immediately before the day three days after the day immediately before the day which comes two days after Sunday?

JIGSAW PUZZLE

Fit the jigsaw together to reveal eight bones of the body.

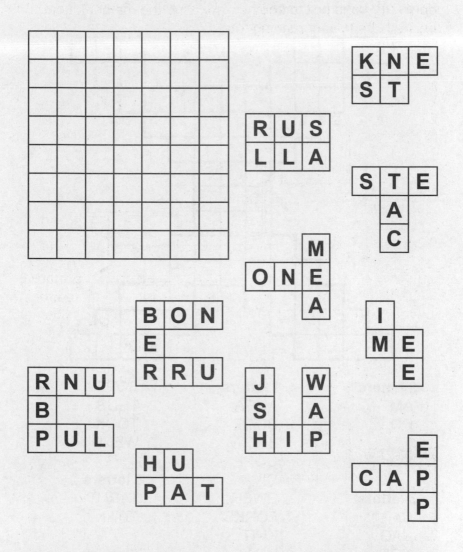

X MARKS THE SPOT

Fill the grid with the listed words, one letter per square. All words are used just once.

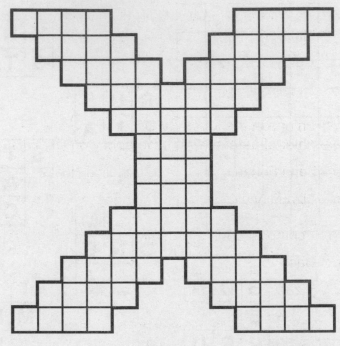

2 letters	4 letters	SOPS
AM	AREA	THUS
DO	BOAR	TOOK
IF	BROW	WEND
SO	COPE	
	DIVA	**5 letters**
	EWER	TAROT
3 letters	FORK	TITAN
CAP	KNIT	
NAG	NEAT	**7 letters**
NOR	NEWS	AIRCREW
OIL	NOUN	CHASTEN
OVA	POET	CRAVATS
RIO	POOL	
VOW	PORE	**9 letters**
	PRIM	DRACONIAN
	SAID	PROPAGATE

GENERAL KNOWLEDGE QUIZ

Can you identify which one of the multiple-choice answers
(a, b, c or d) is correct for each of the questions below?

1   Of the following English monarchs, which one reigned
    the longest?

    a   Edward III   b   Henry III

    c   Richard III   d   William III

2   Which one of the following Oscar winners is the
    daughter of parents who have both won Oscars?

    a   Jane Fonda   b   Anjelica Huston

    c   Liza Minnelli   d   Vanessa Redgrave

3   Who composed the *Academic Festival Overture*?

    a   Bach   b   Beethoven

    c   Bizet   d   Brahms

4   In 1959, Alaska and Hawaii became the 49th and 50th
    states of the USA. On 14 February 1912, which had
    become the 48th?

    a   Arizona   b   Montana

    c   New Mexico   d   Utah

5   In which year were women allowed to compete in
    athletics events at the Olympic Games for the first
    time?

    a   1908   b   1928

    c   1948   d   1968

6   What first name is shared by the poet Byron, actor and
    director Orson Welles and singer Van Morrison?

    a   George   b   John

    c   Robert   d   William

DOUBLE-CROSSER

Two crossword puzzles, but you have to decide which of the solutions to each clue fits into each grid. In both cases, one word has been entered to give you a start.

DOUBLE-CROSSER

Across

1 Headlong plunge into water; Quick lowering of the head or body, a jerky bow (4)

3 Delilah's partner; Redemption money (6)

6 Migratory game fish; Mouth fluid (6)

7 Item of currency; Raised platform (4)

8 Form of speech; Imbecile (5)

10 Gains; Number indicated by the Roman VII (5)

13 Do something; No longer fashionable (3)

14 Country of the Arabian Peninsula; Written composition (5)

17 Capital of Ghana; Racing vessel (5)

19 Requests; Stopper (4)

20 Less difficult; United (6)

21 Division of Ireland; Harsh or corrosive in tone (6)

22 Eye secretion; Repast (4)

Down

1 Fortune, lot; Notwithstanding (7)

2 Capital of Lithuania; White metallic element that burns with a brilliant light (7)

3 Fine grit; Lion's call (4)

4 Place of pilgrimage for Muslims; Prod (5)

5 Fruit, an important source of oil; Pungent vegetable (5)

9 Adult male person; Plaything (3)

10 Enclosure for swine; Seventh letter of the Greek alphabet (3)

11 Come into possession of; Substance injected to prevent disease (7)

12 Non-synthetic; Verbal defamation (7)

15 Exactly matched; Rice and raw fish wrapped in seaweed (5)

16 Number signified by the Roman VIII; Thing of value (5)

18 Ale; Dense growth located on the head, for example (4)

ROUND THE BLOCK

Each eight-letter word in the list is hidden in a square around a central letter that is not a part of the word itself, as shown by the example in the grid. The word may start anywhere within its 'square' and go either clockwise or anticlockwise. When all the listed words are found, the central letters spell out the name of a movie star.

```
M A L B R N C A B E C L
R S T A A O H E R R U B
L A M B T R C I A B E L
F V E E R E I D L L A P
O C N K E L H N E R C E
T A T C A M E O D R E P
E Z I W E A S H S H A B
D P S W A N H C Z E D N
C A P E P D W I N I B A
M A H C T E R O G I U H
C I E O A D Y E T I D
A S D T H S A L D D N
I N L R H A D E T E N A
K I A U I K X S Q C K H
S B M B N C O T A M A C
```

ALLEGORY ✓	LAMBSKIN
BARBECUE	MACKEREL
CAPSIZED	RECALLED
DECKHAND	SANDWICH
FLAMENCO	STOCKADE
HERALDIC	THATCHED

ROUND THE BEND

Instead of each word being hidden in a straight, continuous line, every word has one bend in it. This bend will not necessarily go off at a right angle; it may go in any direction at all! One word is given as an example.

E	D	G	E	T	Q	R	Q	O	G	T	A
L	Z	F	H	S	D	R	U	Y	V	P	Y
W	R	E	R	X	T	L	C	M	R	E	X
O	R	H	E	D	D	O	G	I	X	H	R
N	E	T	V	Y	N	K	C	N	W	R	S
K	F	A	E	T	A	E	T	A	L	U	I
F	O	E	N	R	I	D	E	T	L	M	G
E	R	N	E	H	W	N	P	E	F	I	H
F	E	R	O	Z	L	O	U	F	M	T	T
G	I	E	T	I	S	J	P	A	X	S	X
Z	U	D	T	G	S	R	R	H	L	P	I
B	N	Z	O	H	E	H	E	V	Y	B	D
U	V	S	G	T	S	E	T	L	L	B	N
Z	I	R	N	E	S	S	E	E	X	K	A
R	F	I	N	N	W	V	R	S	K	B	M

APRICOTS ✓   POSSESS

CONTINUAL   RISOTTO

ENLIGHTEN   RUMINATE

INTERPRETER   STIMULATE

KNOWLEDGE   THEREFORE

MANDIBLE   UNDERNEATH

OVERSIGHT   WHENEVER

WORDSEARCH: WEIGHTS AND MEASURES

Can you find all of the listed weights and measures hidden in the grid below? Words run forwards or backwards, in either a horizontal, vertical or diagonal direction.

```
S L S P K R Z E H O D C D R A
J T P Z X I R P W J F J Z C E
T J O R U C L A Q T W K D G W
H Y O N A S D O A S H D N A M
G S N L E K P E G J Y O T I D
I P F G C U R Y T R L T L O N
E H U P W A H P D R A E N E A
W C L B T F M A U P D M C F H
D N B C O N E F M H M N A Y D
E I E U G H O R P E U T A C R
R H O U S M E L W O H Z T A A
D O B G G H D B L O U R A R M
N R O V T A E W M A A N K A Z
U H A D K G E L F U G E D T X
H M K Y G I L L Q N I R U G S
```

ACRE	HAND	OUNCE
BUSHEL	HECTARE	POUND
CARAT	HOGSHEAD	QUART
DRAM	HUNDRED-WEIGHT	SPOONFUL
FATHOM		STONE
	INCH	
FURLONG		THERM
	KILOGRAM	
GALLON		WATT
	LEAGUE	
GILL		YARD
	MILE	

BREAK-TIME CROSSWORD

Across
1 Watching (7)
8 Ill-fitting (5)
9 Bring back into original position (9)
10 Broker (5)
11 Hold in high regard (6)
14 Animal of Arctic regions (5,4)
17 Social policy of racial segregation (9)
19 Postpones (6)
21 Molten rock in the Earth's crust (5)
24 Very steep cliff (9)
25 Series of hills or mountains (5)
26 Perpetually young (7)

Down
1 Spinal bone (8)
2 Decree (5)
3 Arch of the foot (6)
4 Caprine animal (4)
5 Bloodsucking parasite (4)
6 Eternally (7)
7 Converge (4)
12 Nocturnal creatures (5)
13 Biblical shepherd who slew Goliath (5)
15 Revise an evaluation (8)
16 Suspended (7)
18 Want strongly (6)
20 Mexican friend (5)
21 Female equine animal (4)
22 Highest point (4)
23 Queen of the gods in Greek mythology (4)

HEXAFIT

Place the listed words into the hexagons, one letter per cell, starting in any of those surrounding a black circle, so that words read clockwise. Some letters are already in place.

The letter is the same in any cell that shares a common border with a cell in a touching hexagon.

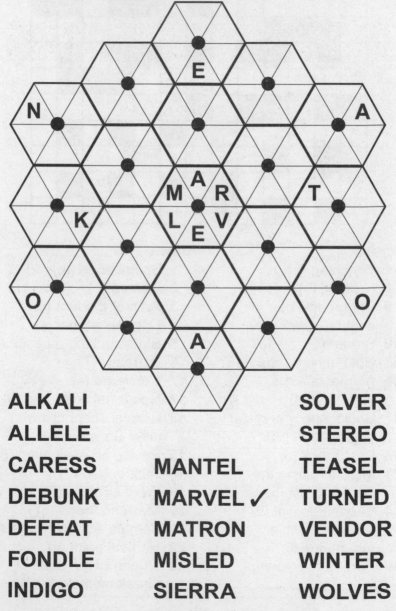

ALKALI		SOLVER
ALLELE		STEREO
CARESS	MANTEL	TEASEL
DEBUNK	MARVEL ✓	TURNED
DEFEAT	MATRON	VENDOR
FONDLE	MISLED	WINTER
INDIGO	SIERRA	WOLVES

KAKURO

Fill the grid so that each block adds up to the total in the box above or to the left of it.

You can only use the digits 1-9, one per square, but the same digit must not be used twice in a block. The same digit may occur more than once in any row or column, but it must be in a separate block.

With mirth and laughter let old wrinkles come.

William Shakespeare

SUDOKU

Place one of the numbers from 1 to 9 into every empty cell so that each row, each column and each 3x3 block contains all the numbers from 1 to 9.

2	4				9			8
		7	1				4	
		1	8					
1	7		4	2				
				8	6		5	1
					4	6		
	6				8	7		
7			9				2	3

Life can only be understood backwards;

but it must be lived forwards.

Søren Kierkegaard

DOMINO PLACEMENT

A standard set of twenty-eight dominoes has been laid out as shown below. Can you draw in the edges of them all? One is already in place.

It may be helpful to use the check-box to tick off the dominoes as they are found.

6	4	4	1	0	2	1	0
6	3	6	1	1	1	3	0
1	5	6	3	2	0	3	3
3	5	4	6	2	4	5	2
5	0	0	4	6	2	6	3
0	1	4	6	0	5	5	4
3	2	2	4	5	1	2	5

0-0	0-1	0-2	0-3	0-4	0-5	0-6	1-1

1-2	1-3	1-4	1-5	1-6	2-2	2-3	2-4	2-5	2-6

3-3	3-4	3-5	3-6	4-4	4-5	4-6	5-5	5-6	6-6
					✓				

ALPHAFILL

Place 25 different letters of the alphabet, one per circle, in order to spell out the listed words. Words are formed by moving between adjacent circles along the connecting lines, either horizontally, vertically or diagonally in any direction.

Begin by crossing out the letters already in place, together with the one letter which doesn't appear in any of the words.

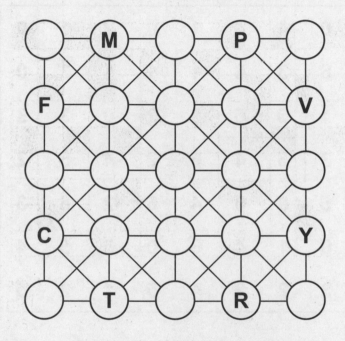

A B C D E F G H I J K L M

N O P Q R S T U V W X Y Z

BOW	MINGLE	RUSE
CLERK	PANDER	SAW
FINDING	PANEL	TENCH
INDEX	POSY	VOWING
JINGLE	QUERY	WINDOW

NUMBER FILLER

Can you fit all of the listed numbers into the grid? One is already in place, to get you off to a good start!

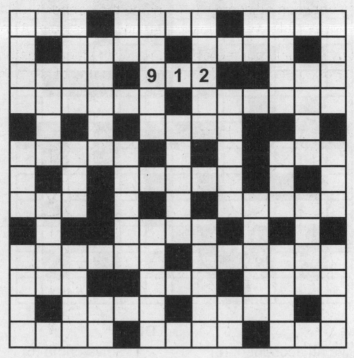

2 digits	693	3487	5 digits	6 digits
26	726	3564	12333	188105
38	912 ✓	4217	15268	281455
60	916	5356	21139	602349
89		5667	42320	680024
	4 digits	5896	44937	
3 digits	1084	6076	45262	
143	1420	6859	47377	
185	1476	7161	50991	
213	2691	7288	73320	
336	2849	8055	77590	
453	2980	8500	80001	
470	3243	8760	91363	
593	3254	9174		
677	3262	9974		

BREAK-TIME CROSSWORD

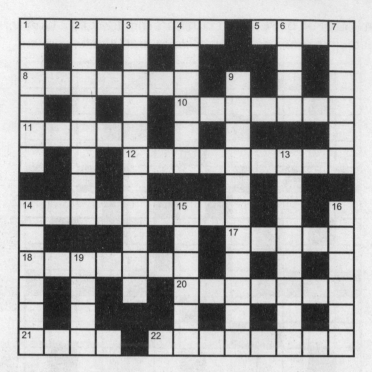

Across

1 Give an account of (8)
5 Those people (4)
8 Agrees, corresponds (7)
10 Number in one century (7)
11 Asian dish eaten with rice (5)
12 Month of the year (9)
14 Officer in charge of a military unit (9)
17 Drama set to music (5)
18 Traditions, habits (7)
20 Desert, leave (7)
21 Look for (4)
22 Protected (8)

Down

1 Solve crime (6)
2 Sunroom (8)
3 Annual period of wet weather (5,6)
4 Chess piece (6)
6 Period of time (4)
7 Unlawful killing (6)
9 Question closely (11)
13 Decapitated (8)
14 Spine-bearing, succulent plant (6)
15 Quantity of medication taken at any one time (6)
16 Sighed with tiredness (6)
19 Item of footwear (4)

CODEWORD

Every letter in this puzzle has been replaced by a number, the number remaining the same for that letter wherever it occurs. Every letter of the alphabet has been used. Substitute numbers for letters to complete the codeword.

It may help to cross off the letters beneath the grid to keep a track of progress, and to use the reference box showing which numbers have been decoded. Three letters have already been entered into the grid, to help you on your way.

23		1		9		10		24	18	4	24	18
15	2	21	23	18	12	23	1		26		17	
2		17		26		21		20	26	13	14	2
23	26	17	6	8	23	14	2		23		17	
21		19		23		13		19	21	17	16	22
	24		19		11	18	24		4		13	
4	18	25	23	7	17		17	9	23	21	1	17
	14		18		22	18	3		14		23	
7	13	21	5	10		24		7		23		24
	5		23		1	18	2	18	7	18	15	23
6	8	18	20	20		25		4		2 T		18
	21		8		9	23	10	23	24	23 E	14	2
7	23	26	26	22		1		26		14 N		22

A B C D E F G H I J K L M
N O P Q R S T U V W X Y Z

1	2 T	3	4	5	6	7	8	9	10	11	12	13
14 N	15	16	17	18	19	20	21	22	23 E	24	25	26

267

ROUND DOZEN

First solve the clues. All of the solutions begin with the letter in the centre of the circle. When the puzzle is complete, you can then go on to discover the twelve-letter word reading clockwise around the outermost ring of letters.

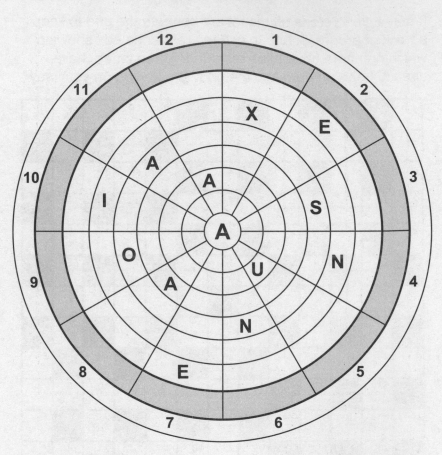

1 Suffocation
2 Large blood vessels
3 Fireproof material
4 Boa-like snake of South America
5 Water-bearer in astrology
6 Legendary oceanic island

7 Part of the Roman Catholic mass (5,3)
8 Aeronautics
9 Food of the Greek gods
10 Fire starter
11 Clapping
12 Spider

The twelve-letter word is: _____

JIGSAW SUDOKU

Fit the numbers 1, 2, 3, 4, 5 and 6 into the grid in such a way that each horizontal row, each vertical column and each of the heavily outlined sections of six squares each contains a different number. Some numbers are already in place.

WHAT DOES IT MEAN?

Which of the following is the correct definition of the word:

RETUSE

1 Having a broad or rounded end with a shallow central notch
2 Having an angle that is greater than a right angle but less than 180 degrees
3 To formulate a policy directed towards recovery of territory lost to an enemy

SPIDOKU

In the spider's web below, each of the eight segments should be filled with a different number from 1 to 8, in such a way that every ring also contains a different number from 1 to 8.

The segments run from the outside of the spider's web to the centre, and the rings run all the way around. So that you can see the rings more clearly, we've shaded them grey and white.

Some numbers are already in place. Can you fill in the rest?

CUBE ROUTES

Fill the words into the grid (one letter is ready in place), changing route where necessary, as with this example:

ASPECT   ENDURE   SPED
CARE   REASON   WRITHE
CASE   ROE

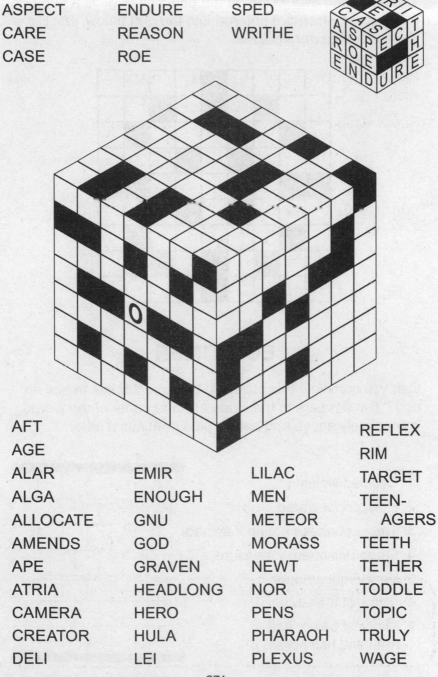

AFT			REFLEX
AGE			RIM
ALAR	EMIR	LILAC	TARGET
ALGA	ENOUGH	MEN	TEEN-
ALLOCATE	GNU	METEOR	AGERS
AMENDS	GOD	MORASS	TEETH
APE	GRAVEN	NEWT	TETHER
ATRIA	HEADLONG	NOR	TODDLE
CAMERA	HERO	PENS	TOPIC
CREATOR	HULA	PHARAOH	TRULY
DELI	LEI	PLEXUS	WAGE

NUMBER CRUNCHER CROSSWORD

A little mathematical crossword, where a little knowledge of mathematics will come in very handy!

The answer to every clue on the opposite page is a number, the digits of which are entered into the grid below, just like a standard crossword puzzle.

1	2		3	■	4		5	6
7		■	■			■	8	
■		9		10		11		■
12			■		■	13		
■		14					■	■
15			■			16		17
	■	18	19		20		■	
21	22	■		■		■	23	
24				■	25			

EGG TIMER

Can you complete this puzzle in the time it takes to boil an egg? The answers to the clues are anagrams of the words immediately above and below, plus or minus a letter.

1 Collided violently

2 Holy, consecrated

3 Tree, Lebanese national symbol

4 Large unit of area measure

5 Very slight amount

6 'Drink of the Gods'

7 Mythical being, half man and half horse

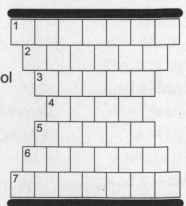

272

NUMBER CRUNCHER CROSSWORD

Across

1 16 Across multiplied by three (4)

4 13 Across multiplied by three (4)

7 2 Down minus three eighths of 2 Down (2)

8 22 Down minus one third of 5 Down (2)

9 237 squared plus 8 Across plus 22 Down (5)

12 Yards in four furlongs (3)

13 12 Across plus one (3)

14 6 Down multiplied by four (5)

15 28 squared (3)

16 One thirteenth of 25 Across (3)

18 193 squared plus 22 Down plus double 7 Across (5)

21 One sixteenth of 15 Across (2)

23 Months in seven years (2)

24 94 squared plus 112 (4)

25 12 Across plus 15 Down minus 11 (4)

Down

1 Ounces in 98 pounds (4)

2 One eleventh of 12 Across (2)

3 15 Across plus two (3)

4 22 Down plus 5 Down plus 23 Across plus four (3)

5 Pints in six gallons (2)

6 1 Across plus 1 Down minus four (4)

9 224 squared minus one third of 22 Down (5)

10 21 Across multiplied by 3 Down (5)

11 136 squared minus one third of 23 Across (5)

15 13 Across multiplied by eight (4)

17 97 squared plus 38 (4)

19 3 Down plus one quarter of 5 Down (3)

20 16 Across minus double 23 Down (3)

22 8 Across plus one third of 5 Down (2)

23 23 Across minus three (2)

LINK WORDS

Fit eight different words into the grid, so that each one links up with the words on either side, eg table - lamp - shade.

When finished, read down the letters in the shaded squares to reveal another word, solving the clue.

SUGAR					ROOT
SPEED					KNOWN
COMMON					COMFORT
MOON					ENGINE
FLIPPED					TAKEN
WIDE					SESAME
RESPECT					BODIED
DUCK					CAST

Clue: Capital city _____

BERMUDA TRIANGLE

Travel through the 'Bermuda Triangle', collecting a letter from each area. You can visit any area once only, and you must enter and exit through the holes in the walls between them. The starting letter may appear in any area.

When you've completed your tour, the 15 letters (in order) will spell out the name of an author (6,3,6).

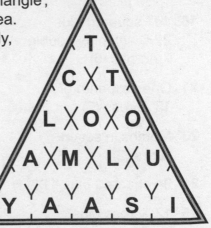

Author: _____

WORD LADDER

Change one letter at a time (but not the position of any letter) to make a new word – and move from the word at the top of the ladder to the word at the bottom using the exact number of rungs provided.

MEMORY TEST

Study the picture below for a few moments, then turn to page 311.

O	O	X
X	O	X
X	X	O

GENERAL KNOWLEDGE CROSSWORD

Across

1 Former French coin (5)

8 Of undeclared authorship (9)

9 Titled peers of the realm (5)

10 Position on a baseball team (7)

11 Covered and often columned entrance to a building (7)

12 Defeats in battle (5)

13 Inflammation of the kidneys (9)

17 Basic monetary unit of Uruguay (4)

20 Round-backed instrument similar to a lute (7)

21 Hemispherical roof (4)

22 Adult male deer (4)

23 Johann ____, Austrian composer of waltzes (1804–49) (7)

24 Group of islands, capital Suva (4)

25 Predatory carnivorous canine (4)

26 Monetary unit equal to one-hundredth of a peso in Chile, Colombia, Cuba, Mexico, etc (7)

27 Piece of furniture with a writing surface (4)

30 Plaintiff's opponent in a court of law (9)

34 Wood used to make piano keys (5)

35 Exhausting routine that leaves no time for relaxation (3,4)

36 Save from ruin, destruction or harm (7)

37 Popeye's girlfriend (5)

38 Constellation of Ursa Major (5,4)

39 Australian marsupial (5)

Down

1 Native of Manila, for example (8)

2 Delivery from a plane or helicopter (7)

3 Bank employee (7)

4 Mixture of decaying vegetation and manure (7)

5 Molluscs from which pearls are obtained (7)

6 Kennel (8)

7 Strong black coffee (8)

14 Longing to return to one's place of residence (8)

15 Lack of knowledge or education (9)

16 Immunise (9)

17 Secret phrase (8)

18 Building for housing horses (6)

19 Law force (6)

GENERAL KNOWLEDGE CROSSWORD

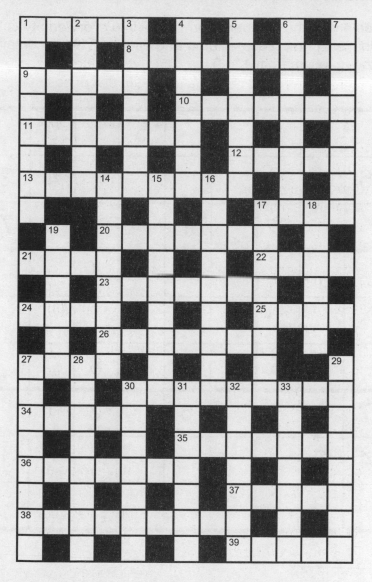

27 Equestrian display (8)

28 Part of the body between the neck and the upper arm (8)

29 And so on (Latin) (2,6)

30 Powerful family (7)

31 Front limb (7)

32 Interconnected system (7)

33 Shrub that yields coffee beans (7)

SUDOKU

Place one of the numbers from 1 to 9 into every empty cell so that each row, each column and each 3x3 block contains all the numbers from 1 to 9.

					8		9	
6							4	2
		3		1				7
		1		3		4		
			8		9			
		5		2		8		
7				6		3		
4	2							1
	3		9					

I don't deserve this award, but I have arthritis

and I don't deserve that either.

Jack Benny

JIGWORD

A symmetrical crossword has been cut into pieces. Can you put it back together? Three pieces are already in position.

RING-WORDS

From the 32 segments below, find 16 eight-letter words by pairing one set of four letters with another.

All of the segments must be used once only.

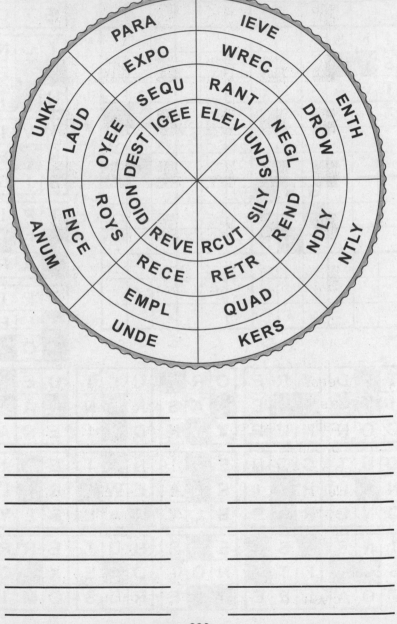

AROUND THE SQUARES

The answer to each clue is a four-letter word, to be entered in the four squares surrounding the corresponding number in the grid. The word can start in any of the four squares and read either clockwise or anticlockwise. The first has already been entered.

	H								
D	1 A	2		3		4		5	
	R								
	6		7		8		9		10
	11		12		13		14		15
	16		17		18		19		20
	21		22		23		24		25

1 Difficult
2 Unit of land area
3 Outer covering on cheese
4 Snake's tooth
5 Application document
6 Item of cutlery
7 Large piece of stone
8 Not illuminated
9 Hinged barrier
10 Verse form
11 Resist, disobey
12 Tall woody plant
13 Public vehicle on rails

14 Story
15 A single time
16 Biblical first man
17 Make watertight
18 Red planet
19 Young sheep
20 Edible marine crustacean
21 Green citrus fruit
22 Incline, slant
23 Close by
24 Moist, humid
25 Magnetic recording medium

WORDSEARCH: CONTAINERS

Can you find all of the listed containers in the grid opposite? Words run forwards or backwards, in either a horizontal, vertical or diagonal direction.

BARREL	ENVELOPE	PURSE
BASIN	EWER	QUIVER
BASKET	FLAGON	RAMEKIN
BATH	FLASK	RECEPTACLE
BEAKER	FOLDER	RELIQUARY
BOTTLE	GLASS	SACK
BOWL	GOBLET	SAMOVAR
BOX	HAMPER	SATCHEL
BUCKET	HANDBAG	SAUCEPAN
BUNKER	HOLDALL	SCHOONER
CANISTER	HOPPER	SCUTTLE
CANTEEN	JAR	SHEATH
CAPSULE	JUG	STEIN
CARRIER BAG	KEG	TANK
CARTON	KETTLE	THIMBLE
CASE	LADLE	TIN CAN
CASKET	LOCKER	TRASH CAN
CHALICE	LOCKET	TRAY
CHEST	MAILBAG	TROUGH
CHURN	MANGER	TRUNK
CISTERN	MORTAR	TUMBLER
CRATE	NOSEBAG	TUREEN
DECANTER	PANNIER	VALISE
DEMIJOHN	PHIAL	VASE
DISH	PIGGY BANK	VAULT
DRAWER	PITCHER	VESSEL
DRUM	POT	WALLET
DUSTBIN	POUCH	WORKBAG

WORDSEARCH: CONTAINERS

```
R E V I U Q E C E P O L E V N E B
E C A O M L R X T E K C U B U L A
L I S J B A P P O D R A W E R C S
B L E M T T I O Q B E A K E R A I
M A I E N R G L T X H C B M C T N
U H T M H A N D B A G A A K G P R
T C U H B Y U O C A S N M N Q E C
D R Z E T A N K X K G I W P T C A
D U S T B I N Y E E E S U N E E R
K O C A S E H T R T A T E G L R R
N R C X T I N C A N U E T E C N I
A E R I S C Y J V T T R R L H D E
B W K S S C H O O N E R E O E T R
Y E A D H T N E A Q A L J E H R B
G L D I E E E C L B P I L C N A A
G W K S A L F R S A M O V A R S G
I O J H T A G Y N E C U U P W H A
P B B F H D X N D K K F S S G C B
J Q E L D L I F E T N F O U E A K
A A S A E E B R S Y U G O L Q N R
E B R G R T R E R R R R T E D H O
L N U O P A H A I L T T T R W E W
T I P N T C U R L N U E E R S Q R
T K G R K Q F A O C K H E I R M T
O E O U I E D T S C C P L T E N E
B M D L J L R R O T P A L A I A K
W A E W O A L L I O V U U E M N S
N R U H C U O P H I A L T B D A A
N A P E C U A S P V E S S E L P C
```

283

RED HERRING

Five of the words below must be entered in the grid, reading across, so as to create five more words reading down. Can you spot the red herring?

ADORN   **MATED**

CRESS   **PRESS**

LAMIA   **STRUT**

LETTER TRACKER

Starting at the top left corner and ending at the bottom right, track a path from letter to letter, in any direction except diagonally, in order to find 15 hidden tools. All of the letters must be used, but none more than once.

S	H	O	V	T	S	C	R	B	A	S	S	C
M	M	A	E	E	A	W	O	W	R	R	E	R
E	R	H	L	R	F	K	R	W	T	E	W	D
C	S	E	P	I	T	C	O	E	E	Z	I	R
A	L	G	D	E	L	H	F	T	E	H	V	E
E	P	C	K	S	S	O	H	D	R	C	T	R
L	C	A	W	A	K	O	L	L	I	L	A	H
I	H	H	S	N	N	C	U	I	B	L	T	O
S	E	L	P	A	E	R	L	T	I	V	A	R

DO IT YOURSELF!

In this crossword puzzle, the clues are in alphabetical order and there are no black squares in the grid. Black out the unwanted squares, to produce a symmetrically-patterned grid containing words that can be matched to the clues.

B	I	S	E	C	T	E	A	B	A	T	E	D
A	R	C	S	U	M	P	R	O	P	U	R	R
N	E	A	A	R	E	A	R	R	A	N	G	E
T	I	M	E	S	O	R	E	I	N	D	I	A
E	V	E	R	O	T	T	E	N	G	R	I	D
R	A	Z	O	R	A	Y	E	G	R	A	S	S
O	D	A	D	A	Y	D	R	E	A	M	E	R
C	O	M	E	T	H	A	T	C	I	G	A	R
I	R	I	S	H	U	B	R	I	S	I	G	H
N	O	N	E	A	T	U	A	R	E	P	L	Y
E	N	I	G	M	A	T	I	C	K	A	E	M
M	I	N	U	E	T	S	D	L	E	G	E	E
A	U	G	U	S	T	Y	S	E	V	E	R	S

Answer
Arrogance
Arrow on a
  computer
  screen
Become ground
  down
Body of salt
  water
Convivial
  gathering
Cut in two
Cuts off from a
  whole
Decayed
Died down

Excavation
Flurry
Gentle teasing
Hoax
Is afraid of, fears
Lawn plant
Lies adjacent to
Main river of
  London
Moments,
  periods
Month
Mysterious
Part of a book
Pay increase

Pieces of poetry
  or verse
Place in a
  different order
Place where
  films are
  shown
Ring
Shaving tool
Tailed heavenly
  body
Tedious
Treeless Arctic
  plain
Tobacco product

DICE SECTION

Printed onto every one of the six numbered dice are six letters (one per side), which can be rearranged to form the answer to each clue; however, some sides are invisible to you. Use the clues and write every answer into the grid. When correctly filled, the letters in the shaded squares, reading in the order 1 to 6, will spell out the name of a herb.

1 Famous tower in Paris

2 Inhalation

3 Alloy of copper and tin

4 European principality

5 Slumbering

6 Missile fired from a gun

JIGSAW PUZZLE

Fit the jigsaw together to reveal eight articles of clothing.

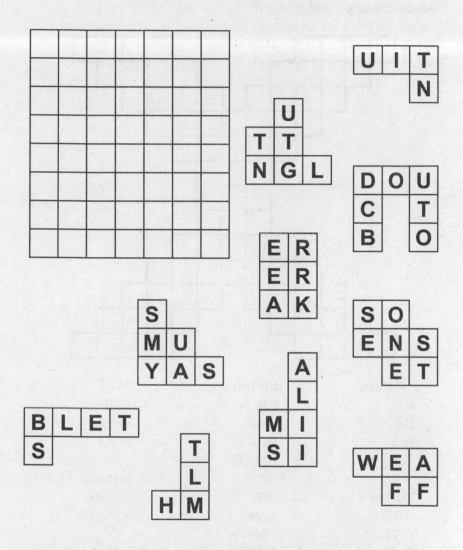

X MARKS THE SPOT

Fill the grid with the listed words, one letter per square. All words are used just once.

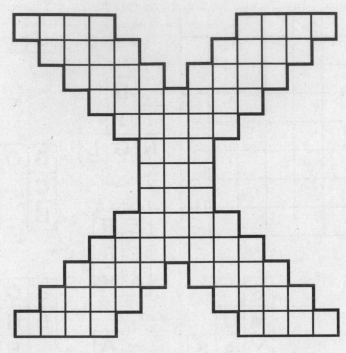

2 letters	4 letters	ORAL
AT	ARIA	TAMP
BE	ASIA	TAPS
NO	BABY	TARO
TO	BORE	
	CAPS	**5 letters**
3 letters	DIRT	ADORE
ARE	EMIR	LARVA
ART	FAST	
DUE	FIRE	**7 letters**
FAT	FORE	CONSIST
NED	GNAT	POSEURS
RIP	JOTS	PREPARE
USE	LIAR	
	LIRA	**9 letters**
	LOSS	DAREDEVIL
	OPTS	REDUNDANT

HALF AND HALF

Pair off these groups of three letters to name eight metals and alloys, each comprising six letters.

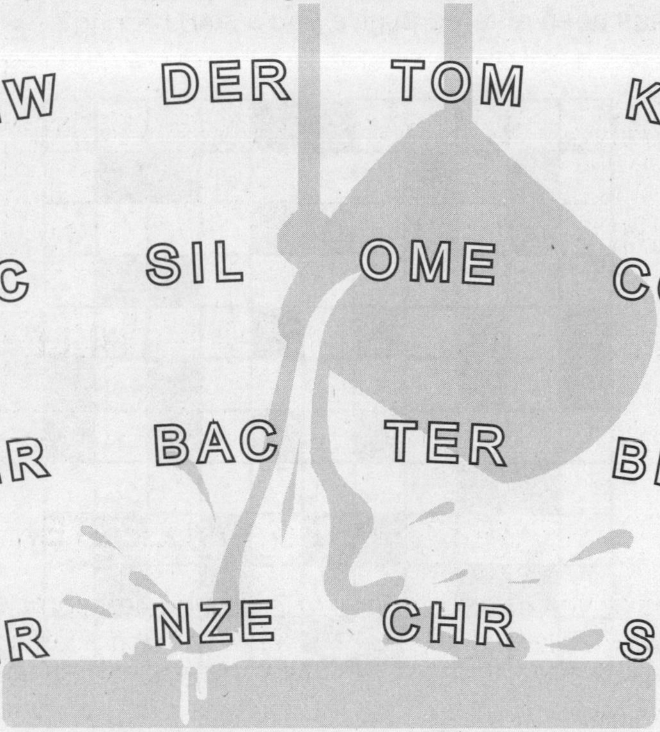

PEW   DER   TOM   KEL

NIC   SIL   OME   COP

VER   BAC   TER   BRO

PER   NZE   CHR   SOL

_____   _____
_____   _____
_____   _____
_____   _____

She said she was approaching forty, and I couldn't

help wondering from what direction.

Bob Hope

DOUBLE-CROSSER

Two crossword puzzles, but you have to decide which of the solutions to each clue fits into each grid. In both cases, one word has been entered to give you a start.

DOUBLE-CROSSER

Across

1 Items of footwear; Range (5)
4 Ride the waves of the sea on a board; Smut from a fire (4)
6 Assist in crime; Curved gateway (4)
7 City, site of the Taj Mahal; Thought (4)
8 Official who evaluates property for the purpose of taxing it; Short tube attached to the muzzle of a gun (8)
12 Partially carbonised vegetable matter, used in gardening; Peruse text (4)
14 Appearing earlier in the same text; Garlic mayonnaise (5)
15 Quiet, serene; Stylish (4)
16 Official emblems; Took a firm stand (8)
20 Chief port of Yemen; Verdi opera with an Egyptian theme (4)
21 British nobleman; High in stature (4)
22 Citrus fruit; Repair (4)
23 Artist's tripod; Part of a flower's calyx (5)

Down

1 Becomes firm, solidifies; Long detailed story (4)
2 Prison room; Rowing poles (4)
3 Cut, as of wood; Takes in food (4)
4 Agitating; Puts a finer edge or point on (8)
5 Criminal deception; Crisp bread (5)
9 One-twelfth of a foot; Seat for more than one person (4)
10 Analysed; Cause to grow thin or weak (8)
11 Footwear usually with wooden soles; Retail establishments (5)
13 Fourth wife of Henry VIII, ___ of Cleves; Opposed to (4)
15 Enchant; Grovel (5)
17 Ailments; Offshore territory (4)
18 Lowest range of tides; The object here (4)
19 Cain's brother; Prearranged fight between two people (4)

ROUND THE BLOCK

Each eight-letter word in the list is hidden in a square around a central letter that is not a part of the word itself, as shown by the example in the grid. The word may start anywhere within its 'square' and go either clockwise or anticlockwise. When all the listed words are found, the central letters spell out the name of a movie star.

CORRIDOR ✓   MONASTIC

DESPATCH   OVERCOAT

ELIGIBLE
              PROPOSAL
HIJACKED

INVASION   SHAMROCK

LAVISHLY   TENTACLE

ROUND THE BEND

Instead of each word being hidden in a straight, continuous line, every word has one bend in it. This bend will not necessarily go off at a right angle; it may go in any direction at all! One word is given as an example.

```
N A T C E R Z Y R T S E
H D N W W V Y D D G Q P
B N C G C U E R G R M A
G O S O L B S N A A I T
Z Y R R R E I C V T L J
H P T D E R L U F E I A
U C A Y E T R A U Q L J
O S H M N X R T N I O C
O W C Y L O W E R J P B
D P J L D A I N S R E R
E R O U E M S L I N G E
W F C S Q A Z G T A S D
O E W D M Z G N X R L D
L A S I U E E N E C I S
L O R P N M N R I M D A
```

ADMIRERS   INTRODUCE

AMAZEMENT   MILITARY

BORDERING   PUZZLING ✓

CORPUSCLE   QUARTERS

ENVELOPE   RECTANGLE

FOLLOWER   SWALLOWED

GRATEFUL   TAPESTRY

WORDSEARCH: THINGS WITH WINGS

Can you find all of the listed things that have wings hidden in the grid below? Words run forwards or backwards, in either a horizontal, vertical or diagonal direction.

```
N P Q B W M L G Z Z F B H S F
B L E K O S T R I C H U A F Q
V E N G R Y P H O N L R R H U
A G A E C X B B R V Y E P M M
H N R E A G L E M L Z H Y D A
Q A C Q S N V Y F O Z C R R U
D J W D Z Y R R Z N T A W S U
A W R K W I E E H M G H P K D
W I N T A T E T I O O H R I G
B A M F T R Z D N K I O P O C
Y X S U I V G F L N T U O J E
R R B P L E L U X S C S U E N
G S M V Z Y N J Q B E X U A A
B A C U I C K R A F N N H S L
V Y D L Y T C A D O R E T P P
```

ANGEL   EAGLE   OSTRICH

BIRDS   FAIRY   PLANE

BUTTERFLY   GOOSE   PTERODACTYL

CHERUB   GRYPHON   SPHINX

CRANE   HARPY   STORK

CROW   HAWK   VAMPIRE

CUPID   MIDGE   WASP

DRAGONFLY   MOTH   WYVERN

BREAK-TIME CROSSWORD

Across

1 European country (6)
7 Sea bordering Italy (8)
8 Very cold (4)
10 Grave, dignified (6)
11 Examine by touching (4)
12 Drying cloth (5)
13 China, Japan, etc (3,4)
16 Flower associated with alpine regions (7)
18 Take part in a row (5)
20 Bluish-white metallic element (4)
21 Substance covering the crown of a tooth (6)
23 Female operatic star (4)
24 Period of unusually warm weather (8)
25 Noisy disturbance (6)

Down

1 Label showing the cost of an article (5,3)
2 Sediment in wine (4)
3 Stunned (5)
4 Native of Tehran, for example (7)
5 Showing little interest or enthusiasm (4-7)
6 Underground workers (6)
9 Tame (11)
14 Enter unlawfully onto someone's property (8)
15 Prehistoric human male (7)
17 Revised before printing (6)
19 Keen (5)
22 Hobble (4)

HEXAFIT

Place the listed words into the hexagons, one letter per cell, starting in any of those surrounding a black circle, so that words read clockwise. Some letters are already in place.

The letter is the same in any cell that shares a common border with a cell in a touching hexagon.

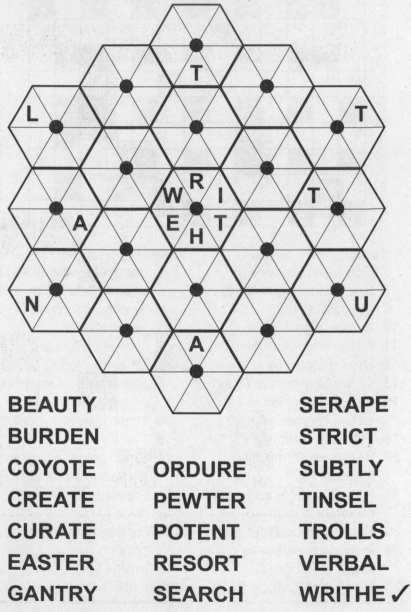

BEAUTY		SERAPE
BURDEN		STRICT
COYOTE	ORDURE	SUBTLY
CREATE	PEWTER	TINSEL
CURATE	POTENT	TROLLS
EASTER	RESORT	VERBAL
GANTRY	SEARCH	WRITHE ✓

296

KAKURO

Fill the grid so that each block adds up to the total in the box above or to the left of it.

You can only use the digits 1-9, one per square, but the same digit must not be used twice in a block. The same digit may occur more than once in any row or column, but it must be in a separate block.

SUDOKU

Place one of the numbers from 1 to 9 into every empty cell so that each row, each column and each 3x3 block contains all the numbers from 1 to 9.

					4			
			2	9	5			
	7							8
						5	4	
	9			1			3	
	8	6						
4							2	
			7	8	3			
			6					

SAY WHAT YOU SEE

DOMINO PLACEMENT

A standard set of twenty-eight dominoes has been laid out as shown below. Can you draw in the edges of them all? One is already in place.

It may be helpful to use the check-box to tick off the dominoes as they are found.

4	3	1	4	4	3	1	1
0	3	1	5	5	0	6	4
5	3	1	4	6	4	3	6
2	4	0	2	6	5	4	2
2	6	0	0	5	6	5	2
3	3	0	3	2	5	5	6
2	1	2	1	6	1	0	0

0 - 0	0 - 1	0 - 2	0 - 3	0 - 4	0 - 5	0 - 6	1 - 1

1 - 2	1 - 3	1 - 4	1 - 5	1 - 6	2 - 2	2 - 3	2 - 4	2 - 5	2 - 6
						✓			

3 - 3	3 - 4	3 - 5	3 - 6	4 - 4	4 - 5	4 - 6	5 - 5	5 - 6	6 - 6

ALPHAFILL

Place 25 different letters of the alphabet, one per circle, in order to spell out the listed words. Words are formed by moving between adjacent circles along the connecting lines, either horizontally, vertically or diagonally in any direction.

Begin by crossing out the letters already in place, together with the one letter which doesn't appear in any of the words.

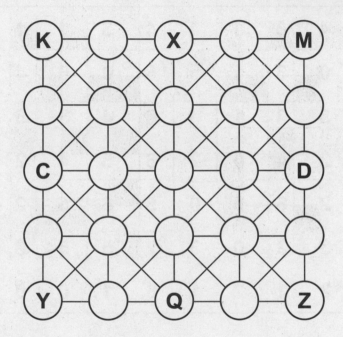

A B C D E F G H I J K L M

N O P Q R S T U V W X Y Z

CARAVAN	JUTE	RESTED
CAREFUL	KNITS	TOXIN
DOING	MOTH	WHO
FEZ	PLURAL	WINK
JULY	QUARTS	WIRED

NUMBER FILLER

Can you fit all of the listed numbers into the grid? One is already in place, to get you off to a good start!

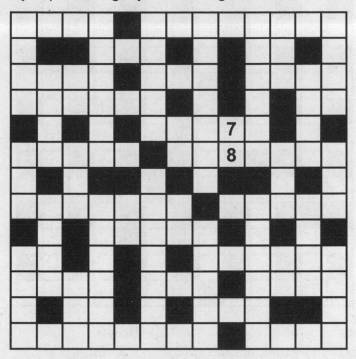

2 digits	3 digits	4 digits	5 digits	7 digits
12	111	1998	13680	1315778
40	150	2315	27166	3084291
43	246	3069	28147	4419009
52	264	3852	29902	4576839
63	367	5287	66071	
69	463	5489	76979	**8 digits**
78 ✓	729	5526		23476879
80	765	5712	**6 digits**	84348839
88	808	5829	310255	
94	957	8356	621594	
		8571	630479	
		9020	643314	
		9582	736340	
		9645	902376	

BREAK-TIME CROSSWORD

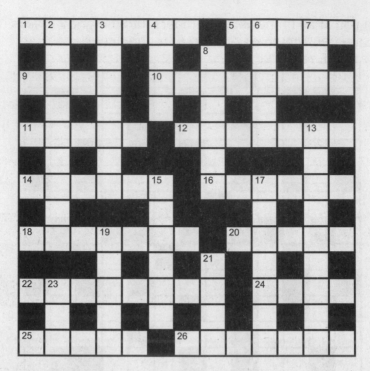

Across

1 Extremely bad, appalling (7)
5 Light narrow boat (5)
9 Land force of a nation (4)
10 Country, capital Bratislava (8)
11 Donated (5)
12 Raise an objection (7)
14 Annoy continually or chronically (6)
16 Submissive to training or direction (6)
18 In a murderous frenzy (7)
20 Cloak, often knitted (5)
22 Animal or plant that lives in or on a host (8)
24 Cut off with the teeth (4)
25 Item of bed linen (5)
26 Deliver a talk (7)

Down

2 Temporary defensive barrier (9)
3 Timidity (7)
4 As well (4)
6 At a distance (5)
7 Kimono sash (3)
8 Secured in a dock (6)
13 Brine (4,5)
15 Insect with large pincers at the rear of the abdomen (6)
17 Live together (7)
19 Left over, superfluous (5)
21 In this place (4)
23 Burned remains (3)

CODEWORD

Every letter in this puzzle has been replaced by a number, the number remaining the same for that letter wherever it occurs. Every letter of the alphabet has been used. Substitute numbers for letters to complete the codeword.

It may help to cross off the letters beneath the grid to keep a track of progress, and to use the reference box showing which numbers have been decoded. Three letters have already been entered into the grid, to help you on your way.

22 C	11	6	16	20	19	19	■	4	5	7	22	23
20 A	■	20	■	14	■	4	■	25	■	22	■	25
4 T	21	14	7	22	■	20	14	9	7	25	4	26
5	■	17	■	5	■	4	■	4	■	16	■	■
25	22	11	14	11	6	7	22	■	18	7	25	24
3	■	■	■	12	■	22	■	19	■	22	■	11
12	11	11	4	25	3	■	14	7	22	23	25	1
20	■	12	■	3	■	15	■	1	■	■	■	10
1	25	17	19	■	12	25	19	25	20	12	22	5
■	■	20	■	22	■	1	■	14	■	5	■	11
8	11	14	2	21	7	1	■	22	11	26	16	21
20	■	13	■	15	■	11	■	25	■	6	■	14
15	12	20	18	25	■	24	20	12	5	25	20	3

A B C D E F G H I J K L M

N O P Q R S T U V W X Y Z

1	2	3	4 T	5	6	7	8	9	10	11	12	13
14	15	16	17	18	19	20 A	21	22 C	23	24	25	26

SUM TOTAL

Fill each empty square so that every row contains ten different numbers from 0 to 9. In columns, the numbers may be repeated. The black squares show the sum total of the numbers in each column.

Wherever one square touches another either vertically or diagonally, the numbers must be different. Some are already in place.

3	2	0		8	7		5		6
	8				1	9		3	2
0	9	2	1				6		
8		7			1	0		9	
		0		9			2		6
9		7	5			4		8	
30	**29**	**20**	**18**	**27**	**21**	**33**	**29**	**41**	**22**

TRY SOMETHING NEW

It's easy to get into a rut as the years advance, and routine can be reassuring as we get older, but there's no reason why you can't try something new.

Take books, for example: if you always read romance novels, try a mystery – and if your taste is for westerns, try a science-fiction novel instead.

Who knows, you may discover a whole library of books out there, just waiting to be read!

JIGSAW SUDOKU

Fit the numbers 1, 2, 3, 4, 5 and 6 into the grid in such a way that each horizontal row, each vertical column and each of the heavily outlined sections of six squares each contains a different number. Some numbers are already in place.

				1	
	3				
		6			
		5			
			3		
4					2

WHAT DOES IT MEAN?

Which of the following is the correct definition of the word:

PRESCIENT

1 Having practical ability or skill; expert, clever

2 Knowing or anticipating the outcome of events before they happen

3 Cut off beforehand, prematurely, or abruptly

SPIDOKU

In the spider's web below, each of the eight segments should be filled with a different number from 1 to 8, in such a way that every ring also contains a different number from 1 to 8.

The segments run from the outside of the spider's web to the centre, and the rings run all the way around. So that you can see the rings more clearly, we've shaded them grey and white.

Some numbers are already in place. Can you fill in the rest?

CUBE ROUTES

Fill the words into the grid (one letter is ready in place), changing route where necessary, as with this example:

ASPECT   ENDURE   SPED
CARE   REASON   WRITHE
CASE   ROE

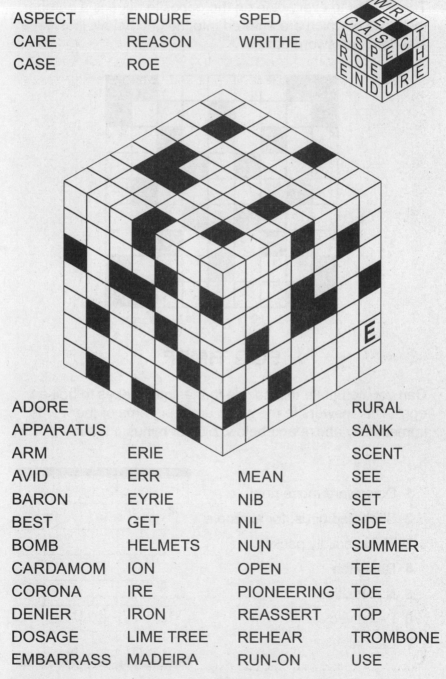

ADORE

APPARATUS

ARM   ERIE

AVID   ERR   MEAN

BARON   EYRIE   NIB

BEST   GET   NIL

BOMB   HELMETS NUN

CARDAMOM ION   OPEN

CORONA   IRE   PIONEERING

DENIER   IRON   REASSERT

DOSAGE   LIME TREE REHEAR

EMBARRASS MADEIRA RUN-ON

RURAL

SANK

SCENT

SEE

SET

SIDE

SUMMER

TEE

TOE

TOP

TROMBONE

USE

307

NUMBER CRUNCHER CROSSWORD

A little mathematical crossword, where a little knowledge of mathematics will come in very handy!

The answer to every clue on the opposite page is a number, the digits of which are entered into the grid below, just like a standard crossword puzzle.

EGG TIMER

Can you complete this puzzle in the time it takes to boil an egg? The answers to the clues are anagrams of the words immediately above and below, plus or minus a letter.

1 Downward movement

2 Sheltered birds, for example

3 Thick, solidly packed

4 Despatch

5 Necessities

6 Perceived

7 Eternal

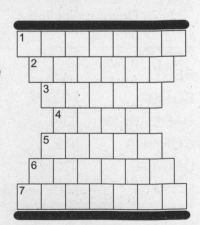

NUMBER CRUNCHER CROSSWORD

Across

1 2 Down multiplied by 9 Across (5)

5 19 Across plus 21 Across plus two (3)

6 13 Across minus 13 (3)

8 One seventh of 25 Across (2)

9 Inches in 12 feet (3)

11 Four squared (2)

13 2 Down multiplied by five (3)

15 Ounces in seven pounds (3)

16 205 squared plus 3 Down plus four (5)

17 15 Across multiplied by five (3)

19 4 Down multiplied by 18 (3)

21 28 Down plus 13 (2)

22 26 Down multiplied by nine (3)

24 One twelfth of 19 Across (2)

25 24 Across plus 14 Down plus 38 (3)

27 Six cubed plus 1 Down (3)

29 15 Across squared minus 26 (5)

Down

1 Square root of 625 (2)

2 Five per cent of 3020 (3)

3 22 Across plus 15 Down minus 32 (3)

4 Number of hours equal to 158,400 seconds (2)

5 6 Across plus 8 Across minus nine (3)

7 27 Across minus 30 (3)

8 312 squared plus 7 Down plus one (5)

10 204 squared minus 40 (5)

12 250 squared minus 74 (5)

14 Minutes in nine hours (3)

15 2 Down minus 14 (3)

18 4 Down multiplied by 14 (3)

20 31 squared (3)

22 3 Down minus 132 (3)

23 9 Across plus 13 Across plus 22 (3)

26 11 Across plus 1 Down (2)

28 Inches in four feet (2)

BRICKWORK

Fill each empty square with a single-digit number from 1 to 8. No number may appear twice in any row or column.

In any set of two squares separated by dotted lines, one square contains an odd number and the other contains an even number.

	1	2		8		
			6			
3		6		1		
	7	1	8		6	3
6	3					8
1		2		4	7	6
7		8			6	1
	1	8		7	4	

In 100 years we have gone from teaching Latin and Greek

in high school to teaching Remedial English in college.

Joseph Sobran

CHAIN LETTERS

Fill each empty circle with one of the letters A, B, C, D or E.

Every horizontal row, vertical column, set of five linked circles, and diagonal line of five circles should contain five different letters.

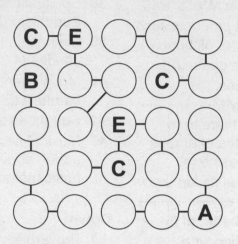

MEMORY TEST

Which of the following is a smaller version of the image on page 275? Make a choice, then turn back to page 275 to see if it is correct.

X	X	O
X	O	X
O	X	X

A

O	O	X
X	O	X
O	X	X

B

X	O	X
X	X	O
O	O	X

C

O	O	X
X	O	X
X	X	O

D

GENERAL KNOWLEDGE CROSSWORD

Across

1 Marine plant (7)
5 Donor (5)
8 Nickname of Corporal O'Reilly in M*A*S*H (5)
9 Sell illicit products such as drugs or alcohol (7)
10 Southern ocean (9)
11 At all times, poetically (3)
12 Brandy made from the residue of grapes after pressing (4)
15 Traditional Italian straw-covered wine bottle (6)
17 Get the better of (5)
19 Mr Redding who sang *(Sittin' on) The Dock of the Bay* (4)
20 Character whose adventures are written in rhyme, ___ Bear (6)
21 Number of sides of a triangle (5)
22 Elaborate song for a solo voice (4)
23 Tatters (4)
25 John Quincy ___, sixth president of the USA (5)
26 Propelling with oars (6)
27 Athletic breed of horse from the Middle East (4)
28 Frequently (5)
29 Ancient country and place of pilgrimage in south-west Asia on the Mediterranean (6)

32 Name given to 6 June 1944 (1-3)
37 Overnight condensation (3)
38 Spiritual head of Tibetan Buddhism (5,4)
39 Extinguish (a candle) (4,3)
40 Moved gently or carefully (5)
41 Sought an answer to (5)
42 Musical accompaniment added above a basic melody (7)

Down

1 Proverbially, the lowest form of wit (7)
2 Accounts checker (7)
3 Mistakes (6)
4 Public discussion (6)
5 Shaped and stuffed pasta dumplings (7)
6 Long depressions in the surface of the land (7)
7 Muscular stiffness occurring after death (5,6)
13 Stage-player (5)
14 Republic in Central America (5,4)
15 Prediction (8)
16 Punctuation mark written as '&' (9)
18 Herb with leaves often used in vinegar (8)

GENERAL KNOWLEDGE CROSSWORD

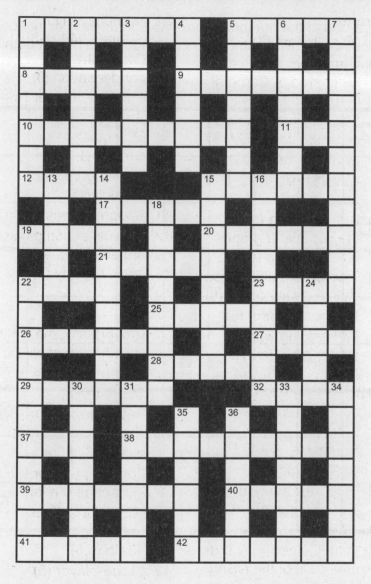

22 Magic word used in a spell or in conjuring (11)

24 Pear-shaped tropical fruit (5)

30 American city (3,4)

31 Human-like robot (7)

33 Body of water between Israel and Jordan (4,3)

34 Beginning of time (4,3)

35 Jubilant (6)

36 Muscle that flexes the forearm (6)

SUDOKU

Place one of the numbers from 1 to 9 into every empty cell so that each row, each column and each 3x3 block contains all the numbers from 1 to 9.

2			7		8			
	8		1	5				
5	7	3						
	9		3	8				
		7				4		
				9	5		6	
						1	8	3
				2	1		4	
			6		4			5

What a wonderful life I've had! I only wish I'd realised it sooner.

Colette

JIGWORD

A symmetrical crossword has been cut into pieces. Can you put it back together? Three pieces are already in position.

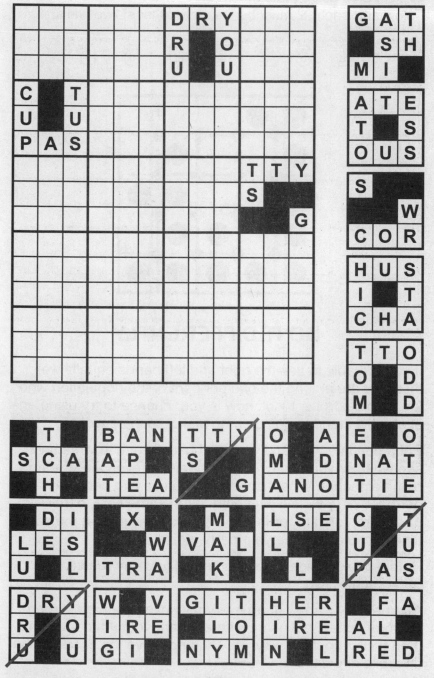

ISOLATE

Draw walls to partition the grid into areas (some walls are already drawn in for you). Each area must contain two circles, area sizes must match those shown by the numbers below and each '+' must be linked to at least two walls.

2 3 3 3 4 5 5

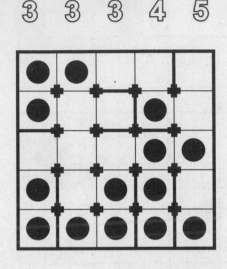

DO IT DIFFERENTLY

If you are able to use the right and left hands equally well, then you are among the one per cent of the population who are ambidextrous. If not, now is your chance to try using an alternative hand to do common tasks, such as writing.

Put a pen into the hand you don't usually use to write and see whether you can write your name, or even a few letters of the alphabet. What happens if you use two pens, one per hand? Try writing with both at the same time, either backward, forward, or in two different directions at the same time. It could become your party trick!

Hold a book upside down, and see if you can read a paragraph or two.

Alternatively, carry out an everyday action such as stirring a cup of coffee, but use a different hand to hold the spoon: then think about the way you stir, and move the spoon in the opposite direction.

WELL SPOTTED

Some of the circles in this puzzle are already black. Fill in more white circles, so that the number of black circles totals the number inside the area they surround.

Every black circle surrounding an area with a number higher than '1' needs to be next to another black circle surrounding the same area.

When solving, it may help to put a small dot into any circle you know should not be filled.

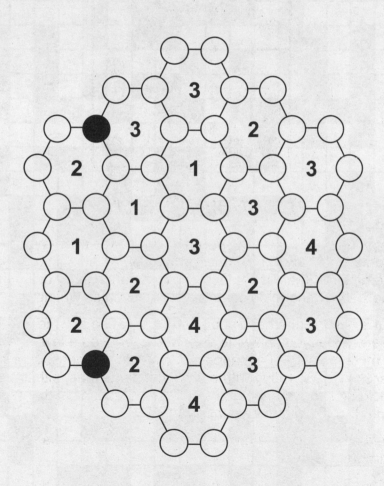

WORD FILLER

On the opposite page is a poem by Rudyard Kipling, with Leander Starr Jameson, a former prime minister of the Cape Colony, in mind as an inspiration for the characteristics he recommended young people to live by (notably Kipling's son, to whom the poem is addressed in the last line).

All of the underlined words will fit into the grid below. One letter is already in place: complete the puzzle!

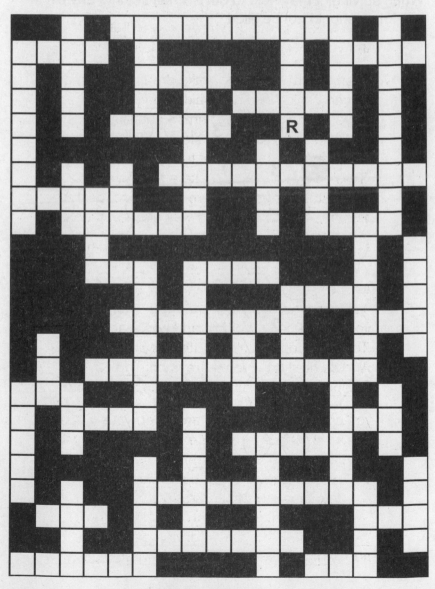

WORD FILLER

If

If you can keep your head when all about you
Are <u>losing</u> <u>theirs</u> and blaming it on you,
If you can trust yourself when all <u>men</u> doubt you,
<u>But</u> make <u>allowance</u> for <u>their</u> doubting too;
If you can wait and <u>not</u> be tired by waiting,
Or <u>being</u> lied about, don't deal in lies,
Or being hated, don't give way to <u>hating</u>,
And <u>yet</u> don't look <u>too</u> good, <u>nor</u> talk too wise.

If you can <u>dream</u> – and not <u>make</u> dreams your master;
If you can <u>think</u> – and not make <u>thoughts</u> your <u>aim</u>;
If you can <u>meet</u> with Triumph and Disaster
And treat those <u>two</u> impostors just the <u>same</u>;
If you can bear to hear the <u>truth</u> you've <u>spoken</u>
<u>Twisted</u> by knaves to make a <u>trap</u> for fools,
Or <u>watch</u> the things you <u>gave</u> your <u>life</u> to, broken,
And stoop and build 'em up with worn-out tools.

If you can make <u>one</u> heap of all your winnings
And <u>risk</u> it on one turn of <u>pitch-and-toss</u>,
And lose, and <u>start</u> again at your <u>beginnings</u>
And <u>never</u> breathe a <u>word</u> about your loss;
If you can force your heart and <u>nerve</u> and sinew
To serve your <u>turn</u> long after <u>they</u> <u>are</u> gone,
And so hold on when there is <u>nothing</u> in you
<u>Except</u> the <u>Will</u> which <u>says</u> to them: 'Hold on!'

If you can <u>talk</u> with crowds and keep your virtue,
Or <u>walk</u> with Kings – nor lose <u>the</u> common touch,
If neither foes nor loving <u>friends</u> can hurt you,
If all men count with you, but <u>none</u> too much;
If you can fill the <u>unforgiving</u> minute
With sixty <u>seconds'</u> worth of <u>distance</u> run,
<u>Yours</u> is the <u>Earth</u> and <u>everything</u> that's in it,
And – <u>which</u> is more – you'll be a <u>Man</u>, my son!

RED HERRING

Five of the words below must be entered in the grid, reading across, so as to create five more words reading down. Can you spot the red herring?

EARNS   STEAM

INUIT   TREND

LEDGE   TULLE

LETTER TRACKER

Starting at the top left corner and ending at the bottom right, track a path from letter to letter, in any direction except diagonally, in order to find 15 hidden birds. All of the letters must be used, but none more than once.

O	R	I	P	A	R	A	K	K	Y	S	T	A
S	T	C	L	I	A	T	E	S	L	K	L	R
A	M	H	B	U	A	G	E	T	A	R	I	N
G	P	I	E	D	W	E	L	A	G	U	P	G
R	C	G	I	G	N	T	P	H	N	F	F	I
O	R	A	R	E	A	R	O	E	I	T	B	N
S	L	K	E	L	O	C	M	A	G	H	U	Z
S	L	E	R	D	N	K	R	S	I	N	A	Z
B	I	S	T	U	N	C	O	A	N	T	R	D

DO IT YOURSELF!

In this crossword puzzle, the clues are in alphabetical order and there are no black squares in the grid. Black out the unwanted squares, to produce a symmetrically-patterned grid containing words that can be matched to the clues.

M	U	S	I	C	A	L	A	C	R	U	D	E
U	N	C	O	Y	E	A	R	L	A	N	E	I
S	C	A	L	P	A	R	E	A	D	I	N	G
T	O	N	E	R	A	G	E	N	E	F	E	H
A	U	S	T	E	R	E	G	G	H	O	S	T
R	N	O	I	S	E	R	T	H	I	R	T	Y
D	R	O	W	S	E	O	S	T	A	M	E	N
V	I	C	A	R	S	W	O	O	P	I	N	E
P	E	A	C	E	T	A	P	P	E	A	S	E
I	E	R	R	R	E	P	A	I	D	L	A	D
O	R	I	G	A	M	I	N	C	H	I	L	L
U	I	N	O	S	E	T	H	A	N	K	E	E
S	P	A	T	E	D	I	L	L	N	E	S	S

Apparition

Consistent

Cool down

Egg-shaped and flutey-toned instrument

Evergreen conifer

Flood, rush

Flower part

Glances over

Greater

In the news

Jangle

Japanese paper-folding art

Knitting implements

Large North American deer

Malady

Mollify

Number

Perusing text

Play featuring singing and dancing

Popular hot condiment

Remove by rubbing

Severely simple

Silence

Similar

Skin on the top of the head

Snooze

Unrefined

Very religious

CALCUDOKU

Each row and column should contain the numbers 1-6. The numbers placed in a heavily outlined set of squares may be repeated, but must produce the calculation in the top left corner, using the mathematical symbol provided. So, for example, when multiplied, the numbers 3 and 4 total 12:

x12	
4	**3**

Any block of one square will contain the number in the top left corner.

x72	/2		+12		
		/4	/5	x36	
x90					x8
	x100	/3			
/2			x6		x15
	−1		+10		

YOU KNOW YOU'RE GETTING OLD WHEN …

Your list of complaints is longer than your memory.

You've given up all your bad habits, but you still don't feel any better.

JIGSAW PUZZLE

Fit the jigsaw together to reveal eight currencies.

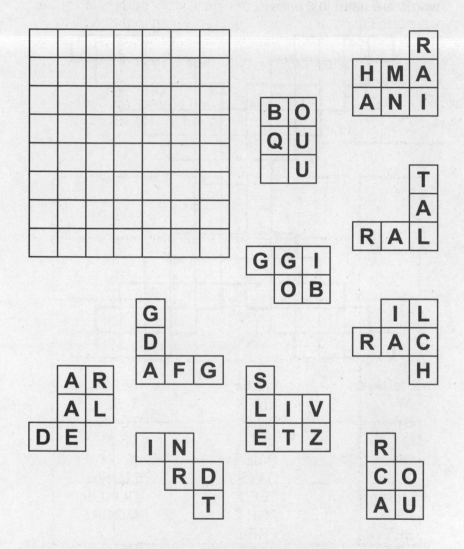

X MARKS THE SPOT

Fill the grid with the listed words, one letter per square. All words are used just once.

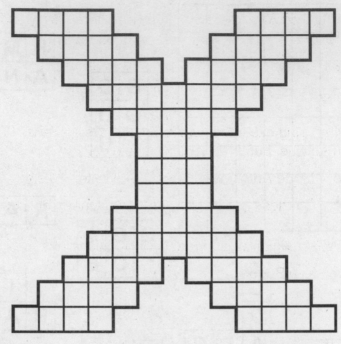

2 letters
AT
BY
MY
OF

3 letters
ART
BET
LEA
NOR
OUT
SLY
TAB

4 letters
BEES
BRIE
BYTE
DAIS
DAYS
FEED
FORT
FREE
FRET
LIED
LOAF
RARE
RIOT
ROAR
TAUT
TEEM

TERM
TOIL
TOSS
TRIM

5 letters
DONOR
MOORS

7 letters
COOLANT
DIOCESE
FANTAIL

9 letters
FERRYBOAT
MOONSTONE

GENERAL KNOWLEDGE QUIZ

Can you identify which one of the multiple-choice answers (a, b, c or d) is correct for each of the questions below?

1 The Sea Swallow is an alternative name for which bird?

   a Seagull   **b** Penguin

   c Tern   **d** Cormorant

2 On being executed, who said: "This is a sharp medicine, but it will cure all diseases."?

   a Marie Antoinette   **b** Sir Walter Raleigh

   c Charles I   **d** Mary Queen of Scots

3 What religion was founded by Bodhidhama?

   a Zen Buddhism   **b** Islam

   c Hinduism   **d** Sikhism

4 Of what is Tribology the study?

   a Hormones   **b** Tissues of organisms

   c Sea creatures   **d** Lubrication and friction

5 In what sport would you see a Western Roll?

   a Ten pin bowling   **b** Wrestling

   c High jump   **d** Judo

6 Who, when he was murdered whilst playing poker, held two aces and two eights, a hand which from then on was known as a Dead Man's Hand?

   a Wyatt Earp   **b** Jesse James

   c Billy the Kid   **d** Wild Bill Hickok

DOUBLE-CROSSER

Two crossword puzzles, but you have to decide which of the solutions to each clue fits into each grid. In both cases, one word has been entered to give you a start.

DOUBLE-CROSSER

Across

1 Frolic; Narrow towards a point (5)
4 Amusement or pastime; Movable barrier in a fence (4)
6 Deficient in beauty; Leer (4)
8 Flightless bird; One who is playfully mischievous (3)
10 Capacious; Coral reef (5)
11 Bus garage; Small and light boat (5)
12 Penetrate gradually; Rope used to restrain an animal (5)
15 Cliff-dwelling, gull-like seabird; Scottish island (4)
17 Chief Norse god; Image or representation of a god (4)
19 Govern; Ringo ___, former Beatle (5)
22 Love intensely; Maxim (5)
24 Causing laughter; Specified value (5)
26 Large edible mushroom; Young seal (3)
27 Organ of smell; Stockings, socks and tights (4)
28 Brought into existence; Consistency (4)
29 Burn superficially or lightly; Number indicated by the Roman LX (5)

Down

1 Baby birds; Does business (6)
2 Acute discomfort; Quick look (4)
3 Divert in a specified direction; Indian currency unit (5)
4 Fetch; Place to work out (3)
5 African republic; Spanish city famous for steel and swords (6)
7 Characteristic of those who are not members of the clergy; Communist state of Asia (4)
9 Grinding tooth; Pigmented spots on the skin (5)
13 ___ Baba, fictional character; ___ Khan (3)
14 Believer in a major religion; Large crowd of people (5)
16 Balkan country, capital Priština; Japanese robe (6)
18 Knitting tool; Tolerance (6)
20 Filled tortilla; Persistence of a sound after its source has stopped (4)
21 Goes along at great speed; Yawns wide (5)
23 Blatant; Peak (4)
25 Archaic form of the word 'your'; Hostel (3)

ROUND THE BLOCK

Each eight-letter word in the list is hidden in a square around a central letter that is not a part of the word itself, as shown by the example in the grid. The word may start anywhere within its 'square' and go either clockwise or anticlockwise. When all the listed words are found, the central letters spell out the name of a movie star.

H	E	D	I	S	L	O	C	R	A	T	K
M	A	E	C	T	E	H	M	I	S	L	A
L	A	C	N	A	R	E	F	A	C	T	U
G	M	E	Q	U	A	R	E	I	H	Y	T
N	I	W	R	V	T	E	P	U	R	A	W
V	I	E	J	N	O	R	O	A	T	R	L
E	K	U	D	I	E	L	S	E	S	R	E
R	E	O	H	R	U	I	N	G	E	R	S
Y	A	R	C	E	A	T	N	B	T	R	A
D	I	L	D	K	I	T	O	L	W	L	E
I	D	O	L	S	B	I	C	R	K	I	U
T	Y	S	O	L	L	I	U	K	I	N	G
B	A	C	P	L	E	G	R	E	K	A	S
E	L	I	Z	A	N	V	J	K	A	E	P
R	E	N	O	T	Y	O	U	T	H	F	U

ARCHDUKE   OPERATOR

BLOTTING

    PLATONIC

CRUCIBLE ✓

    SOLIDITY

DISTANCE

LACEWING   SPEAKING

MISCHIEF   TRAWLERS

ROUND THE BEND

Instead of each word being hidden in a straight, continuous line, every word has one bend in it. This bend will not necessarily go off at a right angle; it may go in any direction at all! One word is given as an example.

```
O P X E N T A T Y I N G
E S P G Y F E L A V H I
N E U J D E N L E T N L
O K G R N F E E I W E
P V A I E L V D A V C D
T G T N E L A V Z Y I Z
S O P F L E E T K S Q N
D I T R T P H B I C U V
E B A A T U O O E M A I
L D R L L N N A B L M B
I E N L E U E E U T F O
B V S Y T C N C R K Q F
E I G O N V K S L E R U
D X Y A L U T I O N D H
X L R G A R F C S G U S
```

BACKBONE	HEAVENLY
CENTRALLY	NUMBERED
DELIBERATE	POSTPONE
DELIGHTED	SHUFFLE
EXPOSURE	SOLUTION
FRAGRANCE	TELEVISION
GARDENIA ✓	VALENTINE

HAND AND EYE CO-ORDINATION

Draw in the missing sides of each picture, so that the two giraffes are exact reflections of one another.

Nobody can go back and start a new beginning, but

anyone can start today and make a new ending.

Maria Robinson

Solutions

Page 6

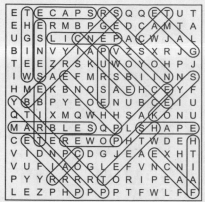

Page 7

Page 7 crossword letters:
- D I S P L E A S U R E
- A G I N H E U
- S A L U T E D R I S E N
- S O Y E A P N
- I C O N S A P P H I R E
- G D R N R C
- N U T M E G D E L E T E
- A O P C L S
- T H R I L L E D P L U S
- I N O L B I A
- O N A I R L E A R N E R
- N D E A L K Y
- H O R S E R A D I S H

Page 8

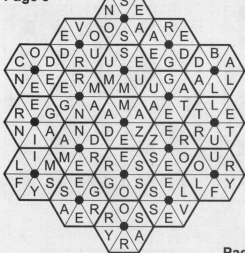

Page 9

2	6		4	1	2		3	1
1	5	2	9	6	3		9	6
	4	8			1	4	2	3
8	2		3	1	9	7		
2	1		7	5	6	8	9	3
9	7	5	8		8	9	7	6
7	3	2	1	5	4		4	2
		1	4	9	7		3	1
7	1	3	2			3	5	
9	7		5	7	9	8	6	4
8	3		6	9	8		8	1

Page 10

1	5	3	9	7	2	6	4	8
8	9	6	3	4	5	7	2	1
4	7	2	1	6	8	9	3	5
9	1	4	8	5	3	2	6	7
7	2	8	4	1	6	5	9	3
3	6	5	7	2	9	8	1	4
6	4	7	2	8	1	3	5	9
5	3	1	6	9	7	4	8	2
2	8	9	5	3	4	1	7	6

Page 11

1	0	1	1	2	3	3	1
2	0	0	1	2	6	6	3
6	6	1	2	5	1	4	1
0	6	4	5	5	6	0	6
5	5	4	6	4	3	0	0
2	3	5	2	0	4	4	3
3	2	5	5	4	3	4	2

Solutions

Page 12

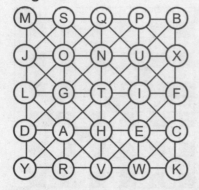

Page 13

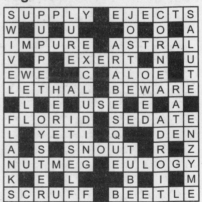

Page 14

```
M A T I N E E   A   C   F
U   R   I   S   G U A V A
S T A L E M A T E   B   C
H   P   C   U   S P A C E
R U S S E T   U     R
O       S H A P E L E S S
O   V   E   S     T   M
M A I L O R D E R       A
  E   E   T E A S E R
A L T E R   K   A   P   T
I   N   O V E R S T A T E
D R A M A   P   O   D   S
E   M   D   T A N G E N T
```

Page 15

```
S U P P L Y   E J E C T S
W   U   U     O   O   A
I M P U R E   A S T R A L
V   P   E X E R T   N   U
E W E   C   A L O E   T
L E T H A L   B E W A R E
  L   E   U S E   E   A
F L O R I D   S E D A T E
L   Y E T I   Q   D E N
A   S   S N O U T   R   Z
N U T M E G   E U L O G Y
K   E   L     B   I   M
S C R U F F   B E E T L E
```

Page 16

1 Dyslexia, 2 Doorknob,
3 Damascus, 4 Deadline,
5 Downtown, 6 Dominant,
7 Disclaim, 8 Daiquiri,
9 Division, 10 Defeated,
11 Dynamite, 12 Drunkard.
The twelve-letter word is:
ABSENT-MINDED

Page 17

1	4	5	3	6	2
2	3	4	1	5	6
6	2	3	5	4	1
5	6	2	4	1	3
4	1	6	2	3	5
3	5	1	6	2	4

Page 17

1

Solutions

Page 18

Page 19

Pages 20/21

1	3	4	4			7	8	4	1
9	0		7		3			9	9
6			7	3	7	9	3		6
5	4	0		0			3	6	0
				7	0	5	6	9	
3	9	2			6		8	2	8
3		7	3	0	1	7			6
1	6			0		9		5	4
2	4	8	4			6	1	7	0

Page 20

1 Algebra, 2 Arable,
3 Blare, 4 Real,
5 Clear, 6 Cradle,
7 Crawled.

333

Solutions

Page 22
Death - wiSh - list
After - gLow - worm
Bath - roOm - service
True - loVe - letter
Middle - East - Africa
Marching - baNd - wagon
Cast - Iron - curtain
Super - novA - Scotia
Answer: SLOVENIA

Page 22
Author: BARBARA CARTLAND

Page 23
DISH – dash – bash – bass –
boss – bows – BOWL
(Other solutions are possible)

Page 23
The nine-letter word is:
SHARPENED

Pages 24/25

R	U	N	U	P		O		D		M		H
E		U		I	M	P	R	E	C	A	T	E
A	T	T	I	C		E		P		L		A
C		C		C	A	R	E	R		A		T
T	O	R	S	O		E		E	A	R	T	H
I		A		L	O	T	U	S		I		E
N	A	C	H	O		T		S	P	A	W	N
G		K			T	A	X	I			H	
	G	E	N	I	E			N	Y	L	O	N
W	E	R	E		A	D	A	G	E		E	
	S		W		C		P		A		V	
	T		E	T	H	E	R		S	T	E	M
E	A	R	L	Y			O	T	T	E	R	
	P		P	L	A	N			R		A	
P	O	S	S	E		G		C	U	R	E	S
E		U		W	A	I	V	E		A		T
R	O	G	E	R		T		D	E	F	O	E
H		A		I	R	A	Q	I		I		R
A		R		T		T		L	A	R	G	O
P	I	E	C	E	M	E	A	L		M		I
S		D		R		D		A	W	A	R	D

Page 26

2	5	7	1	8	9	6	4	3
8	3	9	5	6	4	1	7	2
6	1	4	2	3	7	8	5	9
4	9	8	6	5	2	7	3	1
7	2	3	4	1	8	5	9	6
1	6	5	7	9	3	2	8	4
5	8	1	9	4	6	3	2	7
3	4	2	8	7	1	9	6	5
9	7	6	3	2	5	4	1	8

Page 27

Page 28

CHILDREN	PROSPERS
CORRODED	RETICULE
ENCIPHER	RIGHTFUL
EULOGIST	SPLUTTER
FLOGGING	TRUTHFUL
LUCIDITY	UNDERPIN
MERINGUE	VEHICLES
NEOPHYTE	WHOMEVER

Solutions

Page 29

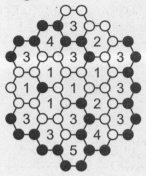

Page 32

G	L	A	R	E
R	O	M	A	N
A	V	O	I	D
D	E	N	S	E
E	D	G	E	D

Page 32

Canada, Belgium, Namibia, Egypt, Italy, Norway, Paraguay, Turkey, Spain, Poland, Senegal, Tunisia, Morocco, Mongolia.

Page 34

$76 - 4 = 72$, $72 \div 8 = 9$, $9^2 = 81$, $81 + 39 = 120$, $120 \div 3 = 40$, $40 - 4 = 36$, $36 \div 4 = 9$

Page 34

Saturday

Pages 30/31

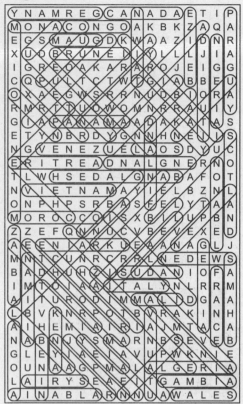

Page 33

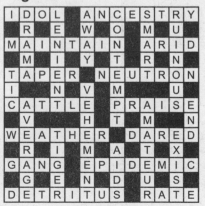

Solutions

Page 35

B	U	F	F	A	L	O
G	I	R	A	F	F	E
L	E	O	P	A	R	D
C	A	R	I	B	O	U
W	A	L	L	A	B	Y
G	A	Z	E	L	L	E
H	A	M	S	T	E	R
C	H	E	E	T	A	H

Page 36

Page 37

1 b, 2 c, 3 d, 4 c, 5 a, 6 d.

Pages 38/39

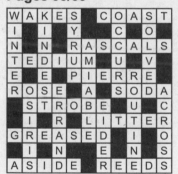

Pages 38/39

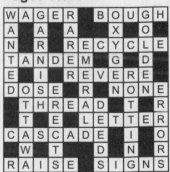

Page 40

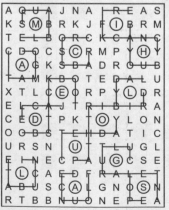

Movie star: MICHAEL DOUGLAS

Page 41

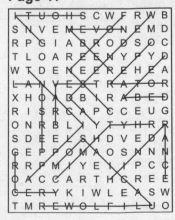

Solutions

Page 42

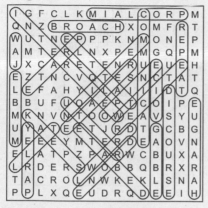

Page 43

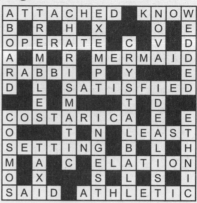

A	T	T	A	C	H	E	D			K	N	O	W
B		R		H		X				O		V	E
O	P	E	R	A	T	E		C		V		V	D
A		M		R		M	E	R	M	A	I	D	
R	A	B	B	I		P		Y				E	
D		L		S	A	T	I	S	F	I	E	D	
		E		M			T		D				
C	O	S	T	A	R	I	C	A		E		E	
O			T		N		L	E	A	S	T		
S	E	T	T	I	N	G		B		L		H	
M		A		C		E	L	A	T	I	O	N	
O		X				S		L		S		I	
S	A	I	D		A	T	H	L	E	T	I	C	

Page 44

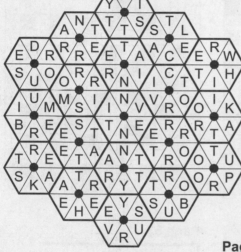

Page 45

7	8		6	8	9		8	2
1	7	4	2	9	5	8	6	3
	3	2	1			4	7	
2	9	7		9	7		4	2
1	6	3	8	2	5	4	9	7
		1	6		9	5		
4	2	6	7	1	8	3	9	5
9	8		9	3		2	5	1
	3	1		9	7	6		
2	4	6	5	9	7	1	8	3
5	1		2	1	4		7	2

Page 46

6	3	1	8	9	7	4	2	5
2	5	8	1	6	4	9	3	7
4	7	9	3	5	2	1	6	8
7	4	6	9	8	5	2	1	3
8	2	3	6	7	1	5	4	9
1	9	5	4	2	3	7	8	6
5	1	4	7	3	6	8	9	2
9	6	2	5	1	8	3	7	4
3	8	7	2	4	9	6	5	1

Page 47

4	4	0	0	0	1	1	6
2	1	1	2	2	3	0	5
3	5	6	2	5	3	2	6
0	2	4	3	0	4	5	0
6	2	1	1	2	4	4	6
1	5	6	0	4	6	6	3
3	3	5	3	5	5	1	4

Solutions

Page 48

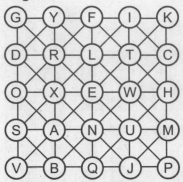

Page 49

2	5	7	■	4	5	8	7	■	8	5	8	3
0	■	4	8	8	1	■	3	2	4	1	■	2
9	1	6	3	■	9	0	4	■	■	4	2	3
9	5	4	7	1	9	■	5	5	7	0	4	9
■	8	■	5	■	9	6	7	2	■	■	7	■
5	3	6	4	8	■	8	■	9	■	9	9	4
3	■	6	■	4	1	2	7	8	■	4	■	5
7	3	2	■	6	■	2	■	7	9	0	8	5
■	1	■	6	1	6	3	■	3	■	4	■	■
8	4	5	0	2	9	■	5	1	3	1	0	3
2	6	7	■	■	4	3	8	■	6	2	0	7
9	■	3	7	3	4	■	8	6	0	1	■	6
6	9	6	9	■	2	7	1	5	■	7	6	5

Page 50

A	P	P	E	A	R	■	C	■	P	■	W	■
G	■	A	■	I	C	E	C	R	E	A	M	■
R	A	S	P	■	V	■	R	■	O	■	I	■
E	■	T	A	L	E	N	T	■	B	E	T	A
E	■	■	R	■	R	■	A	■	A	■	E	■
I	N	D	E	X	■	D	I	S	T	U	R	B
N	■	■	N	■	T	■	N	■	I	■	■	U
G	L	I	T	T	E	R	■	R	O	O	T	S
■	E	■	H	■	A	■	B	■	N	■	■	I
G	A	L	E	■	C	U	R	S	E	D	■	N
■	V	■	S	■	H	■	O	■	R	O	B	E
R	E	D	I	R	E	C	T	■	■	O	■	S
■	S	■	S	■	R	■	H	E	A	R	T	S

Page 51

W	I	D	T	H	■	M	A	S	C	A	R	A
A	■	O	■	A	■	O	■	E	■	L	■	W
S	Q	U	A	L	O	R	■	C	H	I	N	A
P	■	S	■	O	■	B	A	T	■	B	■	K
I	D	E	A	■	K	I	T	■	W	I	F	E
S	■	G	O	N	D	O	L	A	■	U	■	■
H	E	R	O	■	I	■	N	■	L	U	N	G
■	M	■	N	E	G	L	E	C	T	■	■	L
J	U	R	Y	■	H	A	D	■	Z	E	R	O
U	■	U	■	S	T	Y	■	B	■	R	■	A
D	E	L	V	E	■	I	N	E	X	A	C	T
G	■	E	■	A	■	N	■	A	■	S	■	E
E	A	R	P	L	U	G	■	T	R	E	N	D

Page 52

1 Guidance, 2 Gigantic,
3 Geronimo, 4 Grandson,
5 Gazpacho, 6 Glow-worm,
7 Graffiti, 8 Galactic,
9 Gymnasia, 10 Graceful,
11 Germinal, 12 Globally.
The twelve-letter word is:
ECONOMICALLY

Page 53

Page 53

3

Solutions

Page 54

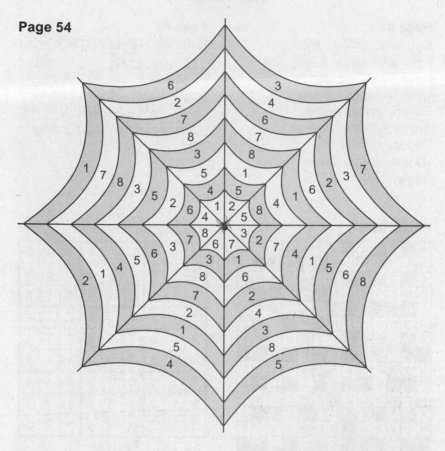

Page 55

Pages 56/57

1	1	2		4		1	1	4
2		5	8	6	3	4		4
8	3		4	7	8		4	8
	3	7		4		8	1	
4	5	7	6		4	8	5	8
	9	9		5		4	9	
1	2		2	4	5		3	9
2		3	4	7	8	4		7
3	5	2		2		1	7	9

Page 56

1 Guarded, 2 Argued,
3 Urged, 4 Rude,
5 Cured, 6 Reduce,
7 Secured.

Solutions

Page 58
Summer - caMp - fire
Fail - sAfe - guard
River - baNk - balance
Under - hanD - some
Fallen - Arch - enemy
Spider - cRab - Nebula
Paper - clIp - art
Sweet - corN - flakes
Answer: MANDARIN

Page 58
Author: ANTHONY TROLLOPE

Page 59
SOFT – sort – sore – core –
care – card – HARD
(Other solutions are possible)

Pages 60/61

B	B	A		U	T	E	N	S	I	L
A	L	U	M	N	U	S		A		O
L	D	T		S	A	L	I	E	N	T
D	O	S	S	I	E	R		L		T
I		P			A	L	S	A	C	E
N	E	W	Y	O	R	K		I	V	R
G	A	D		E	C	O	N	O	M	Y
	R	E		A		N		C		
M	I	N	D	S	E	T		E	M	A	I	L
O		E		S		S		D		A
S	E	A	N	C	E		E	S	C	O	R	T
E		T		L		C		U		T
S	C	E	N	E		H	O	S	T	A	G	E
		L		M		E		T		L
C	H	I	M	E	R	A		A		P		F
I		E		N		P	A	R	A	S	O	L
S	T	R	U	T	S		B			A
T		N		B	I	O	L	O	G	Y
E	R	I	T	R	E	A		A		B		I
R		I		S	U	R	G	E	O	N
N	E	M	E	S	I	S		D		Y		G

Page 62

6	9	8	5	1	7	3	4	2
3	4	7	2	6	8	1	5	9
5	2	1	3	4	9	7	6	8
7	1	9	8	5	6	2	3	4
2	8	6	4	9	3	5	7	1
4	3	5	7	2	1	9	8	6
9	5	4	6	7	2	8	1	3
8	6	2	1	3	5	4	9	7
1	7	3	9	8	4	6	2	5

Page 64

ANTIDOTE	HERMETIC
CLEVERLY	KEYHOLES
DYNAMITE	LECTURER
EGGSHELL	MESMERIC
EMERGING	OPULENCE
EPICYCLE	SCHEMERS
GEOMETRY	SPECIMEN
HEIGHTEN	VIGNETTE

Page 63

D	E	T	A	I	L	S		F	A	C	T
E		O		N		H		A		R
S	A	L	E	S		R	A	B	B	L	E
I		L		I	C	E		L		A
G	U	E	S	S		W	O	E	S		T
N		D	A	T	E	D		D	E	F	Y
E			P	E	R		R		E
R	U	M		N	A	M	E		K	I	D
	A		T		A	G	E			E
B	E	N	T		S	N	I	F	F		C
R		E	A	C	H		S	T	O	O	L
E		C		A	N	T		N		A
W	I	C	K	E	D		R	A	D	A	R
E		L		O		A		L		E
D	I	V	E		W	A	R	H	E	A	D

Solutions

Page 65

1 Rand (c), 2 Tall (a),
3 Cell (c), 4 Race (a),
5 Pair (a), 6 Nile (a),
7 Evil (a), 8 Idle (a),
9 Glen (c), 10 Pawn (c),
11 Lawn (c), 12 Visa (c),
13 Died (a), 14 Edge (c),
15 Weak (a), 16 Thaw (c),
17 Stop (a), 18 Cape (c),
19 Cent (c), 20 Ulna (c),
21 Hate (a), 22 Shoe (a),
23 Thai (c), 24 Stir (a),
25 Slip (c).

Page 68

M	A	G	M	A
A	R	R	A	S
D	E	A	N	S
A	N	I	S	E
M	A	N	E	S

Page 68

Trumpet, Bassoon,
Flute, Harmonica,
Sitar, Clarinet,
Trombone, Harp,
Tuba, Guitar,
Accordion, Piano,
Banjo, Recorder.

Page 70

1 Carpet,
2 Frothy,
3 Almost,
4 Budget,
5 Merlin,
6 Beetle.
Dog: POODLE

Pages 66/67

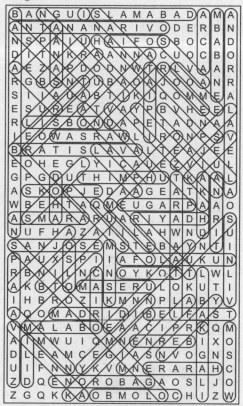

Page 69

Solutions

Page 71

M	A	D	E	I	R	A
V	A	N	U	A	T	U
B	E	R	M	U	D	A
R	E	U	N	I	O	N
I	C	E	L	A	N	D
G	R	E	N	A	D	A
M	I	N	O	R	C	A
S	U	M	A	T	R	A

Page 72

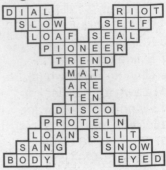

DIAL / RIOT / SLOW / SELF / LOAF / SEAL / PIONEER / TREND / MAT / ARE / TEN / DISCO / PROTEIN / LOAN / SLIT / SANG / SNOW / BODY / EYED

Page 73

Crocus, Dahlia, Mallow, Mimosa, Salvia, Thrift, Violet, Zinnia.

Pages 74/75

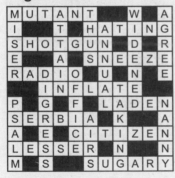

Pages 74/75

Page 76

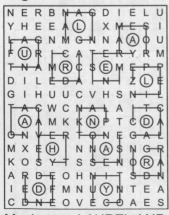

Movie star: LAUREL AND HARDY

Page 77

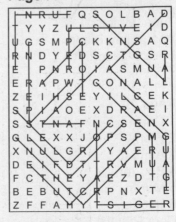

342

Solutions

Page 78

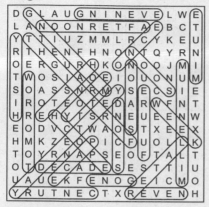

Page 79

Page 80

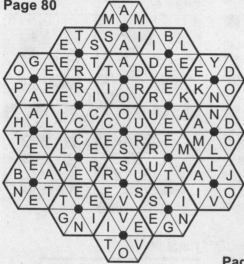

Page 81

6	2	4		8	2	9	6	7
9	6	8		5	1	3	2	4
7	5	6	8	9		8	5	9
3	1	2	6			1	6	
8	3	5	9	1		7	9	8
		3	7	2	1	4		
4	2	1		4	2	5	9	8
9	8			5	8	7	9	
8	4	9		1	3	2	4	6
7	3	1	9	2		1	2	7
5	1	2	7	4		3	1	5

Page 82

4	5	7	3	8	1	6	2	9
1	6	3	2	7	9	8	4	5
9	8	2	4	5	6	1	7	3
8	2	1	7	9	5	4	3	6
5	9	4	1	6	3	2	8	7
7	3	6	8	4	2	5	9	1
3	4	8	6	1	7	9	5	2
6	7	5	9	2	8	3	1	4
2	1	9	5	3	4	7	6	8

Page 83

6	4	5	2	3	2	0	4
6	1	1	1	2	1	1	6
3	5	3	6	5	2	2	1
3	2	5	0	6	0	1	4
4	4	5	2	0	4	0	5
3	6	2	3	3	4	6	4
1	0	0	3	5	0	6	5

Solutions

Page 84

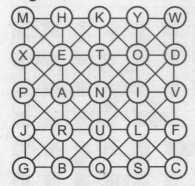

```
M   H   K   Y   W
X   E   T   O   D
P   A   N   I   V
J   R   U   L   F
G   B   Q   S   C
```

Page 85

```
4 8 9 6 ■ 3 4 7 6 1 4 7 8
7 ■ ■ 2 0 0 ■ 8 ■ 8 9 ■ 1
3 7 5 3 ■ 6 9 1 ■ 9 9 2 2
9 7 4 5 5 8 ■ 3 ■ 0 ■ 8 0
■ 6 ■ 4 ■ 3 9 1 5 2 ■ 0 ■
5 0 9 1 3 ■ 6 8 1 7 7 9 2
2 ■ 4 ■ 8 ■ 6 ■ ■ 1 ■ ■ 8
1 8 2 5 7 1 1 ■ 6 3 1 4 5
■ 8 ■ 4 9 2 5 2 ■ 2 ■ 2 ■
9 7 ■ 6 ■ 6 ■ 2 3 3 4 3 5
6 6 1 0 ■ 4 5 0 ■ 7 8 6 0
4 ■ 3 2 ■ 9 ■ 5 4 7 ■ ■ 5
7 1 5 3 5 4 0 7 ■ 6 1 1 3
```

Page 86

```
C O L O R A D O ■ F ■ A
L ■ A ■ B ■ P L E D G E
E P I C ■ B ■ T ■ R ■ I
V ■ D E T E R I O R A T E
E ■ L ■ Y ■ M ■ I ■ A
R A V E L ■ P U L S A T E
■ N ■ B ■ T ■ M ■ W ■ O
M I R R O R S ■ S H A R E
■ M ■ A ■ U ■ V ■ E ■ X
B A D T E M P E R E D ■ C
■ T ■ I ■ P ■ N ■ L I M E
B E C O M E ■ O ■ C ■ S
■ D ■ N ■ T I M E L E S S
```

Page 87

```
S A L I V A ■ J O I N E D
H ■ O ■ ■ L E A ■ M ■ ■ A
A F A R ■ B ■ C O P E ■ I
D ■ D E B U N K ■ S C A N
E ■ T ■ M ■ P ■ ■ H U T
S A T I N ■ Z O O L O G Y
■ G ■ N ■ D ■ T ■ O ■ E
P A R A D O X ■ Q U A R T
E V E ■ ■ O ■ A ■ N ■ ■ A
L E A D ■ R E F U G E ■ S
V ■ D R E W ■ T ■ E A S T
I ■ ■ U ■ A G E ■ ■ C ■ E
C L U M S Y ■ R U S H E D
```

Page 88

```
5  6  7  4  0  1  8  9  3  2
1  4  0  5  3  2  6  7  8  9
5  9  6  2  1  8  3  0  4  7
4  1  7  8  0  9  5  6  2  3
3  0  4  5  6  2  8  1  9  7
9  5  8  2  4  3  7  0  6  1
27 25 32 26 14 25 37 23 32 29
```

Page 89

```
4  2  5  1  3  6
3  6  2  5  1  4
6  4  3  2  5  1
1  5  4  6  2  3
2  3  1  4  6  5
5  1  6  3  4  2
```

Page 89

2

Solutions

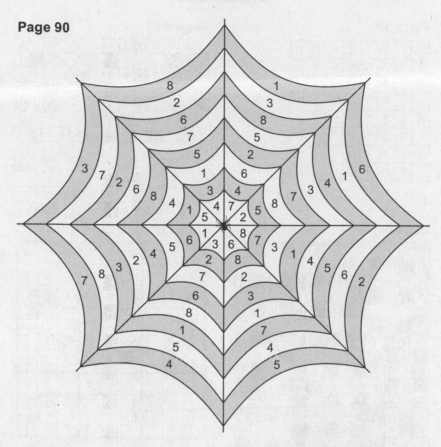

7	2	7	3		1	6	5	3
6	7		6		4		4	8
8		4	0	1	8	1		8
9	7	2		4		6	4	8
			9	6	4	0	0	
7	9	9		0		9	5	7
1		6	1	0	1	5		2
5	2		4		0		3	0
6	6	9	9		8	6	6	0

Page 92

1 Bearing, 2 Regain,
3 Anger, 4, Gear,
5 Agree, 6 Regale,
7 General.

Solutions

Page 94

7	6	2	1	3	4	5	8
2	4	7	6	5	8	3	1
6	5	4	3	8	1	2	7
4	7	8	5	6	2	1	3
5	8	3	4	1	6	7	2
1	2	5	8	7	3	4	6
8	3	1	2	4	7	6	5
3	1	6	7	2	5	8	4

Page 95

C	E	B	A	D
D	B	A	C	E
A	D	E	B	C
E	A	C	D	B
B	C	D	E	A

Pages 96/97

(Crossword solution grid)

Page 98

3	1	2	4	7	5	8	6	9
5	4	6	1	8	9	7	2	3
9	8	7	6	3	2	4	5	1
6	2	8	9	1	3	5	4	7
4	3	5	2	6	7	9	1	8
1	7	9	5	4	8	2	3	6
7	9	4	3	2	6	1	8	5
2	5	3	8	9	1	6	7	4
8	6	1	7	5	4	3	9	2

Page 99

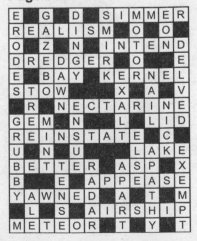

(Crossword solution grid)

Page 100

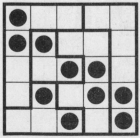

(Grid puzzle solution)

Solutions

Page 101

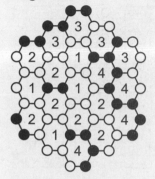

Pages 102/103

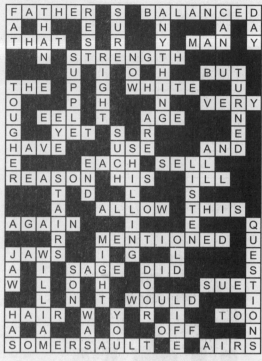

Page 104

P	A	C	T	S
L	I	L	A	C
A	R	O	M	A
N	E	V	E	R
T	R	E	S	S

Page 104

Tulip, Daffodil,
Geranium, Orchid,
Lily, Jasmine,
Iris, Pimpernel,
Hyacinth, Petunia,
Lavender, Primrose,
Marigold.

Page 105

R	E	A	L	L	Y		F	R	A	N	C	E
A			E		A		L		L		H	
I	N	S	O	M	N	I	A		T	O	E	S
N			P		G		M		A		S	
B	R	O	A	D			R	E	F	R	E	S	H
O			R		G		N		A			
W	O	N	D	E	R		C	A	C	T	U	S
		O			E		O		O			U
B	A	R	R	I	E	R		B	O	G	U	S
		L			T		G		K			P
B	O	L	D		I	N	I	T	I	A	T	E
		N			E		N		R			N
B	E	L	O	N	G		L	E	G	E	N	D

Page 106

$36 \div 3 = 12$, $12 - 4 = 8$,
$8^2 = 64$, $64 \times 2 = 128$,
$128 \div 4 = 32$, $32 \div 2 = 16$, $16 - 11 = 5$

Page 106

Tuesday

Solutions

Page 107

P	U	M	P	K	I	N
A	V	O	C	A	D	O
T	A	N	G	E	L	O
F	I	L	B	E	R	T
A	P	R	I	C	O	T
K	U	M	Q	U	A	T
C	O	C	O	N	U	T
S	A	T	S	U	M	A

Page 108

Page 109

1 b, 2 b, 3 d, 4 b, 5 c, 6 a.

Pages 110/111

Pages 110/111

Page 112

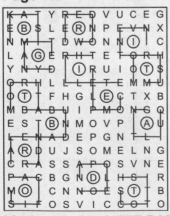

Movie star: BRIGITTE BARDOT

Page 113

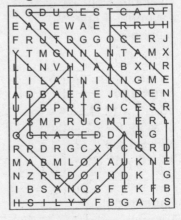

348

Solutions

Page 114

Page 115

Page 116

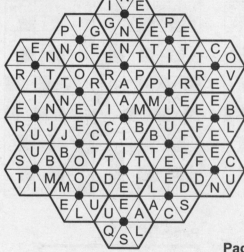

Page 117

	7	6				4	6	
2	8	1	7		9	5	8	7
3	9		2	1	4		5	1
	4	8	1	5	7	6	9	3
		6	5		1	4	3	2
	5	7				8	7	
3	2	5	1		7	9		
6	4	9	5	2	8	7	3	
8	1		2	1	3		1	9
9	3	5	6		9	8	6	7
	8	9				6	2	

Page 118

7	1	4	3	2	5	8	6	9
8	2	5	6	9	4	3	1	7
3	9	6	8	7	1	2	5	4
1	4	9	5	8	7	6	3	2
6	8	2	1	3	9	7	4	5
5	3	7	4	6	2	9	8	1
9	6	1	2	4	3	5	7	8
4	7	8	9	5	6	1	2	3
2	5	3	7	1	8	4	9	6

Page 119

3	6	4	3	0	2	4	1
6	0	2	1	1	0	3	4
3	6	5	6	2	2	3	2
2	0	1	5	0	4	5	1
0	0	6	6	1	0	5	2
6	1	5	4	6	5	3	2
5	4	4	5	3	4	3	1

Solutions

Page 120

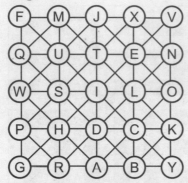

Page 121

Page 122

A	C	C	E	P	T	S		T	H	I	N	G
D		A		E		O	U		D		E	
I	D	L	E	R		B	A	R	G	A	I	N
E		Y		P		B		N		H		E
U	N	P	R	E	T	E	N	T	I	O	U	S
		S		N		D		H				I
C	L	O	U	D	Y		W	E	A	V	E	S
R				I		C		C		I		
I	N	S	E	C	T	I	V	O	R	O	U	S
M		L		T		R		L		T		
S	Q	U	A	L	O	R		N	I	E	C	E
O		N		A		U		E		N		A
N	I	G	E	R		S	T	R	A	T	U	M

Page 123

M	U	S	I	C		P	O	L	Y	G	O	N
E		Q		I	L	L		A		L		I
D	O	U	B	T		E		S	L	A	N	G
A		I		A		A	F	T		Z		H
L	I	B	I	D	O		A	S	P	E	C	T
	R			E	X	I	T		I		O	
V	A	S	T	L	Y		H	A	N	D	L	E
	T		O		G	R	E	W			I	
K	E	T	T	L	E		R	E	J	E	C	T
I		R		I	N	K		S		V		E
C	H	A	N	T		N		O	N	I	O	N
K		I		H		E	L	M		C		O
S	I	N	C	E	R	E		E	N	T	E	R

Page 124

1 Nuisance, 2 Napoleon,
3 Novelist, 4 Negative,
5 November, 6 Nightcap,
7 Narrower, 8 Nagasaki,
9 Nowadays, 10 New Delhi,
11 Nitrogen, 12 Noticing.
The twelve-letter word is:
ENTERPRISING

Page 125

1	4	3	5	2	6
6	2	5	1	4	3
3	5	6	2	1	4
4	3	1	6	5	2
5	6	2	4	3	1
2	1	4	3	6	5

Page 125
2

Solutions

Page 126

Page 127

Pages 128/129

		6	3	7	1	4		
	2	5	9		2	2	5	
4	3		2	6	5		4	8
2	5	6		3		1	1	2
7		3	2	7	5	0		7
2	4	0		9		5	4	0
2	5		2	4	6		8	0
	1	9	6		4	9	2	
		8	2	7	5	0		

Page 128

1 Martian, 2 Tirana,
3 Train, 4 Iran,
5 Brain, 6 Riband,
7 Brigand.

Solutions

Page 130

Blind - Date - line
Gold - rUsh - hour
Alarm - beLl - tower
Citric - aCid - test
Sailing - shIp - shape
Smoke - boMb - shell
For - Ever - green
Movie - staR - board
Answer: DULCIMER

Page 130

Author: MICHAEL CRICHTON

Page 131

FAST – cast – cost – coot –
soot – slot – SLOW
(Other solutions are possible)

Page 131

The nine-letter word is:
LIFESTYLE

Pages 132/133

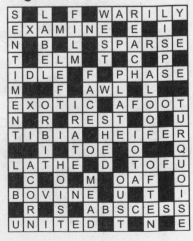

(crossword grid)

```
C R E A M   P   T   S   P
E   N   A L A B A S T E R
R A D A R   R   C   R   E
E   U   T   C U T L A S S
M I S F I R E   I   N   E
O   E   N   L   C E D A R
N A R C I S S U S   E   V
Y     A   E   N   A D Z E
    P   R A M A D A N   I
P I S A   B   E   I O T A
    R   P I L G R I M   H
N A S A   A   M   A M E N
  T   C O N V I C T   R
C E D E   C   N   O     E
A   E   C E L E B R I T Y
T O A D Y   E   A   T   E
A   D   N   A R R E A R S
C O L L I E R   R   L   I
O   I   C   N   I C I N G
M A N G A N E S E   C   H
B   E   L   D   R E S I T
```

Page 134

4	1	5	6	3	9	8	7	2
3	9	6	8	7	2	4	1	5
2	7	8	4	1	5	9	6	3
9	6	3	5	2	1	7	8	4
1	4	7	3	8	6	5	2	9
5	8	2	9	4	7	1	3	6
6	3	4	7	9	8	2	5	1
7	2	9	1	5	3	6	4	8
8	5	1	2	6	4	3	9	7

Page 135

```
S   L   F   W A R I L Y
E X A M I N E   E   I
N   B   L   S P A R S E
T   E L M   T   C   P
I D L E   F   P H A S E
M   F   A W L   L
E X O T I C   A F O O T
N   R   R E S T   O   U
T I B I A   H E I F E R
  I   T O E   O     Q
L A T H E   D   T O F U
  C   O   M   O A F   O
B O V I N E   U   T   I
  R   S   A B S C E S S
U N I T E D   T   N   E
```

Page 136

COMMUTED
CREDITOR
DECRYING
ENRICHED
ENSHRINE
FINISHES
FISSURES
FLUORIDE

MIMICKED
PRESTIGE
PROFILER
THRESHER
UNCORKED
UNFROZEN
VERDICTS
WEIGHING

Solutions

Page 137
1 Walk (c), 2 Alps (c),
3 Spam (a), 4 Mist (c),
5 Slim (a), 6 Lair (a),
7 Star (c), 8 Aunt (c),
9 Tuba (a), 10 Lane (a),
11 Inch (c), 12 Nail (c),
13 Nice (a), 14 Bear (a),
15 Barn (c), 16 Colt (a),
17 Salt (a), 18 Calm (a),
19 Atom (c), 20 Tank (c),
21 Lake (a), 22 Pest (c),
23 Last (c), 24 Coal (a),
25 Sick (c).

Page 140

A	L	P	H	A
S	O	L	O	S
T	I	E	R	S
E	R	A	S	E
R	E	S	E	T

Page 140
Helsinki, Lisbon,
Monaco, Warsaw,
Tirana, Budapest,
Madrid, Prague,
Paris, London,
Vilnius, Skopje,
Vienna, Brussels.

Page 142
1 Mascot,
2 Adhere,
3 Appear,
4 Cornet,
5 Zagreb,
6 Anyhow.
Fruit: CHERRY

Pages 138/139

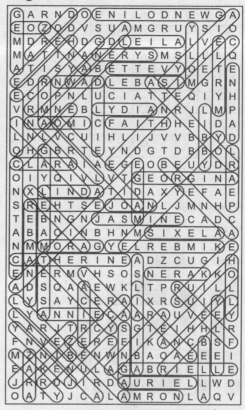

Page 141

353

Solutions

Page 143

E	S	T	U	A	R	Y
P	L	A	T	E	A	U
V	O	L	C	A	N	O
F	I	S	S	U	R	E
C	A	L	D	R	O	N
I	S	T	H	M	U	S
P	R	A	I	R	I	E
G	L	A	C	I	E	R

Page 144

Page 145

Aboard, Anchor, Bridge, Dinghy, Funnel, Galley, Tackle, Vessel.

Pages 146/147

Pages 146/147

Page 148

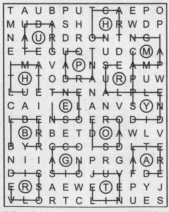

Movie star: HUMPHREY BOGART

Page 149

354

Solutions

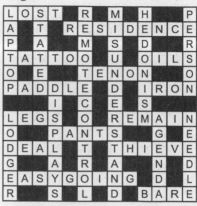

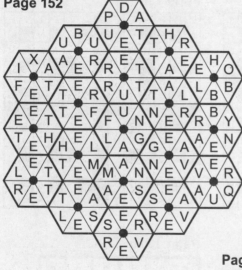

3	9	8		1	9		1	2
1	8	3	5	2	6	4	7	9
	7	9	8	6		3	5	
3	6		9	4	8		9	4
2	4	1		3	7	2	4	1
	9	5		9	8			
3	2	4	1	5		1	3	2
1	3		2	7	1		6	4
	1	2		8	9	5	7	
3	5	4	7	9	6	1	8	2
9	7		1	6		3	9	7

5	3	4	6	7	2	8	9	1
8	2	9	5	3	1	6	7	4
6	1	7	9	8	4	2	5	3
4	6	5	8	2	9	1	3	7
1	8	2	7	4	3	9	6	5
9	7	3	1	5	6	4	2	8
2	4	1	3	6	7	5	8	9
7	9	8	2	1	5	3	4	6
3	5	6	4	9	8	7	1	2

1	2	4	0	0	4	3	6
3	6	6	4	3	0	5	0
1	1	5	4	4	0	2	0
2	3	5	5	3	2	1	1
6	3	2	2	1	5	4	4
6	4	5	3	2	6	2	0
1	1	6	5	6	3	5	0

Solutions

Page 156

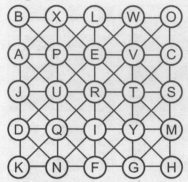

Page 157

8	4	4		3	6	2	4		4	8	8	6
9		2	2	7	0		8	6	9	5		1
4	5	4	4		4	3	3			5	6	3
8	0	5	7	9	5		7	1	0	9	9	0
	5		6		8	1	8	1		7		
4	7	9	9	2		1		5		5	9	4
2		5		5	3	3	9	7		0		2
9	2	2		3		1		6	3	1	7	0
	4		5	9	3	1		2		6		
7	5	1	4	8	2		2	6	7	9	8	2
1	5	3			3	8	5		3	7	7	6
0		6	8	6	4		3	1	2	6		1
1	9	0	6		1	5	3	7		3	2	8

Page 158

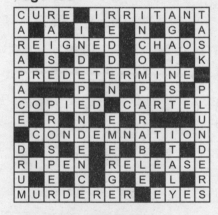

Page 159

Page 160

1 Crossbow, 2 Childish,
3 Cockatoo, 4 Carousel,
5 Creature, 6 Cenotaph,
7 Canticle, 8 Caligula,
9 Circular, 10 Crescent,
11 Convince, 12 Cupboard.
The twelve-letter word is:
WHOLEHEARTED

Page 161

5	2	1	3	4	6
6	3	5	4	2	1
3	4	6	2	1	5
4	1	2	5	6	3
1	5	4	6	3	2
2	6	3	1	5	4

Page 161

3

Solutions

Page 162

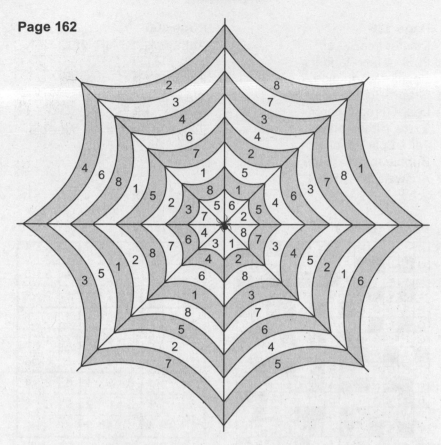

Page 163

Pages 164/165

	4	1	4	6	9		
	2	0	4		7	6	6
5	1		1	1	2		6	2
8	4	5		1		9	3	0
4		5	1	3	6	8		4
7	3	3		9		1	4	4
6	5		1	6	9		7	9
	1	2	1		9	4	1	
		2	7	4	4	8		

Page 164
1 Thermal, 2 *Hamlet*,
3 Metal, 4 Team,
5 Mated, 6 Tandem,
7 Untamed.

Solutions

Page 166
Plaster - caSt - off
Foot - sTep - ladder
Pencil - leAd - pipe
Grand - touR - operator
Leap - Frog - march
Extra - tIme - piece
Tail - Spin - drier
Bubble -batH - towel
Answer: STARFISH

Page 166
Author: ALISTAIR MACLEAN

Page 167
WARM – wars – bars – bats –
bets – sets – SEAS
(Other solutions are possible)

Pages 168/169

B	I	A	S	E	D		P		A		U	
U		U				A	Q	U	A	L	U	N	G
L	A	R	I	A	T		P		G		K	
L		E		M	A	C	A	D	A	M	I	A
D	R	O	O	P		A		A			N	
O		L		L	O	N	G	I	T	U	D	E
G	E	E	S	E		T		Q		S		S
	A		A		S	E	C	U	R	E	S	T
T	R	O	U	T		R		I		F		E
H		N		B		R	E	U	S	E		E
E		M	A	R	S	U	P	I	A	L		M
A	W	A	S	H		R		G				E
T		N		O		Y		B	L	E	E	D
R	I	G	I	D	I	T	Y		E		R	
I		E		E		A		A	S	I	A	N	
C	H	R	Y	S	A	L	I	S		B		U
	A		I		E		T	H	E	I	R	
F	R	I	C	A	S	S	É	E		R		S
	L		A		U		P	R	A	I	S	E
C	O	N	S	O	M	M	É			A		R
	W		E		O		E	V	E	N	L	Y

Page 170

4	3	1	9	5	8	7	6	2
9	8	2	1	7	6	4	5	3
5	6	7	4	2	3	1	9	8
2	4	3	6	8	1	9	7	5
7	5	8	2	4	9	3	1	6
1	9	6	5	3	7	2	8	4
3	7	5	8	9	4	6	2	1
8	1	9	3	6	2	5	4	7
6	2	4	7	1	5	8	3	9

Page 172

ASSEMBLY	KEEPSAKE
BOTANIST	LABURNUM
CAJOLERY	MOISTURE
DECRYING	QUAGMIRE
EXECUTED	SELECTOR
EXEMPTED	SURPRISE
FUGITIVE	TOBOGGAN
HORSEFLY	YOUNGEST

Page 171

	V		P		T	U	S	S	O	C	K
P	A	R	O	D	Y		U		I		I
	L		O		P	I	C	K	L	E	D
D	E	C	R	E	E		C		C		N
A		O		S	K	I		A	G	E	
T	I	N	K	L	E		N	A	N	N	Y
E		G		T	I	C			A		
D	W	A	R	F		T	O	O	T	H	
	A		I	M	P		R			A	
O	G	R	E	S		I	M	P	A	I	R
T	E	A		H	E	N		T		D	
H		T		I		H	E	R	E	B	Y
E	X	T	R	E	M	E		U		U	
R		L		S		A	B	S	O	R	B
S	C	E	N	T	E	D		H		Y	

Solutions

Page 173

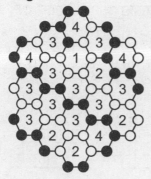

Pages 174/175

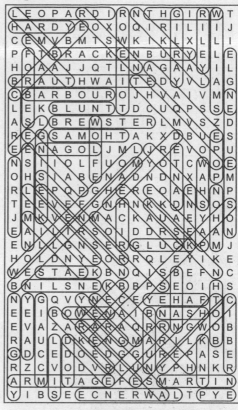

Page 176

P	A	S	T	A
A	G	A	R	S
R	O	L	E	S
K	R	O	N	A
S	A	N	D	Y

Page 176

Grasshopper, Weevil, Hoverfly, Cockchafer, Bedbug, Millipede, Ichneumon, Earwig, Mosquito, Springtail, Silverfish, Mealworm, Locust, Thrip, Flea.

Page 177

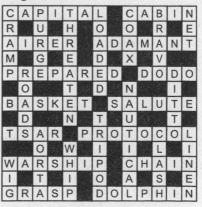

Page 178

5	2	4	1	6	3
3	1	2	6	4	5
6	5	3	2	1	4
1	6	5	4	3	2
4	3	6	5	2	1
2	4	1	3	5	6

Solutions

Page 179

G	L	I	D	I	N	G
N	E	T	B	A	L	L
F	I	S	H	I	N	G
A	R	C	H	E	R	Y
S	N	O	O	K	E	R
F	E	N	C	I	N	G
C	R	O	Q	U	E	T
S	A	I	L	I	N	G

Page 180

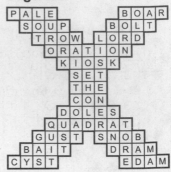

Page 181

1 b, 2 c, 3 c, 4 b, 5 d, 6 d.

Pages 182/183

Page 182/183

Page 184

Movie star: HALLE BERRY

Page 185

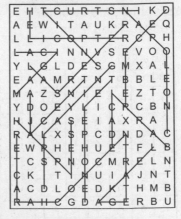

Solutions

Page 186

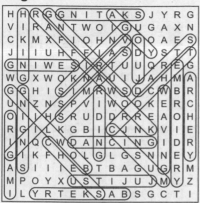

Page 187

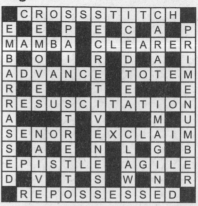

Page 188

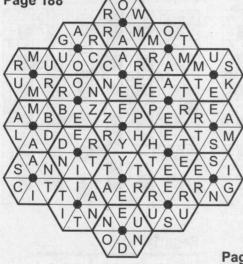

Page 189

1	4	2		4	1		8	2
3	8	4	2	9	6	5	7	1
7	9	8	6		2	1	5	
2	7			3	6			9	8
		6	4	9			6	9
5	3	2	1		3	1	2	4
9	7			8	1	2		
8	6			9	4		7	1
	8	9	6		5	8	9	7
3	9	7	1	4	2	6	8	5
1	5		3	7		1	3	2

Page 190

7	6	9	2	3	4	1	5	8
3	1	5	8	6	7	4	2	9
4	2	8	1	9	5	7	3	6
9	4	7	5	8	3	6	1	2
1	5	3	6	4	2	9	8	7
2	8	6	7	1	9	3	4	5
8	7	1	4	2	6	5	9	3
6	9	2	3	5	1	8	7	4
5	3	4	9	7	8	2	6	1

Page 191

6	5	3	1	6	2	4	5
4	1	0	0	1	3	1	2
3	6	6	6	1	3	2	0
4	1	4	6	1	4	5	5
4	2	4	5	6	2	5	5
5	3	3	2	2	6	3	3
0	2	0	1	4	0	0	0

361

Solutions

Page 192

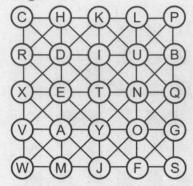

Page 193

Page 194

Page 195

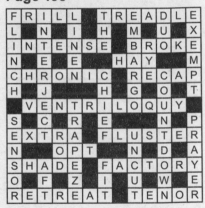

Page 196

3	2	5	7	4	8	1	6	0	9
6	1	4	9	5	3	0	2	8	7
5	0	3	6	7	8	1	4	9	2
8	1	7	9	2	6	3	0	5	4
5	0	8	4	3	7	1	9	6	2
3	2	9	7	6	5	0	8	4	1
30	6	36	42	27	37	6	29	32	25

Page 197

3	6	4	1	5	2
5	1	2	6	3	4
2	4	3	5	1	6
4	5	1	2	6	3
1	2	6	3	4	5
6	3	5	4	2	1

Page 197

2

Solutions

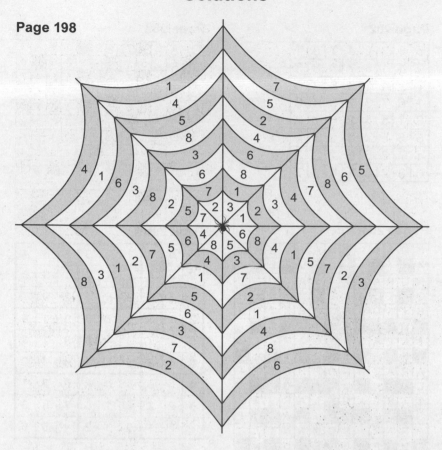

8	5	8		8		8	3	8
9		1	2	0	7	3		5
9	4		8	0	9		3	0
	1	8		0		5	4	
7	6	5	0		1	6	2	0
	5	3		9		2	1	
1	0		1	0	8		2	7
4		1	5	4	4	4		1
3	2	4		8		9	0	5

1 Respite, 2 Priest,
3 Tripe, 4 Pert, 5 Taper,
6 Entrap, 7 Panther.

363

Solutions

Page 202

5	8	3	2	4	7	6	1
2	4	1	6	7	3	8	5
7	2	4	1	5	8	3	6
1	6	7	3	2	5	4	8
8	1	5	4	3	6	7	2
3	5	6	7	8	2	1	4
4	7	8	5	6	1	2	3
6	3	2	8	1	4	5	7

Page 203

```
D A B C E
E B C D A
C E A B D
A C D E B
B D E A C
```

Pages 204/205

```
C H A M P . M A I L B A G
A . I . I . O . M . L . U
R U R A L . V I A D U C T
O . E . A P E . G . N . H
B I S Q U E . D E B T O R
. D . . R . I . E . . R I
A L P A C A . G I R D L E
. E . R . N . U . I . E .
A R A C H N O P H O B I A
E . . H . U . . G . . . B
S T R E A M . L A R V A E
O . . T . . . I . A . . T
P R A Y I N G M A N T I S
. U . P . E . E . D . N .
M E T E O R . R H E S U S
A . S . V . . I . . . R .
G L A S S Y . C A N C E R
N . R . H . E K E . R . U
E P I G R A M . G R A I N
T . S . U . I . I . N . I
O C T O B E R . S K E I N
```

Page 206

3	5	7	1	2	9	8	6	4
9	2	4	6	8	7	1	3	5
1	6	8	3	5	4	2	9	7
2	1	6	8	7	3	5	4	9
5	7	9	2	4	6	3	1	8
8	4	3	5	9	1	6	7	2
4	3	5	7	6	8	9	2	1
6	9	2	4	1	5	7	8	3
7	8	1	9	3	2	4	5	6

Page 207

Page 208

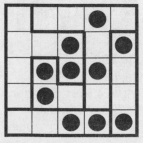

Solutions

Page 209

1 Tent (c), 2 Name (c),
3 Farm (a), 4 Smug (a),
5 Gang (c/a), 6 Numb (a),
7 Beam (a), 8 Riga (c),
9 Ruin (a), 10 Rung (a),
11 Milk (c), 12 Diet (c),
13 Gift (c), 14 Coin (c),
15 Duck (a), 16 Pool (c),
17 Prod (a), 18 Fool (a),
19 Floe (c), 20 Kelp (a),
21 Zoom (c/a), 22 Torn (c),
23 Noon (c/a), 24 Sofa (c),
25 Talc (c).

Page 212

P	A	P	A	W
S	L	A	V	E
A	G	R	E	E
L	A	I	R	D
M	E	S	S	Y

Page 212

Platinum, Rhodium,
Electrum, Bronze,
Manganese, Copper,
Titanium, Steel,
Wolfram, Zirconium,
Mercury, Brass, Zinc,
Pewter, Nickel, Iron,
Lead, Tungsten.

Page 214

1 Flower,
2 Abacus,
3 Dragon,
4 Runway,
5 Rarest,
6 Carrot.
Composer: WAGNER

Pages 210/211

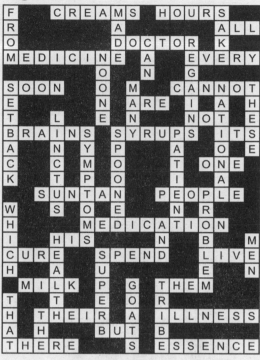

Page 213

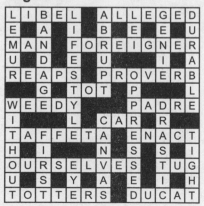

365

Solutions

Page 215

T	R	I	U	M	P	H
L	A	G	O	N	D	A
B	U	G	A	T	T	I
P	O	R	S	C	H	E
D	A	I	M	L	E	R
P	E	U	G	E	O	T
B	E	N	T	L	E	Y
C	I	T	R	O	E	N

Page 216

Page 217

Bright, Chilly, Cloudy, Frosty, Squall, Stormy, Torrid, Warmer.

Pages 218/219

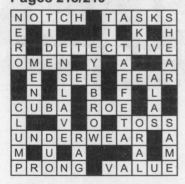

Pages 218/219

Page 220

Movie star: NICOLAS CAGE

Page 221

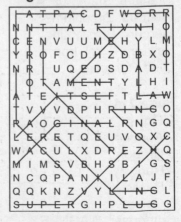

Solutions

Page 222

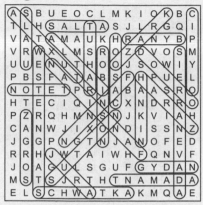

Page 223

Page 224

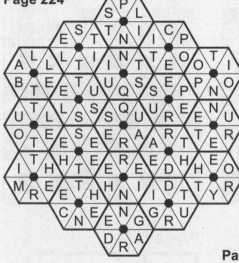

Page 225

5	9		4	9		9	8	7
2	8		1	7		8	2	1
1	5	9	3	8	7	6	4	2
		3	2	4	1	5		
9	7	8	6		9	7	5	8
2	1						3	9
8	5	9	3		2	3	1	6
		6	9	4	7	8		
5	1	7	4	2	8	9	6	3
1	2	3		3	9		5	1
9	4	8		1	3		9	7

Page 226

1	7	2	9	4	6	5	3	8
4	6	3	8	1	5	7	9	2
5	8	9	3	2	7	1	4	6
3	9	7	2	5	1	6	8	4
8	1	6	4	7	3	2	5	9
2	4	5	6	9	8	3	1	7
9	3	4	5	6	2	8	7	1
6	5	1	7	8	9	4	2	3
7	2	8	1	3	4	9	6	5

Page 227

3	3	3	6	6	0	3	0
1	4	2	3	1	1	2	1
5	1	4	6	2	4	5	6
4	4	3	5	1	6	0	2
0	4	5	0	6	5	2	1
3	2	0	2	2	4	4	6
5	6	3	5	5	0	0	1

Solutions

Page 228

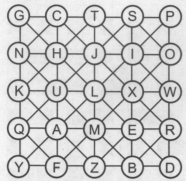

Page 229

1	0	9	9		3	9	7	0	9	5	2	8
0			6	4	7		8		9	1		9
5	4	3	5		7	0	3		2	5	5	3
6	6	5	3	4	8		6		2		5	4
	7		1		2	3	6	9	0		7	
1	6	8	1	0		2	9	2	3	3	7	8
3		2			1		5			2		0
7	9	5	3	6	4	8		5	2	9	3	0
	8		2	6	4	8	4		3		0	
7	1		8		0		9	1	1	4	7	6
6	0	8	2		1	3	6		5	4	1	0
0		1	5		4		4	0	0			8
4	5	6	9	9	2	2	2		7	7	7	8

Page 230

	M	A	T	H	E	M	A	T	I	C	S	
O		L		A		I		H		H		S
B	R	O	T	H	E	R		I	R	A	T	E
S		F		A		R		R		R		E
T	U	T	U		C	O	N	T	R	I	T	E
R			B		R		E		O			Y
U	N	T	R	U	E		B	E	E	T	L	E
C		R		L		E		N				T
T	H	A	I	L	A	N	D		E	C	H	O
I		I		F		D		N		E		E
O	U	T	E	R		U	S	U	A	L	L	Y
N		O		O		R		T		L		E
	P	R	O	G	R	E	S	S	I	O	N	

Page 231

P	H	A	R	A	O	H		B	A	D	G	E
A		D		W		I		U		E		A
C	H	I	N	A		J	U	N	I	P	E	R
K		E		I		A		C		O		L
A	Q	U	A	T	I	C		H	O	T	L	Y
G			E		K		V		I			
E	M	B	O	D	Y		T	R	A	V	E	L
	I		D		Z		I					E
E	X	P	E	L		E	A	S	T	E	R	N
L		R		A		P		K		L		G
F	O	O	L	I	S	H		I	N	E	P	T
I		N		T		Y		N		C		H
N	E	E	D	Y		R	I	G	H	T	L	Y

Page 232

1 Labrador, 2 Liberate,
3 Lessened, 4 Lemonade,
5 Lollipop, 6 Landfill,
7 Leonardo, 8 Lethargy,
9 Lukewarm, 10 Lacerate,
11 Lengthen, 12 Layabout.
The twelve-letter word is:
REDEPLOYMENT

Page 233

Page 233

1

Solutions

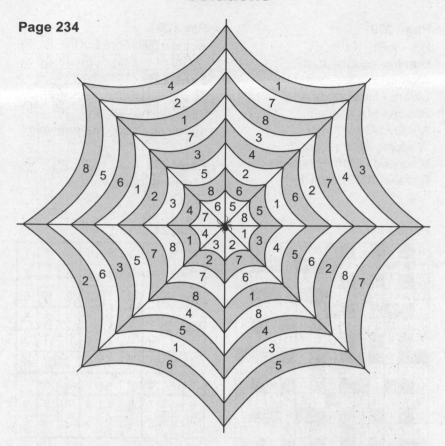

Pages 236/237

8	6	6		2		1	2	9
9		4	2	0	3	2		6
1	7		2	1	6		3	0
	3	9		6		7	5	
9	7	8	6		9	5	2	6
	4	0		9		7	6	
4	8		2	6	4		3	2
1		9	6	8	4	9		3
2	5	6		0		8	6	4

Page 236

1 Enticed, 2 Deceit,
3 Edict, 4 Tied, 5 Tepid,
6 Depict, 7 Predict.

369

Solutions

Page 238

Hill - foRt - Knox
Burning - bUsh - baby
Atomic - maSs - market
Sword - fisH - pond
Bench - Mark - time
Ankle - bOne - meal
Wedding - Ring - leader
Magnetic - tapE - measure
Answer: RUSHMORE

Page 238

Author: CHARLES KINGSLEY

Page 239

TEAR – team – tram – trap –
trip – drip – DROP
(Other solutions are possible)

Page 239

The nine-letter word is:
ENIGMATIC

Pages 240/241

```
S M M   P O R C I N E
P R O V I S O       H     M
E   A   L     S P E E D U P
C A T S E Y E     S     R
I     S     L A S S I E
A M M E T E R     R   Y     S
L   A     O O C T O P U S
    S     N O     I     H
D E S S E R T     S L O T H
U   I     S     T     N     O
M A D R A S   W E A S E L
B   I     P     A     R     E
O V O L O     R I C K E T S
    R     S     E     O     D
P H A E T O N     R     E     C
A   M     L   A M M O N I A
R E A D E R       O     R
E   U     A I R L I F T
S P E N S E R     A     C     O
I   C     M O N S O O N
S P H E R E S     T     N     S
```

Page 242

4	6	2	3	9	8	5	7	1
7	3	8	5	1	6	9	4	2
9	5	1	4	7	2	3	6	8
3	9	4	8	6	1	7	2	5
1	7	5	9	2	4	6	8	3
8	2	6	7	3	5	1	9	4
5	4	3	6	8	9	2	1	7
6	1	7	2	4	3	8	5	9
2	8	9	1	5	7	4	3	6

Page 243

```
P O L Y P   D E F A C E
A   I   R O E     G   X
G L A D E   S   D E E P
O   B   S A I L E D   A
D O L L S   R   L     N
A L E   U N O P E N E D
    D   R   U   T     E
D   O V E R S T E P   D
E   A   A   A   P
R A I N D R O P   J A R
E   I   E   E X I L E
L   S T U F F S   G   N
I N K Y   I   T I G H T
C   I   E A R   L   E
T I N N E D   Y I E L D
```

Page 244

ANIMATOR · LIBERATE
ANTIBODY · MEGABYTE
BEHAVING · MEMBRANE
BOUNDARY · OBSIDIAN
BREAKING · OBTAINED
DREAMING · SATANISM
ENVIABLE · TABLOIDS
GRANULAR · UNBEATEN

Solutions

Page 245

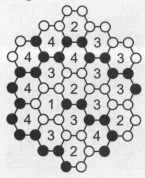

Page 248

C	A	P	R	I
O	R	L	O	N
B	E	A	U	S
R	A	N	G	E
A	S	S	E	T

Page 248

Alsatian, Elkhound, Whippet, Borzoi, Poodle, Staghound, Lurcher, Retriever, Chihuahua, Pekinese, Sheepdog, Samoyed, Greyhound, Doberman, Labrador.

Page 250

$84 \div 7 = 12$, $12^2 = 144$, $144 \div 9 = 16$, square root of $16 = 4$, $4 \times 13 = 52$, $52 \div 2 = 26$, $26 + 45 = 71$

Page 250

Friday

Pages 246/247

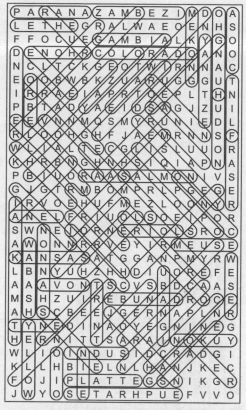

Page 249

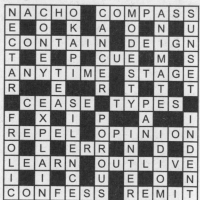

Solutions

Page 251

S	T	E	R	N	U	M
J	A	W	B	O	N	E
S	C	A	P	U	L	A
H	I	P	B	O	N	E
K	N	E	E	C	A	P
S	T	I	R	R	U	P
H	U	M	E	R	U	S
P	A	T	E	L	L	A

Page 252

Page 253

1 b, 2 c, 3 d, 4 a, 5 b, 6 a.

Pages 254/255

Pages 254/255

Page 256

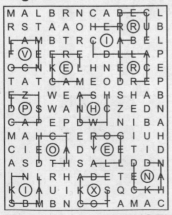

Movie star: RIVER PHOENIX

Page 257

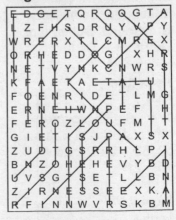

Solutions

Page 258

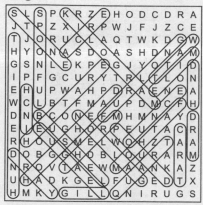

Page 259

Page 260

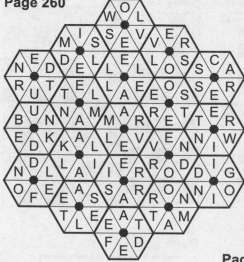

Page 261

4	1	5	2		8	4	9	5
8	3	9	7		5	2	6	4
	6	8	9	5		1	3	2
9	5	7		3	8		8	1
8	2		1	2	4	5	7	3
	6	5	8	7	9			
3	6	1	2	4	5		7	1
2	8		3	1		7	9	3
6	7	9		6	1	3	4	
4	9	8	7		6	9	8	7
1	2	7	3		2	8	6	9

Page 262

2	4	3	6	5	9	1	7	8
6	8	7	1	3	2	5	4	9
9	5	1	8	4	7	3	6	2
1	7	5	4	2	3	9	8	6
8	2	6	5	9	1	4	3	7
4	3	9	7	8	6	2	5	1
3	9	8	2	7	4	6	1	5
5	6	2	3	1	8	7	9	4
7	1	4	9	6	5	8	2	3

Page 263

6	4	4	1	0	2	1	0
6	3	6	1	1	1	3	0
1	5	6	3	2	0	3	3
3	5	4	6	2	4	5	2
5	0	0	4	6	2	6	3
0	1	4	6	0	5	5	4
3	2	2	4	5	1	2	5

Solutions

Page 264

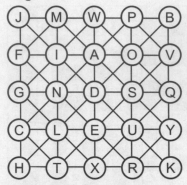

Page 265

Page 266

Page 267

Page 268

1 Asphyxia, 2 Arteries,
3 Asbestos, 4 Anaconda,
5 Aquarius, 6 Atlantis, 7 Agnus
Dei, 8 Aviation, 9 Ambrosia,
10 Arsonist, 11 Applause,
12 Arachnid.
The twelve-letter word is:
ASSASSINATED

Page 269

5	3	4	1	2	6
6	4	1	2	3	5
2	6	3	5	1	4
4	5	2	3	6	1
3	1	6	4	5	2
1	2	5	6	4	3

Page 269

1

Solutions

Page 270

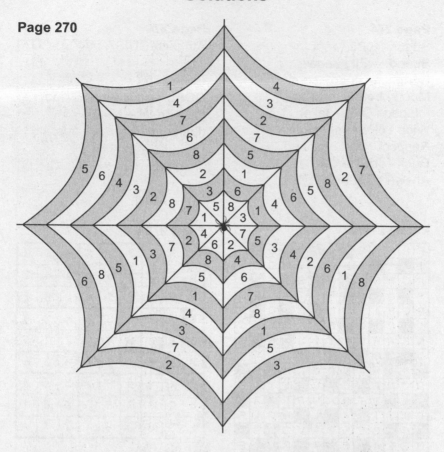

Page 271

Pages 272/273

1	8	2	7		2	6	4	3
5	0		8		3		8	3
6		5	6	3	5	1		9
8	8	0		8		8	8	1
		1	3	5	6	4		
7	8	4		1		6	0	9
0		3	7	4	4	8		4
4	9		9		4		8	4
8	9	4	8		7	9	1	7

Page 272

1 Crashed, 2 Sacred,
3 Cedar, 4 Acre,
5 Trace, 6 Nectar,
7 Centaur.

375

Solutions

Page 274

Sugar - cuBe - root
Speed - wEll - known
Common - coLd - comfort
Moon - beaM - engine
Flipped - Over - taken
Wide - oPen - sesame
Respect - Able - bodied
Duck - dowN - cast
Answer: BELMOPAN

Page 274

Author: LOUISA MAY ALCOTT

Page 275

COAL – coat – moat – most –
mist – mint – MINE
(Other solutions are possible)

Pages 276/277

```
F R A N C   C     O   D   E
I   I   A N O N Y M O U S
L O R D S   M   S   G   P
I   D H   P I T C H E R
P O R T I C O   E   O   E
I   O   E S   R O U T S
N E P H R I T I S   S   S
O     O   G   N   P E S O
  P   M A N D O L A   T
D O M E   O   C   S T A G
  L   S T R A U S S   B
F I J I   A   L   W O L F
  C   C E N T A V O   E
D E S K   C   T   R   E
R   H   D E F E N D A N T
E B O N Y   O   E   R   C
S   U   N   R A T R A C E
S A L V A G E   W   B   T
A   D   S   L   O L I V E
G R E A T B E A R   C   R
E   R   Y   G   K O A L A
```

Page 278

1	5	4	2	7	8	6	9	3
6	8	7	3	9	5	1	4	2
2	9	3	6	1	4	5	8	7
8	7	1	5	3	6	4	2	9
3	6	2	8	4	9	7	1	5
9	4	5	1	2	7	8	3	6
7	1	9	4	6	2	3	5	8
4	2	8	7	5	3	9	6	1
5	3	6	9	8	1	2	7	4

Page 279

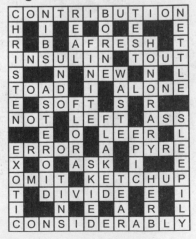

```
C O N T R I B U T I O N
H   I   E   O   E   E
R   B   A F R E S H   T
I N S U L I N   T O U T
S     N   N E W   N   L
T O A D   I   A L O N E
E   S O F T   S   R
N O T   L E F T   A S S
    E   O   L E E R   L
E R R O R   A   P Y R E
X   O   A S K   I   E
O M I T   K E T C H U P
T   D I V I D E   E   I
I     N   E   A R   L
C O N S I D E R A B L Y
```

Page 280

DESTROYS	QUADRANT
DROWSILY	RECENTLY
ELEVENTH	RETRIEVE
EMPLOYEE	REVEREND
EXPOUNDS	SEQUENCE
LAUDANUM	UNDERCUT
NEGLIGEE	UNKINDLY
PARANOID	WRECKERS

Solutions

Page 281

1 Hard (c), 2 Acre (a),
3 Rind (c), 4 Fang (a),
5 Form (c), 6 Fork (a),
7 Rock (c), 8 Dark (c),
9 Gate (a), 10 Poem (c),
11 Defy (a), 12 Tree (a),
13 Tram (c), 14 Tale (a),
15 Once (c), 16 Adam (c/a),
17 Seal (a), 18 Mars (c),
19 Lamb (a), 20 Crab (c),
21 Lime (c), 22 Lean (a),
23 Near (a), 24 Damp (c),
25 Tape (a).

Pages 282/283

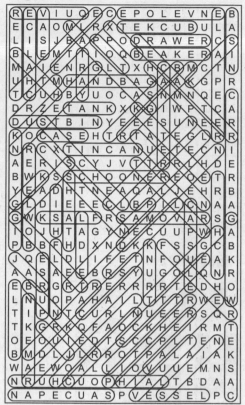

Page 284

C	R	E	S	S
L	A	M	I	A
A	D	O	R	N
M	A	T	E	D
P	R	E	S	S

Page 284

Shovel, Pitchfork,
Fretsaw, Crowbar,
Tweezers, Screwdriver,
Hatchet, Drill, Billhook,
Sledgehammer,
Scalpel, Chisel,
Hacksaw, Spanner,
Cultivator.

Page 285

Page 286

1 Eiffel,
2 Breath,
3 Bronze,
4 Monaco,
5 Asleep,
6 Bullet.
Herb: FENNEL

Solutions

Page 287

S	W	E	A	T	E	R
M	U	F	F	L	E	R
Y	A	S	H	M	A	K
D	O	U	B	L	E	T
C	A	T	S	U	I	T
B	L	O	U	S	O	N
M	I	T	T	E	N	S
S	I	N	G	L	E	T

Page 288

Page 289

Bronze, Chrome, Copper, Nickel, Pewter, Silver, Solder, Tombac.

Pages 290/291

Pages 290/291

Page 292

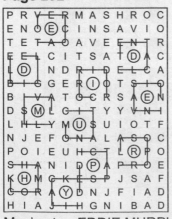

Movie star: EDDIE MURPHY

Page 293

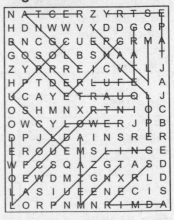

Solutions

Page 294

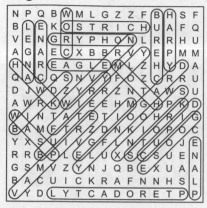

Page 295

P	O	L	A	N	D		I		H		M	
R		E			A	D	R	I	A	T	I	C
I	C	E	D		Z		A		L		N	
C		S	O	L	E	M	N		F	E	E	L
E			M		D		I		H		R	
T	O	W	E	L		F	A	R	E	A	S	T
A			S		C		N		A		R	
G	E	N	T	I	A	N		A	R	G	U	E
	D		I		V		E		T		S	
Z	I	N	C		E	N	A	M	E	L		P
	T		A		M		G		D	I	V	A
H	E	A	T	W	A	V	E			M		S
	D		E		N		R	U	M	P	U	S

Page 296

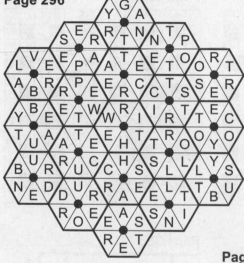

Page 297

9	7	1		3	1			1	9
8	4	2	7	9	5			2	7
5	3		4	8			9	4	8
	1	8	2			1	2	3	5
7	5	9	3	6	4	8			
9	2			9	7	8		6	9
		2	6	9	5	8	7	4	
7	6	9	8		2	1	5		
3	2	1		2	3			4	1
9	1		8	4	6	7	9	3	
8	3		6	1		9	8	6	

Page 298

6	5	1	8	7	4	3	9	2
8	4	3	2	9	5	6	7	1
9	7	2	3	6	1	4	5	8
3	1	7	9	2	8	5	4	6
2	9	4	5	1	6	8	3	7
5	8	6	4	3	7	2	1	9
4	6	8	1	5	9	7	2	3
1	2	5	7	8	3	9	6	4
7	3	9	6	4	2	1	8	5

Page 299

4	3	1	4	4	3	1	1
0	3	1	5	5	0	6	4
5	3	1	4	6	4	3	6
2	4	0	2	6	5	4	2
2	6	0	0	5	6	5	2
3	3	0	3	2	5	5	6
2	1	2	1	6	1	0	0

Solutions

Page 300

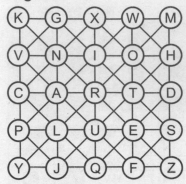

```
K   G   X   W   M
V   N   I   O   H
C   A   R   T   D
P   L   U   E   S
Y   J   Q   F   Z
```

Page 301

```
5 2 8 7 ■ 2 3 4 7 6 8 7 9
4 ■ ■ 3 6 7 ■ 4 ■ 4 0 ■ 0
8 3 5 6 ■ 1 1 1 ■ 3 8 5 2
9 0 2 3 7 6 ■ 9 ■ 3 ■ 8 0
■ 6 ■ 4 ■ 6 6 0 7 1 ■ 2 ■
2 9 9 0 2 ■ 3 0 8 4 2 9 1
6 ■ 5 ■ 1 ■ 9 ■ ■ 4 ■ 5
4 5 7 6 8 3 9 ■ 1 3 6 8 0
■ 5 ■ 2 8 1 4 7 ■ 1 ■ 5 ■
1 2 ■ 1 ■ 5 ■ 6 3 0 4 7 9
9 6 4 5 ■ 7 2 9 ■ 2 3 1 5
9 ■ 6 9 ■ 7 ■ 7 6 5 ■ ■ 8
8 4 3 4 8 8 3 9 ■ 5 7 1 2
```

Page 302

```
A B Y S M A L ■ C A N O E
■ A ■ H ■ L ■ M ■ P ■ B ■
A R M Y ■ S L O V A K I A
■ R ■ N ■ O ■ O ■ R ■ ■ ■
G I V E N ■ P R O T E S T
■ C ■ S ■ ■ E ■ ■ ■ A ■ ■
H A S S L E ■ D O C I L E
■ D ■ ■ A ■ ■ ■ O ■ T ■ ■
B E R S E R K ■ S H A W L
■ ■ P ■ W ■ H ■ A ■ A ■ ■
P A R A S I T E ■ B I T E
■ S ■ R ■ G ■ R ■ I ■ E ■
S H E E T ■ L E C T U R E
```

Page 303

```
C O M P A S S ■ T H I C K
A ■ A ■ N ■ T ■ E ■ C ■ E
T U N I C ■ A N X I E T Y
H ■ G ■ H ■ T ■ T ■ P ■ ■
E C O N O M I C ■ V I E W
D ■ ■ R ■ C ■ S ■ C ■ ■ O
R O O T E D ■ N I C K E L
A ■ R ■ D ■ B ■ L ■ ■ ■ F
L E G S ■ R E S E A R C H
■ ■ A ■ C ■ L ■ N ■ H ■ O
J O N Q U I L ■ C O Y P U
A ■ Z ■ B ■ O ■ E ■ M ■ N
B R A V E ■ W A R H E A D
```

Page 304

```
3  2  0  1  8  7  4  5  9  6
6  8  4  5  0  1  9  7  3  2
0  9  2  1  3  7  8  6  5  4
8  6  7  5  4  1  0  3  9  2
4  3  0  1  9  5  8  2  7  6
9  1  7  5  3  0  4  6  8  2
30 29 20 18 27 21 33 29 41 22
```

Page 305

```
5  2  6  3  1  4
1  3  2  4  5  6
2  1  5  6  4  3
3  6  4  5  2  1
6  4  1  2  3  5
4  5  3  1  6  2
```

Page 305
2

Solutions

Page 306

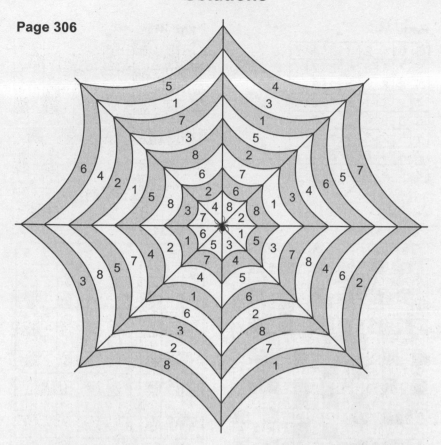

Page 307

Pages 308/309

	2	1	7	4	4		
8	5	5		7	4	2	
9	2		1	4	4		1	6
7	5	5		1		1	1	2
5		4	2	5	0	3		4
5	6	0		7		7	9	2
6	1		3	6	9		6	6
	6	4	4		2	4	1
		1	2	5	1	8	

Page 308

1 Descent, 2 Nested,
3 Dense, 4 Send,
5 Needs, 6 Sensed,
7 Endless.

Solutions

Page 310

5	6	1	2	3	8	4	7
8	7	4	5	6	3	2	1
3	8	6	7	1	2	5	4
4	2	7	1	8	5	6	3
6	3	5	4	2	1	7	8
1	5	2	3	4	7	8	6
7	4	3	8	5	6	1	2
2	1	8	6	7	4	3	5

Page 311

Pages 312/313

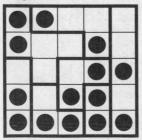

Page 314

2	6	1	7	4	8	5	3	9
9	8	4	1	5	3	6	7	2
5	7	3	9	6	2	8	1	4
4	9	6	3	8	7	2	5	1
3	5	7	2	1	6	4	9	8
1	2	8	4	9	5	3	6	7
6	4	2	5	7	9	1	8	3
7	3	5	8	2	1	9	4	6
8	1	9	6	3	4	7	2	5

Page 315

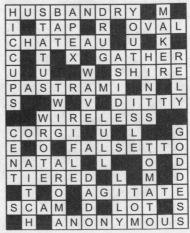

Page 316

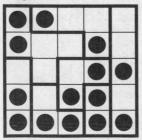

Solutions

Page 317

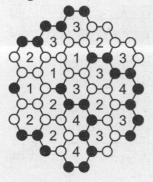

Pages 318/319

Page 320

S	T	E	A	M
T	U	L	L	E
I	N	U	I	T
L	E	D	G	E
T	R	E	N	D

Page 320

Ostrich, Magpie, Budgerigar, Crossbill, Kestrel, Dunnock, Cormorant, Pheasant, Nightingale, Wagtail, Parakeet, Skylark, Starling, Puffin, Buzzard.

Page 322

6	1	2	3	5	4
4	3	1	5	2	6
5	6	4	1	3	2
3	5	6	2	4	1
2	4	5	6	1	3
1	2	3	4	6	5

Page 321

Solutions

Page 323

R	I	N	G	G	I	T
C	O	R	D	O	B	A
A	U	S	T	R	A	L
B	O	L	I	V	A	R
Q	U	E	T	Z	A	L
G	U	I	L	D	E	R
D	R	A	C	H	M	A
A	F	G	H	A	N	I

Page 324

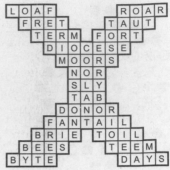

Page 325

1 c, 2 b, 3 a, 4 d, 5 c, 6 d.

Pages 326/327

Pages 326/327

Page 328

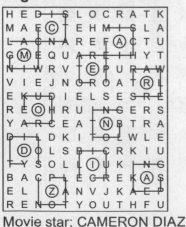

Movie star: CAMERON DIAZ

Page 329

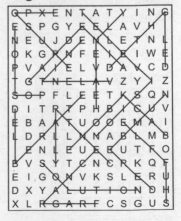

384